SURVIVING
THE NEW ECONOMY

SURVIVING
THE NEW ECONOMY

Edited by
John Amman
Tris Carpenter
Gina Neff

Paradigm Publishers
Boulder • London

Paradigm Publishers is committed to preserving ancient forests and natural resources. We elected to print *Surviving The New Economy* on 50% post consumer recycled paper, processed chlorine free. As a result, for this printing, we have saved:

4 Trees (40' tall and 6-8" diameter)
1,657 Gallons of Wastewater
666 Kilowatt Hours of Electricity
183 Pounds of Solid Waste
359 Pounds of Greenhouse Gases

Paradigm Publishers made this paper choice because our printer, Thomson-Shore, Inc., is a member of Green Press Initiative, a nonprofit program dedicated to supporting authors, publishers, and suppliers in their efforts to reduce their use of fiber obtained from endangered forests.

For more information, visit www.greenpressinitiative.org

Copyright © 2007 Paradigm Publishers

Published in the United States by Paradigm Publishers, 3360 Mitchell Lane Suite E, Boulder, CO 80301 USA.

Paradigm Publishers is the trade name of Birkenkamp & Company, LLC, Dean Birkenkamp, President and Publisher.

Library of Congress Cataloging-in-Publication Data
Surviving the new economy / edited by John Amman, Tris Carpenter, and Gina Neff.
    p. cm.
Includes bibliographical references and index.
ISBN-13: 978-1-59451-249-0 (hardcover : alk. paper)
ISBN-10: 1-59451-249-3 (hardcover : alk. paper) 1. High technology industries—Employees—United States. 2. Professional employees—United States. 3. Work environment—United States. 4. Industrial relations—United States. 5. Labor movement—United States. I. Amman, John, 1954- II. Carpenter, Tris, 1968- III. Neff, Gina, 1971- IV. Title.

HD8039.H542U67 2007
331.10973—dc22

2006031570

Printed and bound in the United States of America on acid free paper that meets the standards of the American National Standard for Permanence of Paper for Printed Library Materials.

Designed by Straight Creek Bookmakers.

11 10 09 08 07   1 2 3 4 5

Contents

Introduction

Surviving in the New Economy: Sharecroppers in the Ownership Society

John Amman, Tris Carpenter, and Gina Neff

For many Americans, the promise of thriving in the new economy has been replaced with the realities of survival. The dot-com boom of the late 1990s marked the coming of age of the much-heralded *new economy*, an economic, technological, and social transformation that had been in progress for decades. The same entrepreneurial spirit that characterized the stock market frenzy is still expected of high-tech employees. A highly mobile and in many cases highly compensated workforce face a multitude of new risks: Jobs are no longer secure nor insulated from global competition, employer-provided health benefits are drying up, and retirement planning is almost entirely the responsibility of employees themselves. These changes are not restricted to the high-tech elite. American workers now face a restructured labor market that asks individuals to bear more responsibility for their jobs, training, and benefits; a global labor market that pushes real wages down; and a broken social contract that replaces the promise of security with the hollow rhetoric of ownership. This book brings together people who are thinking about the challenges that workers face in this new economic environment. While this collection focuses primarily on work in high-tech industries, the implications of these economic changes reach workers at all pay levels and in all sectors, as more Americans find themselves struggling to survive in the new economy.

Several writers have addressed the financial changes of the dot-com era and its aftermath (Cassidy, 2002; Brenner, 2002; Henwood, 2003), but there have been few opportunities for activists and academics to debate how these financial changes affect the people who must work within them and what strategies in general will be effective for organizing. The chapters in this book begin that conversation by describing people's efforts to survive in the new economy through traditional union organizing and, perhaps more importantly, through innovative forms of collective action, political mobilization, community organizing, and social support.

American workers must now navigate changes to the relationship between working people and the economy itself. Initially, the dot-com revolution and the new economy were touted as a new era of personal and economic freedom. The Internet, wireless computers, and cell phones were supposed to free white-collar workers from their nine-to-five routines, but instead have blurred the lines between home and office; leisure and work. After years of uncertainty, factory layoffs, and manufacturing jobs moving overseas, the American dream of the new economy promised jobs with stock options, humane workplaces, and creativity and autonomy for individual workers. Those bold enough to join Internet start-ups thought that they would not only own stock in their company, they would be able to act like company owners with increased power over the day-to-day decisions in their workplaces—in short, they felt like they *were* owners of their own companies. The dot-com bust showed how little power these dot-com "partners" actually wielded against the grip of financial capital and how much the Internet's liberating changes also wrought a darker side of surveillance and overwork.

The term *new economy* has been with us since the early 1990s, and, although it has already lost much of the hope and excitement that it conveyed before the dot-com bubble burst, it is still difficult to remember that the term was first used in the Democratic Party platform during Bill Clinton's 1992 campaign for president—years before the first dot-com stock was ever sold. In the "New Covenant with Americans," the "new economy" meant that workers would accept "added responsibilities" and join in "cooperative efforts to increase productivity, flexibility and quality," in exchange "for an increased voice and greater stake in the success of their enterprises." Flexible adaptation was always at the heart of the new economy, and nowhere was this trade-off between increased flexibility and rewards made more explicit than in technology industries. It seemed that the new emphasis on high-tech computer skills provided the antidote to the massive loss of industrial jobs that had once helped to create the American middle class.

The rise of the new economy marked other losses of the security workers enjoyed during the industrial era. With the stock market booming in the late 1990s, many employees did not mind the shift from traditional pension plans with their conservative investment strategies and government oversight to more flexible 401(k) and other individual savings plans. Individually managed risk—be it in a retirement plan or at the workplace—seemed somehow smarter, and certainly more lucrative, than old-fashioned collective approaches like Social Security. The rapid rise in technology stock prices fueled fantasies and myths of dotcom millionaires and luxurious early retirements funded by mushrooming mutual fund balances. Stock analysts became celebrities as investment gurus, like Peter Lynch of Fidelity who regularly appeared on Fidelity ads in the 1990s, assured us all that in the long run the market always outperformed other forms of investment. The risks of these investments became clear when historically high stock market valuations plummeted.

There also was an enduring social cost for this market euphoria in the form of a protoconservative, individualistic approach to social problems. This idea of individual responsibility for wealth creation and job security continues in the ownership society rhetoric favored by the political Right. Within the ownership society ethos of the new economy, though, many people feel less like the "CEO of Me, Inc." (as quoted in Ross, 2003), with the empowerment and agency that being one's own boss implies, than like sharecroppers who bear the burden of risks in exchange for the opportunity to work. The term *sharecropper society* might well describe the state of many Americans better than *ownership society* ever would, as many people lack company-provided job security, income security, retirement security, and health insurance. The reality of the ownership society may be nothing more than another attempt to throw the burden of social and economic security in the laps of individual employees already struggling to get by.

High-tech professionals have already faced difficult lessons in the vagaries of irrational exuberance. Once the darlings of the dot-com era, high-tech workers are not immune from global economic forces. As with their blue-collar counterparts, technology workers, too, must now contend with outsourcing, layoffs, age discrimination, and job insecurity. Many of them work as freelancers or contractors who are rarely with one employer for long. Technological change requires continual training and retraining. And since they rarely work in any one place for long, high-tech workers must develop elaborate networking skills in order to get their next job (Batt et al., 2001). Many fear that there are only two possible futures: good jobs with promises of stock options and early retirement or bad ones in a de-skilled, high-tech Wal-Mart for increasingly lower wages and globally outsourced work.

THE ROAD TO THE NEW ECONOMY

The new economy did not come about simply because of a technological innovation. For twenty years before the rise of the new economy, the United States had already undergone a massive shift from an industrial to a service, or postindustrial, economy. Global economics, geopolitics, changes in corporate governance and political philosophy, and the decline of U.S. labor unions' strength and density conspired throughout the 1970s and 1980s to change the unwritten social compact that major corporations had with their employees (Harrison and Bluestone, 1988; Osterman et al., 2002). While many high-tech professionals do not belong to labor unions and may even see unions as vestiges of the old industrial economy, labor's decline wrought the cavalier relationship their companies have with them. The authors of an analysis of national longitudinal data show that young male college graduates in almost every occupational field in the United States now earn less in real dollars than young men with the same education a generation ago, and they attribute this decline in part to the loss of union density that pushes up wages across the economy (Bernhardt et al., 2001).

Transitions within the American economy have a powerful effect on the lives of workers and on the ability of unions to organize. In the mid-1970s European and Asian countries, recovered from the effects of World War II, began to flood the world market with less expensive but high-quality manufactured goods. American manufacturers had become so used to their hegemony in the marketplace that they could not easily respond to the jolt that the new competition gave them. Unable to recapture market share or unable to quickly produce higher-quality goods, many American corporations began looking to cost cutting in order to maintain profits. The massive armies of workers employed on the factory floor who had felt safe and comfortable in their jobs suddenly faced layoffs, plant closings, and moving factories. Initially, the American South with its historic animus toward labor unions and lower cost of living proved many manufacturers with an attractive alternative to the highly unionized Rust Belt of the Northeast and Midwest. Later, firms began building manufacturing plants outside the United States to take advantage of lower labor costs. Companies began to downsize nonessential functions to subcontractors and to hire contingent or temporary workers to perform tasks once done by full-time employees (Harrison and Bluestone, 1988; Osterman et al., 2002; Stone, 2001).

High inflation and rising oil prices added to the economic difficulties of the late 1970s. Firms in industries like heavy manufacturing and steel production turned to unions for help through concessions in collective bargaining agreements. Unions agreed to wage freezes, two-tiered wage structures, benefits cuts, and other contract concessions to bolster struggling manufacturing firms. At Chrysler, for example, the combination of union concessions, government loans, and new management saved the corporation. Nonetheless, concession bargaining, which began to salvage firms that were in financial trouble, became the norm in major areas of collective bargaining. Even healthier firms could exact concessions simply by threatening to move unionized work to the South or outside the United States. Nonunion companies made similar veiled or direct threats to employees considering a union organizing drive. With manufacturing leaving the United States and the economy shifting from an industrial to a service economy, labor unions saw membership drop at a steady pace.

The deregulation of specific industries that began in Jimmy Carter's administration in the 1970s continued with a vengeance during the Reagan administration. Reagan did not see "big government" as the solution to the nation's economic problems, and the federal government began to entertain the more conservative economic theories of Milton Friedman. Instead of Keynesian economic strategies to increase macroeconomic demand, such as government spending to create employment Reagan cut taxes to corporations and individuals in an effort to stimulate the so-called supply side of the economy. Reagan believed that economic stimulus came through fewer restrictions on the private sector and that without government restrictions and with fewer taxes corporations would invest money in research and development, in infrastructure, and ultimately in their employees. As a consequence, even the government put on the appearance of becoming "lean and mean" (Harrison, 1994) with the loss of federally funded social programs and the privatization of government jobs. Unemployment increased during Reagan's first administration, but job losses were seen as part of the necessary adjustment to the changing economy, short-term pain in order to achieve long-term gain.

The 1980s proved to be an even more difficult decade for U.S. labor. Membership in labor unions continued to drop as did unions' influence with lawmakers. Reagan's firing and replacement of striking air-traffic controllers during his first administration demonstrated that the federal government would not negotiate with the nation's labor unions, and the strike became the seminal event of the rapid decline of the U.S. labor movement (Harrison and Bluestone, 1988). In the twenty years that followed the air-traffic controllers' strike, organized labor continued to lose membership and influence. Democratic Party leaders, although grateful for the AFL-CIO's ability to walk precincts and get votes out for their candidates, failed to reward this work by putting labor issues at the top of their agenda. If anything, in the post-Reagan years Democrats leaned toward the right, as "moderate" centrist politicians replaced the party's old liberal leadership.

A number of academics and labor leaders argue that corporate and government leaders during this period abandoned a social contract with American workers (Osterman, et al., 2002). American workers during post-World War II economic expansion came to expect that profitable employers would pass on a part of profits as a reward for hard work and loyalty. While this social contract seemed like a fair deal, it could not withstand global competition, mainly because the contract never truly existed. The "old psychological contract" promised "long-term job security, orderly promotional opportunities, longevity-linked pay and benefits, and long-term pension vesting" in exchange for worker loyalty, but it was "psychological" in that workers and their employers perceived this implicit contract differently, the latter of whom simply changed the contract when worker loyalty was no longer required (Stone, 2001, 524). Industrial-era firms trained workers, provided them with job security, and negotiated with their unions simply because they needed them to do the work. When the old psychological contract was broken, American workers had limited options for securing social benefits. The American labor movement made no concerted effort to create the type of welfare state that exists in Western Europe, in part because American trade unionists favored government intervention only in ensuring the rights of workers to organize and providing mediation, and they argued instead that workers should secure health care and pensions through collective bargaining. With few laws to aid them and little willingness on the part of government to write new legislation that would, American workers found themselves handed a new psychological contract and facing the new economy with limited options.

THE PROMISE OF QUALITY JOBS AND HUMANE WORK

The expansion of the technology sector seemingly provided assurance that the American labor market would improve. For example, during the debates over the North American Free Trade Agreement, supporters claimed that the loss of manufacturing jobs to Mexico would be more than made up for by high-paying jobs in technology. Robert Reich argued that "symbolic analysts"—highly educated, globally oriented, and uniquely skilled—would be able to best navigate the challenges of the twenty-first century labor market (Reich, 1991). The rise of the World Wide Web and the dot-com boom that followed Netscape's historic initial public stock offering seemed to provide a road to new economy riches for a risk-loving, smart, young, entrepreneurial workforce. The feverish growth of the prices of Internet-related stocks only fueled the frenzy. But when the Internet stock market bubble burst, thousands of Americans who thought they had solved the challenges of the new economy found themselves unemployed.

In his chapter, Derek Schultz debunks the pernicious and persistent myths about high-tech work that emerged out of the heady days of the dot-com boom. Schultz has worked for nearly three decades as a computer programmer and consultant, and in his chapter he richly describes from a first-hand perspective the economic realities facing high-tech professionals. The five myths that Schultz exposes promulgate "unrealistic visions of high-tech worker utopias" and, he argues, prevent high-tech workers from seeking collective voice and collective action to the ongoing problems within the industry.

Information technology continues to be an essential sector of the U.S. economy, and it clearly is the key to much of America's economic future. However, the relatively freelance and entrepreneurial nature of the work provides, as Rosabeth Moss Kanter (1995) argued, a "new career model" for future professional work. Flexibility and contingency, though, are volatile forces in an economy that bases benefits on long-term, full-time, and permanent employment. What happens when workers must rely on relationships with a number of different employers as opposed to daily work in one workplace? In a nation that relied on the good will of corporations to provide social benefits like health insurance and pensions, what happens to the free-lance professionals who are unable to work for any one employer long enough to obtain health insurance or vest in a pension plan?

The dot-com era also promised a new, humane workplace where employees were rewarded not merely for hard work, but for creativity, individualism, and boldness. Work in the new economy was supposed to flatten the old hierarchies of boss versus worker and replace the *Organization Man* grind with meaningful work. Dot-com workers did not consider themselves employees as much as they considered themselves partners with the company owners in creating computer programs, software, games, and Web sites. People worked long hours, but were often paid well for their efforts. Compensation often included stock options, further signifying that they were partners in the Internet ventures they worked in, and not merely cogs in the corporate system. The history of Razorfish, the company that Andrew Ross profiled in *No-Collar*, shows the unique relationship that technology workers had with entrepreneurs during the tech boom. The people at Razorfish believed that they were not only creating a new business venture and developing a new form of media and communication, but that they were creating a new, more creative, more engaging, and more humane workplace. Work relations in the new economy were thought to be the antithesis of the old corporate culture, in which "the work rules, hierarchies, and rituals of corporate organization were condemned for stifling initiative and creativity and for stunting the appetite of employees for opportunity and meaningful self-application" (Ross, 2003). Dot-commers saw their companies and the industry that they were creating as the replacement for the old, stodgy corporations. Where the corporate world demanded conformity, the new economy world of dot-coms inspired individuality. Where the corporate world insisted on rigid hierarchies, the dot-com world purportedly broke down the barriers between company owners and the workforce. The willingness to drop formal hierarchies and communicate openly promised to make dot-com firms more productive, responsive, and efficient.

The relationship between creativity and a sense of workplace empowerment has long been linked to greater levels of productivity (Heckscher, 1996). In the case of the dot-com firms that Ross studied, creativity was essential to their allure for both workers and clients alike who expected dot-com consultants to appear a bit bohemian. In New York, for example, Internet companies often located themselves in downtown lofts, where workplaces "imitated all the attributes of artists—their habitats, lifestyles, clothing, work patterns and custom individuality" (Ross, 2003). In Manhattan's trendiest bars and nightclubs, dot-coms sponsored parties that became key social networking events for people who worked in the industry (Neff, 2005). "Neobohemias" sprouted across the country, proving the lure of artistic cultural capital to high-tech firms (Lloyd, 2006) and ready access to the labor services of the "creative class" (Florida, 2004). This context, though, of creative, artistic, and relatively autonomous labor further complicates technology professionals' abilities to understand themselves as employees, as work in creative industries merges artistic and entrepreneurial drives (Neff et al., 2005). How can professional workers ever find a home in traditional unions if they change jobs many times throughout their careers, think of themselves as full-fledged team members on par with their employers, and think of themselves as creative talent instead of employees? Does the classic industrial union structure even make sense in the context of the new economy?

WHAT SURVIVED THE CRASH

The new economy dream of the creative and humane workplace did not survive the dot-com crash. New technologies, rather than liberating employees from the office, allow employers to monitor employee behavior and productivity on a minute-to-minute basis (Head, 2003). In high-tech industries, countless professionals lost their jobs with little to show for their start-up experience but worthless stock options. Companies that did survive the crash adopted aspects of the corporate culture that they once derided. Many technology companies laid off employees, cut back salaries, and outsourced jobs overseas. In the few cases in which employees participated in union organizing drives, employers vehemently resisted.

In his chapter in this collection, Simon Head argues that despite the rhetoric of liberated workers, the information technology revolution has instead renewed industrial-era practices of Taylorism and scientific management. Corporations are using information technologies not to liberate the workforce, but to control workers—speeding up the work process and using advanced management tools for surveillance. Wal-Mart and Toyota, heralded as new economy models for their expansive use and profitable integration of information technology, both use a form of Taylorism that devalue workers' "skills, erodes their job security, and undermines their bargaining power in the workplace," as Head writes. The practice of scientific management reaches beyond the proletarian ghetto of Wal-Mart "associates" and auto assembly-line workers, and, as Head argues, now invades the gated, professional world of middle managers, administrators, and even doctors. In this way of thinking about the new economy as a continuation of the drive toward ever-greater efficiency, Head argues that the principles of the new system are "deeply embedded in the economic and business history of the United States."

The hope for quality jobs and human workplaces is fading as the economic recovery provides little evidence that average Americans are recovering. With rising health care costs and increased burdens for retirement savings, Americans are earning less in real expendable wages. In 2005, the *Financial Times* reported the fastest drop in real wages in fourteen years (Swann, 2005). Yet, as incomes are dropping, worker productivity in the United States continues to rise. The Economic Policy Institute reported in its April 2005 "Economic Snapshot" that there is a growing gap between worker productivity and the growth of real wages. These findings run counter to the long-held view that increased productivity leads to wage increases.

Benefits, too, as we have said, continue to be more, not less insecure in the new economy. Compared to traditional union pensions, individual retirement savings programs like 401(k) plans lack government protection and oversight. Recent reports have also shown that corporations increasingly underfund traditional pension plans or avoid pension obligations altogether when they file for bankruptcy protection. Even the Pension Benefit Guarantee Corporation (PBGC), which is responsible for meeting the responsibilities of failed pension plans, is itself $30 million in the red.

Despite the fact that individual savings programs were never meant to entirely replace pensions, they do fit neatly with the neoconservative ideology of personal responsibility within the economy. George W. Bush, in describing the "ownership society" in his 2005 inaugural speech, said that individuals should be the stewards of their economic destinies, and this rhetoric shored up his later attempts to begin privatizing Social Security. While neoconservative economists, pundits, and politicians applauded, the nation as a whole did not, and it soon became clear that the American public wants some measure of income stability into their old age. The Social Security battle was the latest skirmish in the ongoing ideological war about how individuals relate to the market in the new economy.

The entrepreneurial fervor of the dot-com era played a significant role in this ideological war. Most people working in Internet start-ups were not entrepreneurs, even if they were entrepreneurial. Entrepreneurship is fine if one actually has a modicum of control over a company's destiny. It is quite another thing if entrepreneurship is imposed, when companies' platitudes about ownership and partnership become means to avoid their responsibilities to their employees. As Gina Neff argues in her chapter, "The Lure of Risk," the dot-com boom made taking economic risks more appealing and in turn provided ideological support for notions like the ownership society. Neff writes that high-tech workers "willingly accepted and seemingly welcomed risk," because risk "offered choices" as opposed to the "uncertainties" of the new economy that seem out of the control of ordinary employees. The attraction to personal economic risk that dot-com entrepreneurship inspired survived the dot-com crash all too well.

GLOBAL CHALLENGES

Clearly, work in the new economy is even more global in nature. American firms still dominate wide swaths of the world's economy, but communication technologies have enabled them to outsource operations outside the United States. There is certainly nothing new about outsourcing, but one of the hopes of the 1990's tech boom was that the United States would emerge as a vibrant center for knowledge work as "new forms of centrality" emerged in the coordination of business services (Sassen, 1996). Training in computer technology was supposed to be the ticket to job security, but American tech workers increasingly must compete with a global, often lower-paid workforce. Naive protectionist rhetoric, however, often misses the complexities of the global challenges that labor faces. Careful analyses of the labor market in countries that do outsourced work call into question images of a specter of low-wage labor in India and China.

In his contribution, Andrew Ross reminds us that it is too simplistic when American workers place blame on "the faceless foreigner for 'taking' their job" rather than holding "companies accountable for paying Third World wages and asking First World prices." In fact, Ross's research shows that recent increases in Chinese job loss are just as much the result of corporate globalization and neoliberal privatization as is U.S. job loss. Employers in Shanghai also use the same threats of lower-paid employees abroad (in this case, India) to encourage employees to work harder. These threats have long been a form of "intimidation to speed up the work rate, or win concessions, in labor-intensive industries," and employers now apply them to white-collar work. China represents a threat to the income security in the West, not so much because of low wages, but because, Ross warns, "it is the biggest and weakest link in the communication network aimed at combating the trade in what economists euphemistically refer to as 'global labor arbitrage,' and what contrarians call 'the race to the bottom.'" Only "if workers are able to communicate with the same ease, trust, and conviction that their employers do" will a network emerge of "workers and employees sharing knowledge, tactics, and goals across national borders" who can respond to the challenges of corporate globalization.

Even international flows of capital within globalized direct investment are not exempt from some local influence. Seán Ó Riain in his chapter argues that the Irish case of information technology development is more than "a simple story of neo-liberal globalization" as foreign investment *and* indigenous industry, as well as local demand, were central to the creation of the "Celtic Tiger" information technology (IT) boom in the 1980s and 1990s. Although the institutional arrangements that supported rapid growth in Ireland were different from those in other high-tech regions, working conditions in the Irish tech boom converged toward a global standard, so that working in Dublin became a lot like working in Silicon Valley. As Ó Riain writes, "High turnover, individualized human resource management strategies, and non-union approaches to workers" dominated Irish high tech, making it look "a great deal like Silicon Valley for workers—perhaps not surprisingly given the massive influence of U.S. and Silicon Valley companies such as HP and Intel" in Ireland.

Even for workers who get the coveted jobs in the global labor market for high-tech workers, there is no guarantee of quick wealth or even steady incomes, as Immanuel Ness shows in his examination of the relationship between Indian H-1B visa holders in the United States and those who return to India. Quite simply, Ness contends that, in addition to workers in the United States, "foreign workers are also exploited while working for U.S. firms," as often they work for companies that charge U.S. rates for products and services but pay foreign workers lower wages. Guest worker programs in this country can "evoke the essence of nonstandard contracting jobs: low-wage labor, social isolation from the general workforce, indentured servitude, and upon completion of the job, forced deportation to one's home country." Ness follows the movement of high-tech workers who are organizing against these conditions. High-tech workers are forming organizations across the country, especially in regions with large high-technology workforces, that are independent of labor unions; address global concerns by resisting crude protectionist rhetoric; and incorporate multiple political, technological, and social strategies for organizing.

LOCAL RESPONSES; LABOR REFORMS

There are many innovative responses to these challenges and models for future directions in maintaining good work in creative and high-tech industries. In his chapter, Chris Benner looks to localized political power that the labor movement can have in high-tech regions. Through his examination of cooperative efforts among the local central labor council in Silicon Valley, community organizations, and local political initiatives, Benner describes one model of confronting the challenges of the new economy and reestablishing the political importance of place in a globalized world. Benner reminds us that globalization has led to one sort of recentralization, one that presents possibilities for organizing: production is increasingly "organized around smaller workplaces connected together in complex, constantly shifting networks operating at multiple spatial scales, from the local to the global" that supersede "the centralization of production in large enterprises that was the dominant feature of the industrial era." These changing locations of production—from centralized factory to smaller, globally connected offices—reestablish the importance of local economic development initiatives, which can improve the quality of life in high-tech regions and the conditions for high-tech workers. In this landscape, unions and central labor councils can "improve the quality of jobs through engaging in a variety of community-based economic development strategies." Although this social mobilization can improve the quality of jobs in the region, it is, Benner argues, no substitute for workers organizing within high-tech industries themselves. Still, Benner's case study of Silicon Valley shows that labor movement can reinvent its role in improving the lives of workers through an approach that provides solutions for local problems.

Social mobilization brings up issues of the models for unions themselves. There have been several innovative approaches to solving workplace issues of the new economy—such as the "Freelancers Union" established by Working Today and other associations that address the specific concerns of the high-tech workforce. Danielle van Jaarsveld provides an in-depth look at one of these emerging models, WashTech, a union created by computer programmers and technicians working in Washington State. She compares WashTech with the case of unionized high-tech employees within Dow Jones. From these case studies van Jaarsveld finds "that new economy jobs are not so different from old economy jobs   the need for representation and protection in the workplace remains," but that the multifaceted needs of tech workers and contingent workers require "an organizational structure that can deploy a variety of strategies to represent the demands of constituent employees." Two of these strategies use models of organizing that are outside the traditional union structure that entails a collective bargaining agreement with one particular employer. WashTech gains support, van Jaarsveld argues, by using the models of associational unionism (Heckscher, 1996) to "advocate on behalf of its constituents" and by using features of a "citizenship unionism" model (Stone, 2001) to address more global concerns.

There are other lessons to be learned from different representational structures. John Amman argues in his chapter that the high-tech workforce would be wise to closely examine how entertainment industry unions work, particularly those in film and television. Freelance television and film workers deal with many of the same issues as freelance high-tech workers. Both are "well-trained, highly skilled and largely freelance," "rely heavily on similar types of networking relationships with employers and co-workers in order to maintain their careers," and must adapt to ever-changing technologies. Credentialing, training, work schedules, and celebrating best practices are challenges that "old media" unions have addressed; Amman carefully describes the ways in which their strategies could be applied by "new media" workers. One "old media" tactic Amman identifies is organizing "employer members." Organizing around the "profession, not the workplace," means that some members will also occasionally be consultants or employers on jobs. Amman shows that the entertainment industries have actually increased their strength by including these employer-members into their constituencies.

"Freelancers can organize," Tris Carpenter argues from his own experiences organizing film and television editors working on reality television shows, a format that had been considered difficult to organize. Carpenter offers advice for high-tech workers who "wish to move forward collectively," and gives several examples of the models entertainment industry unions created for portable benefit systems that can be carried over during slow times, restrictions on long or unpaid hours, and assistance for people who wish to train on new and evolving technologies. Carpenter's chapter reminds readers "rough coalition victories that provide some results may be the best way to begin" organizing, and he points out that trade guilds without legal standing had been doing that in periods of American history. While an agreement for collective bargaining is clearly the strongest protection American workers can earn, the obstacles to a full contract, Carpenter argues, should not stand in the way of making advances.

Surviving in the New Economy brings together these chapters in order to present the challenges and obstacles, the strategies and tactics, and the successes and shortcomings of providing for collective approaches to security for people who must now work in a vastly changed economic environment.

1

Myths and Realities about High-Tech Work in the New Economy—A Personal View

Derek W. Schultz

This chapter offers a first-person view of high-tech work and workers—a window into the world of high-tech work as I've observed it for more than a quarter century as an employee, an independent consultant, and a subcontractor to consulting companies. I started my career at Bell Labs working on usability engineering for software systems—how to make the large computer programs that ran the telephone network easier to understand and use. Five years later I started consulting. I've worked with many projects—both short and long term and in both the private and public sectors—to solve problems or build products in telecommunications, environmental sciences, consumer electronics, Web-based applications, and process analysis and improvement.

My training and experience in research management centered on teamwork in R & D projects—creating environments where a team of talented people could excel. But this knowledge became moot as companies actively pursued policies that devalued and demoralized workers, such as downsizing merely to inflate stock prices, offshoring to cut short-term costs at the long-run expense of communities, and replacing long-term employees with foreign workers on temporary visas (H-1B, L-1). I've talked to dozens of high-tech workers, and read e-mails and postings from hundreds more, who have been abused and abandoned in this "new economy." The more I watched these and similar disturbing trends, and the more I studied business and labor history, the more I came to believe that unions—reinvented for the realities of the twenty-first century—are crucial for correcting these policies and restoring economic justice.

Let me offer two caveats. First, I've made no attempt to conceal personal viewpoints and biases. Second, I'm not going to recount recent trends surrounding work and large corporations; it's obvious that the nature of work in our society has been changing for thirty years, and those changes have been accelerating in the past decade.

FIVE MYTHS ABOUT HIGH-TECH WORK

I use the term *high-tech workers* to mean technical and/or professional workers, especially in high-tech arenas. This definition includes engineers, computer scientists, programmers, graphic designers, technical writers, instructional developers, and scientists of all varieties who participate in developing and delivering high-tech products or systems.

The conventional wisdom about these workers and the work they do is based largely on five myths:

1. It's-Not-So-Bad Myth
2. Loyalty-Pays Myth
3. Training-as-Panacea Myth
4. Old-and-in-the-Way Myth
5. Individualism Myth

This chapter explores the realities of these myths. To provide context for our exploration, let me offer a few generalizations. The main thing to understand is that there's nothing wrong with high-tech work that isn't also wrong in nearly every other arena of work in our society—it's just that technical/professional workers arrived at their mistreatment later than most other workers. Also, at least for white males, the realities of high-tech work today aren't all that different from the realities of clerical or white-collar work in the 1950s, or the 1920s, or the 1880s: It's not that high-tech work (or white-collar work more generally) has suddenly gotten so bad; rather, it's that high-tech work in a few selected arenas has lost its temporary and largely unprecedented patina of congeniality and returned to the more dismal realities that most workers have experienced all along.

Like most myths, the myths discussed here have some underlying kernels of truth, but those kernels have been overblown into unrealistic visions of high-tech worker utopias. During the course of the twentieth century, a few enlightened companies (that is, enlightened compared to the standards at that time) such as Bell Labs, General

Electric, and Hewlett-Packard hired some very talented people and treated them rather well overall, especially compared with workers in other industries.[1] Those exceptional "old high-tech" work environments, and a few other exceptional "new high-tech" companies that blossomed during the Internet boom of the late 1990s, became the models from which many myths about high-tech work and workers arose. In reality, most workers (regardless of talent) in the vast majority of tech-related companies had work lives that were less than idyllic.

MYTH #1: THE IT'S-NOT-SO-BAD MYTH

The first myth worth debunking goes like this: *Tech workers are just spoiled, whiny babies—they've come to expect Foosball tables, stocked refrigerators, and BMWs as signing bonuses. Tech workers get good salaries and stock options, so any discomforts they encounter are offset by high rewards. Besides, tech workers love being "on" all the time, so they don't mind working long hours and they often work from home via the Web. Tech workers don't know how good they really have it.*

This myth really has four underlying parts: 1) tech work is easy, at least compared with other jobs; 2) tech workers are spoiled by perks and flexibility they've come to expect; 3) tech workers are well compensated; and 4) tech workers really prefer to work all the time. Let's examine each part in turn.

Part 1: Tech work is easy. On most criteria, tech work seems better than mining coal or picking lettuce, but that doesn't mean tech work is easy. Most tech work requires months or years of training, and makes demands both mentally and physically. Unpaid overtime is the norm in most tech work, and is nearly out of control in some tech arenas (e.g., in computer game design/development, 80-hour weeks seem to be the industry standard). Nor is it without stress: I've known tech workers who suffered depression, ulcers, migraines, sleeplessness, and alcohol abuse. Tech work also is not without risk of physical harm: I've known tech workers with carpal tunnel/repetitive stress injuries, and at least one worker who had to shift from programming to testing because of her injury. (Although the Clinton administration established Occupational Safety and Health Administration [OSHA] guidelines to prevent such injuries, President Bush rescinded those guidelines as one of his earliest acts in office.) Suicide is not unheard of and worker rage ("going postal") has been on the rise.

Part 2: Tech workers are spoiled by perks and flexibility. In some companies, although far fewer now than in 2000, some tech workers do have benefits and perks not available to most other workers. But most perks, if they existed at all, disappeared during the course of the 2001 recession and never reappeared. Most tech workers never enjoyed stocked refrigerators, Aeron chairs, or company game rooms, and the flexible hours portion of the myth is best refuted by a saying attributed to workers at Microsoft: "Sure, we have flextime—you can work any 18 hours a day that you want."

Part 3: Tech workers are well compensated. Compared with some workers, this is undoubtedly true. But the myth conveys images of salaries typically exceeding $100,000 and stock options that create 28-year-old multimillionaires. In fact, neither is common. Granted, most tech-worker salaries, commensurate with tech-workers' education and training, are above the U.S. median household income (which is roughly $45,000), and some do exceed $100,000. But the norm for nonsupervisory tech workers, especially after the 2001 recession and ongoing wage stagnation, is more like $60,000–$70,000.[2] Unpaid overtime that's expected, which often surpasses 12 hours/week and can exceed 40 hours/week in some start-ups and in the computer game industry, further dilutes the real hourly wage.

As for "insta-millionaires," the myth far surpasses the reality. The only workers who ever got rich were those who got in relatively early (say, within the first 200 or so employees), whose company succeeded wildly (e.g., Microsoft, Netscape), and who were able to cash out before the Internet bubble burst. Sure, some people got rich and a few became very wealthy, but most never saw any significant return on their stock, especially after paying taxes on their options. In fact, some lost money after taxes, and many who hold options in companies still afloat find that their options are "under water"—the company's stock is trading at a lower price than their options to buy. The exception is executives—boards of directors often reprice the executives' options so that the revised option price is still lower than the now-low trading price of the company's stock.

Tech workers used to be assured of a comfortable, middle-class lifestyle but the same was true of autoworkers in Detroit during the latter half of the twentieth century. A unionized autoworker could expect middle-class wages (roughly $25/hour or more), good health insurance with no or low copayments, and a comfortable pension. That American dream has evaporated, first for factory workers and now for tech workers. Ironically, as factory jobs ran offshore over the past two decades, workers were told to get more training, especially in computer-related fields. Many did, only to find that the tech jobs they're currently chasing are following their old factory jobs offshore.

Part 4: Tech workers prefer to work all the time. This is the most pernicious part of the myth. Sure, tech workers are professionals who, by and large, like their work. For these reasons, they often choose to stay late or work on a weekend if project deadlines demand it. Because tech work requires creativity, just like work in many other professions, a tech worker may get up in the middle of the night to pursue an insight or inspiration. Some tech workers, like some workers in nearly any field, choose to work long hours for their own satisfaction or for personal reasons, but it doesn't follow that all tech workers *prefer* to work long hours all the time for their entire careers.

Quite simply, most tech workers like working, but also like not working. Most like to be able to work on the spur of the moment (say, to pursue a sudden insight), but don't want to be required to work into the wee hours of every morning. Typically, tech workers view long hours as an early-career right of passage or as a big push to a start-up's initial public offering (IPO), not as a life-long commitment. In short, most tech workers are much like workers in other white-collar or professional or creative arenas—work is an important part of who they are, but it's not their sole defining characteristic. The myth of "geeks want to work all the time" is a glib mischaracterization used by managers and executives to justify overworking salaried tech workers in order to meet unreasonable deadlines on badly managed projects or to over-inflate productivity statistics (which typically assume 40-hour weeks). In short, the It's-Not-So-Bad Myth serves as window dressing for high-tech sweatshops.

MYTH #2: THE LOYALTY-PAYS MYTH

This myth goes as follows: *Loyalty to the company pays off: As your company does better, you will, too. If your work is good, your job is safe. And remember that wages and benefits may fluctuate, and a few jobs may disappear, but pensions are paid already and will remain secure.*

This myth is easy to debunk—just look at the number of long-term employees who lost their jobs for no reason other than to cut corporate costs and inflate stock prices. Sure, excuses like "global competition" are usually offered, but that doesn't change the reality: No matter how long you've worked there, no matter how good your work has been, and no matter how much you've contributed to the company's success, you could lose your job tomorrow—loyalty be damned. In contrast, few executives are hired without protective employment contracts that specify the limited circumstances under which they can be fired (regardless of corporate performance) and that guarantee huge payouts and pensions if they are terminated.

Over the course of twenty-five years, I have worked with hundreds of technical/professional workers and dozens of managers. Late in 2003 I realized that, of all the managers I had worked with over the past quarter century, the five I considered to be the best were all involuntarily unemployed. These were managers whose loyalty and competence were unquestioned, who had successfully managed leading-edge projects on more than one occasion, and who had consistently been rated as outstanding both by their workers and by their superiors. But being terrific wasn't good enough—once they reached their mid- to late-forties they were no longer worth keeping. Sure, each one eventually found employment elsewhere, sometimes even in management, but always with a cut in pay and benefits.

In *I'll Be Short: Essentials for a Decent Working Society,* former Secretary of Labor Robert Reich (2002) argues that the social contract in America has traditionally involved three key promises and that all three promises have been broken and need to be restored (and in some ways expanded):

1. *As companies do better, their employees do, too.* In brief, this covers commitments like no layoffs in profitable years, layoffs only as a last resort, and rehiring of laid-off people as business turns up. Traditionally, layoffs were a blue-collar phenomenon, but the 1990s saw white-collar downsizing become the standard approach for titillating Wall Street analysts.
2. *Workers are paid enough to support themselves and their families.* This means that a person working full time can support a small family without being impoverished (i.e., no working poor) and that companies have commitments to communities as well. Here again, tech companies have abandoned workers, their families, and their communities by exporting jobs to Asia, by importing foreign workers to undercut wages, and by shifting corporate costs onto workers (e.g., health care costs), communities (e.g., pollution, tax rebates/avoidances), and customers (e.g., automated customer service via 800 numbers).
3. *Everyone has an opportunity to develop and use his/her abilities, starting with publicly supported education.* This promise extends to commitments like universal K–14, continuing education, better schools, lower college tuition costs, and broader acceptances into colleges (more opportunity to enroll). We've

heard for years that American public schools are producing students who cannot compete globally—our performance is said to be inferior to that of other countries, especially in math and science—and tech companies seemed eager to bludgeon America's public schools as inferior and incompetent. But rather than step up to the challenge of improving public education, most tech companies simply used reports of lagging educational performance as an excuse for importing foreign workers or for exporting jobs offshore.[3]

No reasonable person can doubt that the mid-twentieth century social contract has been voided, and that the American middle class is worse off for it. Even if you keep your job, your wages are likely to be stagnant or falling. Companies not only are getting stingier on wages, they're also backpedalling on benefits to both employees and retirees. In particular, some companies have opted to abandon health benefits promised to retirees and to cease funding any pension plans (except perhaps for executives). It looks like taxpayers will be forced to pick up the slack: Pension funding shortfalls have risen to unprecedented levels, as have federal guarantees needed to compensate for private sector pension plan shortfalls. The Loyalty-Pays Myth reflects a social contract that was honored once but has long since been abandoned by most American corporations.

MYTH #3: THE TRAINING-AS-PANACEA MYTH

This myth (also known as "Training's the answer; what's the question?") says: *Knowledge has value in this new knowledge-based economy, so the more you know, the more value you have. If you have enough training, along with motivation, you're ensured a job. It follows, conversely, that unemployed tech workers must lack education, so more training is the answer to their problems.*

This myth sounds compelling—after all, what could be better than more training? But not only is this myth dead wrong, it's also misleading. Let's examine this myth in three parts: 1) American tech workers need training, 2) American tech workers can't (or won't) get trained, but 3) if they got trained, tech workers could get jobs.

Part 1: Tech workers need training. This part of the myth is simply wrong. American tech workers have used computers most of their lives, and have consistently moved from one system or language to the next as technologies have evolved. In general, adapting to technology has been central to American life for the past century, especially for the past thirty years. American workplaces were computerized long before those of most other countries, and personal computers have been commonplace in America for nearly twenty years. Many of these "unskilled" American tech workers, ironically, were the people who designed and built the computing and communications technologies on which the latest wave of globalization is enabled—so those who developed the Internet are watching their jobs get offshored via the Internet.

Even if this part of the myth were true, there should be no problem—tech workers who have been riding the wave of change for a generation can easily pick up new methods and technologies. As jobs moved offshore, many tech workers started second careers in secondary education, especially teaching math and science.[4] If they were able to learn a new profession (teaching), they certainly could learn another programming language.

Part 2: American tech workers can't (or won't) get trained. Tech workers like to learn, but need an opportunity to do so. Two obstacles arise: First, many workers can't afford to pay for additional software and training courses, which can cost thousands of dollars and offer no guarantee of finding work as a result. Second, many workers can't afford the time for off-the-job training, especially when they're working significant unpaid overtime or a second job.

Back when American companies honored a social contract, ongoing training was simply part of the job, especially in high-tech fields. Workers were expected—often required—to complete additional training every year in order to get satisfactory job performance ratings. This approach circumvented both obstacles: Workers incurred no cost for training, and could receive training on company time. But if training is so important in a knowledge-based economy, why have corporations gutted their internal training programs? Surely it's cheaper to train a current employee with a new skill than to hire a new employee and bring them up to speed on the whole panoply of company- and industry-related knowledge, especially since the new employee inevitably will need additional training at some time in the future. In fact, it seems the only "training" corporations have consistently endorsed lately is the training that downsized employees are required to give their foreign guest worker replacements as a condition for receiving severance pay.

Sadly, American companies have started a self-fulfilling prophecy of a skilled worker shortage in two ways: First, since 2001 fewer undergraduate students are entering technical and scientific fields, precisely because they've seen high-tech jobs offshored to cheaper labor markets or reserved for foreigners on guest worker visas.

Enrollment in computer science programs has fallen markedly in the past several years, so much so that Bill Gates toured high-tech universities (e.g., MIT, Carnegie-Mellon, Illinois, Stanford), encouraging students to enroll in computer science and related fields. But why should they? No matter how good their training, they'll be left out of the high-tech job market as it runs away to Asia.

Second, as tech workers have been excluded from the labor market, their skills have begun to become outdated. If you want to make sure that American workers are weak on the latest technologies, just make sure they're unemployed for two or three years—it's the planned obsolescence of the American technical workforce.

Part 3: If they got trained, tech workers could get jobs. This part of the Training-as-Panacea Myth not only is wrong but also is tragically misleading—*show me the jobs.* For several years, newspapers have run stories of displaced tech workers, such as the engineer with eighteen Bell Labs patents who is now working at Home Depot and the high-tech marketing whiz who is selling clothes at the Gap. An acquaintance has master's degrees from MIT in both computer science and architecture, but was jobless for nearly two years. No doubt you've read similar stories or know someone in similar circumstances. These are smart people who are fully capable of producing solid work, if the jobs stayed here and weren't filled by imported guest workers.

Although estimates vary and reliable data are scarce, analyses indicate that roughly 500,000–800,000 high-tech jobs have moved off-shore in the past five years, largely to India, China, and the former Soviet bloc.[5] Even worse, the American technical labor market has been flooded with foreign workers on H-1B or L-1 guest worker visas, again mostly from India.[6] Exact counts are not available, but estimates suggest that almost a million guest workers currently reside in the United States on H-1B visas, and another million or more on L-1 visas. If these estimates are accurate, offshoring and guest workers would account for nearly three million jobs that American workers have lost. Historically, tech-worker unemployment has been stable at about 2 percent, but in the past four years the unemployment rate for tech workers has risen dramatically. For example, according to Bureau of Labor Statistics data, unemployment was close to 7 percent for electrical engineers in 2003, and close to 8 percent for computer programmers in 2004. Even worse, the unemployment rate for older tech workers has skyrocketed—some estimates suggest that more than 20 percent of tech workers over fifty are either unemployed or underemployed.

When smokestack industries closed down in the 1980s and 1990s, many workers were retrained for jobs in the shiny new "knowledge-based" economy. Of those retrained, only about 20 percent ever got full-time jobs in their new career fields according to a Department of Labor study in 2001. But those who didn't get jobs were soon joined by some who initially had: It turns out that you don't need retraining if your new high-tech job soon gets de-skilled, or automated, or offshored, or filled by an imported worker.

In truth, Training-as-Panacea is a red herring to divert attention away from corporate cost cutting. Training has been advocated by vested interests (i.e., training companies selling computer language courses or foreign-based consultancies selling H-1B/L-1 workers) and subscribed to by those who should know better (e.g., former Labor Secretary Robert Reich).[7]

To better understand how this myth gets promulgated, let's draw a distinction between skills and knowledge. A skill is the ability to perform a specific task or set of tasks. Knowledge, on the other hand, is richer and entails a number of skill sets as well as a broad and detailed understanding of the job, the company, and the industry: projects, contexts, histories, process interactions, people, customers, successes, failures. A long-time employee or an experienced worker will have more relevant *knowledge*, even though he may not know a specific skill.

For example, a 50-year-old programmer may have learned and successfully used a dozen different programming languages over the course of a career, but may not yet be acquainted with the latest variation on the C language or Java or HTML. Because he has learned and used a dozen languages, many of which are similar to one another, likely he will have no trouble picking up the latest variation given a week or two to do so. Alternatively, a new hire straight out of college may have learned and used the latest programming language variation—she has that skill. But what the new graduate lacks, which the older programmer has abundantly, is a rich and detailed knowledge about the software development life cycle and process, especially as it is practiced in that particular company or division or department.

But there is another crucial difference between the new graduate and the older programmer: The new graduate's salary and benefits, including health insurance costs, are probably only a fraction of those for the older programmer. If the corporate goal is to cut costs with little regard for long-term impacts on the company or its communities, then the easiest way to "maximize shareholder value" is to replace the older programmer with a cheaper programmer—say, a recent graduate or a foreigner on a guest worker visa.[8] Obviously, the way to justify firing the older programmer, while attempting to circumvent age discrimination and other legal liabilities, is to argue that the older employee lacks some special skill, like the latest variation on a programming language.

Of course, the older employee could be retrained, despite arguments to the contrary that older workers can't learn new skills, but doing so wouldn't serve the goal of replacing an expensive older employee with a cheaper new graduate or foreign worker. The older employee could even take training on his own time and at his own expense but, of course, doing so would not guarantee the older employee job security: If the company's goal is simply to cut costs, another excuse for firing the older employee will be found eventually and, adding insult to injury, the older employee will not only be out of a job, but also has spent the money and time for the training he took.

Training-as-Panacea is either the glib response of those who haven't thought the issue through completely, or else the deliberate misdirection of those who simply want cheap labor—workers who are either younger, or foreign, or both. Frankly, back in the early 1990s I naively believed in the Training Myth, and I still think that—back then—most people advocating retraining of the smokestack workforce were sincere in their efforts. But I certainly don't believe the Training Myth now, and neither should you.

MYTH #4: THE OLD-AND-IN-THE-WAY MYTH

This myth says: *Older tech workers just aren't productive, and never contribute as much as younger workers because tech workers get burned out with age. In fact, they actually prefer to get out of the fast-paced "high-tech game" and move into management or some other field entirely. Quite simply, high tech is a young person's game—oldsters can't keep up with the rapid pace of change.*

This is the classic camouflage for age discrimination: Despite any knowledge or dedication the worker may have, in high-tech fields they're usually "finished at forty," not because they can't produce but because they're more expensive than younger workers.

Again, there's a kernel of truth underlying this myth—not that older workers can't learn new skills, but often they'd rather move on to using a broader range of their knowledge and experience. For example, after programming for twenty years in more than a dozen different languages, not all programmers get excited about learning yet another variation on a programming language. They'd rather use their extensive experience in software development to help scope and design the new systems to be built, or plan and manage projects, or mentor new hires.

After a while, learning the umpteenth version of a coding language gets boring for some people.

Granted, many fifty-year-olds aren't eager to work 70 hours/week the way they might have in their twenties, but what they might lack in lemminglike devotion they usually make up in tactical insight—working smarter, not harder. This point goes back to the distinction of knowledge versus skills—the experienced worker has seen all manner of crises before, can sense when the project is starting to slip or go awry, and knows what corrective or preventative actions are needed. This is exactly why project managers typically aren't recent college graduates.

Much of my own work involved forming and leading small teams (roughly eight–twelve people) responsible for the entire range of user interface/support on large software systems—user interface design, online help and tutorials, user guides and other documentation, training and self-instructional guides, and so on. When selecting team members, I always tried to build as much diversity of gender, race, age, disciplinary background, and industry experience into the team as possible. Doing so was the best way to maximize the likelihood that, when a problem was encountered, someone on the team would be able to contribute an outside-the-box insight or solution. Ages on my teams typically ranged from early twenties to mid- to late-sixties; usually I was at the median in the team's age distribution. The outcome? I never had an older team member whose work was unsatisfactory, although I did have some younger team members who were not successful. More importantly, on several occasions I saw older team members contribute crucial solutions or insights based on their experiences from years past. I'm convinced that diversity—of age, gender, race, training, and experience—is essential for optimizing team success in high-tech work.

Among the unemployed tech workers I've known, those over forty are disproportionately represented. Of course, in a "knowledge-based" economy, the trend should be just the opposite: Older tech workers, presumably with the most knowledge, should have the lowest rates of unemployment; younger tech workers, fresh out of school with little real-world experience, should have far higher rates of unemployment. However, the statistics contradict the prediction, and the reason, quite simply, is blatant age discrimination and knee-jerk cost cutting. But don't take my word for it: Look at IBM and other high-tech companies currently fighting age discrimination class action lawsuits. Or ask tech workers over fifty whether they think their age is an advantage or an impediment when interviewing for a job. (For older workers, most job-hunt counselors advise removing any information from a résumé that could suggest or reveal one's age.) Or read Barbara Ehrenreich's *Bait and Switch: The (Futile) Pursuit of the American Dream*, a book about the difficulties middle-aged white-collar workers encounter seeking jobs (2005). In reality, the Old-and-in-the-Way Myth merely puts lipstick on age discrimination.

MYTH #5: THE INDIVIDUALISM MYTH

This final myth says: *Tech workers are individualists who want to control their jobs and lives. In fact, tech workers are loners, almost hermits; managing tech workers has been likened to "herding cats." For this reason, tech workers will never join in a collective action on the job, much less join a union. Thus, unions are obsolete in the twenty-first century, especially for tech workers.*

This myth has two parts: 1) tech workers prefer an "ownership society," and 2) tech workers are loners who will never coalesce into common voice or collective action.

Part 1: Tech workers prefer an "ownership society." In his 2005 State of the Union speech, President Bush alluded to an ownership society that, in part, is built on the argument that workers will do better when they have control over their own benefits—that they will be best served by "owning" their health care and retirement plans. Because tech workers are smart, the argument goes, they would prefer to buy their own pension investments and insurance coverage, believing that they can do a better job at it than government or corporate bureaucrats. In short, tech workers can make it on their own—they don't need a safety net of government or corporate assistance.

Of course, an ownership society shifts the burden of responsibility from corporations onto the backs of workers, who now must become experts in assessing health care providers, comparing alternative medical plans, negotiating premiums and claims, and selecting investments to ensure sufficient returns for retirement. This privatization argument sounded good when the Internet stock bubble was inflating 401(k) plans until workers at companies like Enron and Lucent over-invested in their own companies' stock and lost nearly everything.

Actually, ownership of costs is compatible with Daniel Pink's notion of a "free agent nation" but is not especially comforting to most free agents (2001). Both the Freelancers Union in New York City (www.workingtoday.org) and Working Partnerships in San Francisco (www.wpusa.org) were founded in part to facilitate group health insurance and other benefits for the self-employed. Successful "ownership" of benefits assumes that employees are able to set aside money for the payments required but, as of July 2005, the U.S. savings rate had dropped to zero. In fact, Social Security was established as a mandatory plan precisely because people typically don't save enough for retirement. Of course, if a corporation fails to fund its pensions adequately, the federal government will bail it out (and Wall Street will boost its stock as soon as the bailout is promised). However, if workers fail to fund their "self-owned" pensions, they'll probably end up homeless and hungry, just like many retirees did before Social Security.

Part 2: Tech workers are loners who shun collective action. It's true that tech workers tend to be independent, just as scientists, artists, and top performers in many fields tend to be independent. But "independent" does not mean "antisocial." Most tech workers, especially in the high-tech industries since 1950, are well experienced in working collaboratively on teams in large projects. Project Apollo was not staffed with loners, and neither is the Windows development project at Microsoft. Although a single worker might make an essential insight, implementing that insight as part of a successful project requires cooperation and communication.

The "loner myth" is often used to predict that technical workers will never join unions. It's true that tech workers tend to be more resistant to unions than some other worker groups, probably for two reasons. First, despite overwork and job insecurity, tech workers are fairly well off compared with sweatshop or farm workers, so tech workers feel less motivated to organize. Second, tech workers often grew up in families without a single union member to serve as a model, or in families where the word *union* was anathema. (A friend once observed that we baby boomers grew up when unions meant Jimmy Hoffa, not Samuel Gompers.)

Actually, many professionals are unionized—aerospace engineers, teachers at all levels, nurses, physicians, graduate students, freelance writers, airline pilots, actors on both stage and screen, cinematographers, screen writers, film directors, scientists, and even some computer programmers and systems analysts. In fact, there are so many different unions of professional, scientific, and technical workers that there is an overarching participatory council to coordinate activities and opportunities among them—the Council of Engineers and Scientists Organizations.

Over the past several years, I've had more and more tech workers tell me they've changed their minds about unions: They used to think unions meant bureaucracy and corruption. Now they realize that a revitalized labor movement is essential for creating a collective voice for workers, and for protecting America's increasingly stressed middle class. In fact, over the past few years, several high-tech unions have arisen from grass-roots worker actions aimed at self-preservation. For example, WashTech (CWA Local 37083 in Seattle; www.washtech.org) arose largely because of worker dissatisfaction at Microsoft, and Alliance@IBM (CWA Local 1701 in Endicott, New York; *www.allianceibm.org*) arose because of worker outrage over conversion of pensions to cash balance plans (which unfairly penalized long-time employees). WashTech members helped win the "perma-temps" lawsuit against Microsoft; Alliance@IBM members won a court ruling that reversed the pension conversions. More broadly, tech workers around the country have joined forces in groups like the Programmers Guild (*www.programmersguild.org*) to help pass antioffshoring legislation in several states and to help draft and introduce such legislation in Congress. In short, tech workers don't like getting short-changed any more than anyone else and are perfectly capable of acting collectively to protect their workplace rights and jobs. More often than not, they just need to be shown the way.

For that reason, unions and the labor movement more generally should be actively seeking converts from high-tech fields—people who have "seen the light" of worker solidarity and who are speaking out to help people take back control of their work and their lives. In organizing workers to unite, credibility is crucial. You wouldn't send a computer geek to organize steelworkers. No matter how dedicated, the tech worker wouldn't know about the realities of work in the mill or be able to convince the steelworkers that they should follow his lead. The converse also is true: Unions shouldn't send organizers with no technical/scientific credentials out to organize tech workers. Tech workers won't pay much attention to anyone lacking their particular kind of "street cred."

Union density is lower now than it has been since the 1920s and has been falling for roughly four decades. But the white-collar workforce has been growing steadily and now constitutes the majority of workers in America. Perhaps it's time to focus on organizing technical and professional workers—to target this segment of workers who could bring a spectrum of talents and skills to the struggle—rather than dismissing them as too self-involved to embrace worker solidarity.

We've seen a quarter century of the "cult of the CEO," starting rather benignly with Lee Iacocca but evolving more virulently with the celebrity of Al Dunlop and Jack Welch. The cult-of-CEO atmosphere served as an enabling mechanism that let Chainsaw Al and Neutron Jack (as well as slash-and-burn wannabes like Robert Allen at

AT&T and Rich McGinn at Lucent) wreak havoc on highly talented and dedicated workforces. The suffering of American workers is their legacy, but these trends are reversible. Now is the time to begin celebrating the "cult of the worker"—a culture in which workers of all varieties understand that they share common cause, and that opportunities for America's children and grandchildren can survive only by collective voice and collective action. We need a broad social movement of, by, and for *workers*—exactly what the labor movement started out as a century ago—and we need to get started right away.

The author would like to thank Jim McNeill for his comments on an earlier draft of this chapter.

NOTES

1. This is not to say that these companies are still enlightened—far from it. It only means these companies were enlightened back in the mid-twentieth century, especially compared with companies in general.

2. For a detailed analysis of wages in IT disciplines, see John Mino's December 2005 study *The Bottom of the Pay Scale: Wages for H-1B Computer Programmers,* available at http://www.cis.org/articles/2005/back1305.html, accessed February 22, 2006.

3. Interestingly, after Sputnik 1 was launched in October 1957, the same allegations were cast against American public schools—that we were turning out students who could not compete with the Communist bloc. But back then, a time when the social contract was still honored, America's tech companies committed time, money, resources, and their reputations to improving public education—consider the Westinghouse Talent Search, the GE College Bowl, and the many films produced by Bell Laboratories and distributed to public schools. In fairness, Bill Gates recently announced a talent search and mentoring program among high school students ... except the search will be done in India!

4. A friend who took this route three years ago told me that, in both high schools where he's taught, roughly a quarter of the math/science teaching staff were retooled engineers, programmers, and scientists who had been downsized.

5. Based on confirmed or published announcements, TechsUnite (http://www.techsunite.org) has started tracking the number of tech jobs offshored since 2000. By the end of 2005, TechsUnite had confirmed a total of nearly 470,000 jobs offshored. Given employers' reticence to publicize offshoring of jobs, this total undoubtedly errs conservatively.

6. See Norman Matloff, "On the Need for Reform of the H-1B Non-Immigrant Work Visa in Computer-Related Occupations," available at http://heather.cs.ucdavis.edu/Mich.pdf. This is not to say that American unem-

ployment is the fault of any H-1B/L-1 workers themselves, who are among the most abused and exploited workers in high-tech industries. Rather, it's the fault of corporate managers and executives who seek ever-cheaper labor regardless of the long-term consequences, and of corporate-funded politicians who never met a visa ceiling they didn't want to raise regardless of flooding the labor market and driving wages lower. Despite the cries of "high-tech labor shortage" from Silicon Valley CEOs, the only shortage that ever existed in Silicon Valley was a shortage of Americans with graduate degrees (and often families and mortgages) who were less than thrilled about working for wages not much higher than the federal hourly minimum (especially after factoring in unpaid overtime).

7. For biting rebuttals of the Training-as-Panacea Myth, see Jonathan Tasini's "Workers of The Real World," available at http://www.tompaine.com/print/workers_of_the_real_world.php, accessed February 22, 2006; and see Tasini's "Robert Reich, Are You Listening?" which is available at http://workinglife.typepad.com/daily_blog/2005/08/robert_reich_ar.html, accessed February 22, 2006.

8. Corporations will say that the law requires them to pay guest workers the same as Americans or permanent residents. This is true—the law does require approximate (95 percent) pay parity. Unfortunately, because of loopholes in the law, when an American citizen or permanent resident is replaced by a guest worker on an H-1B or L-1 visa, the guest worker's salary is usually at least 30 percent less than what the job paid before. See John Miano's essay "How To Underpay H-1B Workers," which is available at http://www.programmersguild.org/archives/howtounderpay.htm, accessed April 15, 2006. This means that replacing American tech workers with foreign workers on H-1B/L-1 visas can save significant costs in salaries, not to mention benefits (usually none) and pensions (usually none). Any higher costs that result from importing guest workers—such as loss of corporate knowledge base or bad publicity—are difficult to pinpoint and thus are easy to overlook, especially when corporate executives are pumping up the share price for the sake of their near-term stock options.

2

The Lure of Risk: Surviving and Welcoming Uncertainty in the New Economy

Gina Neff

The new economy made risk and risk taking desirable, and this is one of its enduring social consequences. After decades of growing concern with job security, downsizing, and corporate cutbacks, the lure of risk during the dot-com boom made the lack of security seem like a choice—and a good one at that for those working in the potentially lucrative technology industry. The lure of risk—and by this I mean the idea of *taking* chances—has replaced the fear of uncertainty as the predominant economic rhetoric for the new economy. This shift was subtle, but important as *risk* and *risk taking* in economic life now imply active choices while *uncertainty* connotes economic passivity and forces beyond one's own control. For high-tech firms and start-up Internet companies, skyrocketing stock prices during the late 1990s gave risk the shiny luster of potential wealth for employees, justifying in individual terms both the profits and losses that came with the stock market crash in 2000.

In this chapter, I want to explore the attraction of risk in the new economy and the relationship between risk and the larger, structural economic changes. I argue that people accepted and welcomed risk because taking risks offers a semblance of choice in an era when many things seem out of ordinary employees' control. The subtle discursive distinction between risk and uncertainty serves a powerful function in the new economy, one which has survived all too well after the dot-com crash. What I hope to do in this chapter is to lay out the ways in which the dot-com boom helped to glorify risks—and shifted social and economic uncertainties to individually accounted risks.

Today, security still seems old-fashioned, out of place, and out of date after the employee-driven job hopping and options shopping of the tight labor market for technology workers in the late 1990s. With high skills that were in demand, people working in technology attempted to find their own answer to uncertainty in the U.S. economy by taking risks and chances that they at least felt some modicum of control over. Describing the shift undergoing work in the new economy culture, one headline in 2000 said "risk and reward are key, not job loyalty" (Pham and Stoughton, 2000). High-tech companies seemed to welcome and encourage employees' risk taking as contributing to a more democratic and participatory form of organization, even within a longer trend that devastated a culture of corporate loyalty to employees. Part of this is attributable to the rise of "market populism" with the stock market boom, as Frank (2000) chronicled, but it is, I argue, also part of a larger shift within the U.S. economy.

Job risks and rewards at work are not new, but changes in the organization of work mean that individuals now bear the brunt of the costs of flexibility and are responsible for activities previously thought of as within the purview of companies. Individual workers are less protected by their companies from the economic risks that companies face, and, with the fraying of the social safety nets of union protection and government support, workers are facing these risks alone.

In technology industries, employee risk taking has perhaps been the most visible—and the most attractive—as stock-option millionaires were created by the 1990's lucrative initial public offerings. But there are many other ways that economic risk has increased at work. Within a larger social and political context of flexible work, there is a greater potential for both individual rewards and for individual losses than there is for collective responsibility and group, organizational, or structural causes for either prosperity or poverty.

The notion that risk taking will ultimately be rewarded is a deeply held value within American business culture. Taking risks at work is inexorably linked to the promise of possible wealth, so much so that company founders' stories are rich with the risks that they overcame and outsmarted. Economists have long viewed profits as the returns for taking risks, but as an *ideology* risk taking provides a rationalization for economic stratification that is almost as powerful and complete as the idea of meritocracy: Those who take risks get ahead, and those who don't are left behind. The new economy only cemented this truism.

In the new economy, ordinary employees integrated this acceptance of risk into their own narratives about the choices they made, regardless of the likelihood for their risks to pay out and even in retrospect when it was clear that the risk that they took was a so-called bad one. These narratives were at times almost tautological in nature and often prescriptive: Risks have positive payoffs—thus, people do and should take them. In the words of one New York software engineer whom I interviewed, the stock options that he was given in lieu of salary represented, "just the upside":

> There's really no downside to stock options. They either expire worthless or they become worth something. It's upside potential. If you don't have [stock options] then you're just a worker bee. If you have it, then you're an equity holder in the company and if the company does well, then you'll retire early, I guess.

Rhetorically, the risk represented by stock options—especially those that substituted for part or all of regular salary—had no "downside" in this engineer's assessment of his choices. In fact, at the time of this interview, his stock options *were* worthless, and he had been unemployed for over eight months after his company folded. Even so, for him the idea of employment security with one company had been replaced by his sense of ownership—he was nobody's worker bee—even if that sense of ownership ultimately cost him his job and did not afford him the power that owners have to keep the company running. This engineer welcomed risk in the dot-com era as a way to take control, but clearly he counterpoised financial risk with job security. In his mind, you're either a risk-taking stock-option holder or just a worker bee, and there is little room in between.

Risk taking across the high-tech sector was perceived as being a requirement of working in the industry, not just a lifestyle option. An organizer with Washington Alliance of Technology Workers (Wash-Tech) said, "Most of the workers in this industry think of stability as dead-end," and throughout the boom-time 1990s, taking risks was seen as the only way to get ahead. Highly skilled, highly educated, and mobile workers were able to take on and benefit from these risks and welcomed them as an opportunity for personal challenge and growth. In addition, those who "opt in" for work in this industry (as one employee described the process to me) offered individual-level explanations for and solutions to the problems of risk, regardless of the organizational- and industrial-level uncertainties that they faced. They felt that economic risk taking gave them the power to manage other sorts of risk on their own. One senior producer, who was starting his third job in

less than eighteen months, had the following to say about why he
sought out what he called risky jobs:

> One way I try to offset [risk] is, again, I look at it from an investment
> perspective. If you take the risk, there have to be rewards; otherwise
> why take the risk? So, I think that's one reason I've been able to get
> on the fast-track career, that I've been willing and able to absorb the
> higher risks and, therefore, reap the higher rewards.

When I asked him about what he looked for in companies, he
explained very clearly that his job search was akin to financial
analysis:

> Really, it's what every stock investor would look for in a company.
> Because that's the view I take. Any company that I want to work for I
> should be more than happy to invest money [in] and buy their stock.

He was far from alone in his investor mentality toward work. But this is
part of an approach to jobs creates an ideology that covers more than
the stock market—this approach to economic risk *individualizes* job
security, making security a problem for the individual to solve and
relieving companies, industries, and economic structures of responsibility for workers. Larger social and economic problems become personal
ones. As this senior producer said later in the interview, even having a
job in an economic downturn is a reflection of individual effort and not
luck or circumstance:

> Some people's jobs are more expendable than others, and therefore
> they're at a higher risk. It's really up to you to manage that risk, to
> take precautions, and build up savings, what is psychologically and
> financially [necessary] to handle that [risk]... So, in a way, the wind
> is against everybody in the industry looking for a job right now,
> because the market has taken a downturn, but I've managed well, I
> think.

Even though this interview was conducted after the stock market crash,
he framed risks as choices he had made and things that he had
managed—choices that could pay off like a stock or that he would hold
himself responsible for. His words show just how far attitudes toward
company loyalty have shifted. It is as if the logic of American capitalism has replaced the metaphor of "climbing the ladder" for professional
work with that of jumping aboard a ship that has yet to come in. Risk,
as an idea, supports the ideology that, in the words of the producer
interviewed above, "it is really up to you to manage" the risks of a

market downturn, of losing a job, of becoming technologically obsolete. And the lure of "the upside" of risks supports this individualization among the labor force more generally.

OTHER VIEWS OF RISK AND THE INDIVIDUAL

Within economic literature there is a clear distinction between risk and uncertainty. Frank Knight's (1921) classic formulation, risks are knowable, calculable, and probabilistic. In this sense, someone can hedge against risk and take a risk with knowledge of the possible outcomes, regardless of whether the risk pays out or not. *Uncertainty*, in Knight's theory, is unknowable, like the odds of the complete collapse of the economy. Risk, in Knight's definition, entails careful choice among several options, balancing risks with potential rewards, and balancing safer and riskier options. Knight argued that real entrepreneurial profit came not from managing risks because risks were known, which makes it difficult for one entrepreneur to have an advantage over others or over the market, but from exploiting uncertainties, from figuring out a way to manage the incalculable. But the strategies for managing risk that may work for an investor or in a stock portfolio won't necessarily work for an employee, as we will see next.

Ulrich Beck (1992; 2000) argues that people now see many kinds of risks as their individual responsibility, and indeed this seems to be the case. For Beck, the individualization of risks is reflected in the economic sphere through a shrinking social safety net and the increased exposure of employees to market forces and in the environment through a pervasive exposure to environmental "bads" such as toxins and pollution. Beck predicted the rise of a *risk society* in reaction to the pervasiveness of risk, especially environmental ones. While knowledge about risks and the power to do something may not be equally distributed, the pervasiveness of risks, Beck argued, would lead to increased collective action to prevent and manage risks. But, just as Marx never predicted that capitalism could produce such a large and strong middle class, Beck, writing before the economic downturn that began in 2000, did not foresee how ideologies of economic risk would continue to make risk seem attractive, at least among the U.S. labor force.

Economic and financial risk is not something necessarily natural and innate, but rather constructed in part from the discourses that surround it. As Louise Amoore (2004) has argued, how risk is framed concretely shapes social practices. Management consultants influenced employees' perceptions of the risks of globalization and the actions that the employees took as a consequence of these perceptions. If the risks of globalization seem inevitable, Amoore argues, then there exist a very different range of choices that people feel they can make. While Amoore focused on discussions of globalization, the same holds true for how workers welcomed risk, trumping any discussion of uncertainty or structural change in the U.S. labor market.

In a similar way, discussion of risk in the new economy put a positive spin on the discourse of unforeseen events, one in which people learned to accept that they could profit from uncertainty and should embrace—not fear—the corporate changes underway. Just as managerial doctrines about globalization encouraged employees to be more entrepreneurial, the discourse of risk served a powerful symbolic function to get employees to accept more uncertainty within their jobs and within the economy. The lure of risk—the potential for payout—adds an element of choice, that people are choosing to accept risk rather than merely accepting the consequences of economic structural change.

RISKS ARE WELCOMED, VALUED, AND MANAGED

I'd like to propose this new way of thinking about risk and uncertainty. Risk gives the appearance of choice, power, and individual agency. As such, risk provides a powerful justification for the lack of security in jobs in the new economy. If anything, capitalism's social innovation during the dot-com era was that images of risk made a lack of job security a *good* thing. To those who are surviving the new economy, risk seems to provide a powerful hope of hitting a potential payout. The strong lure of risk combined with its individualization has created a volatile situation in which risk is welcomed and as a means of avoiding the uncertainty facing the collective. This shift of focus away from economic uncertainty and away from collective structures toward individual risk taking, choice, and power hinders the ability to demand and create good stable jobs and workplaces.

Purportedly, the Internet industry attracted people who thought they might get rich quick. However, the majority of the people I interviewed from 1997–2003 sought employment in the industry because it matched their desire for creative, interesting work. People working in the Internet industry reported feeling freer there than they did in other industries—doors were "wide open," as one respondent who had jumped into the industry from book publishing said. The medium itself was "the freest around," as a former documentary filmmaker said of his online job with a corporate media concern. Job openings matched "talents not resumes," in the words of another person interviewed. Growth, at a certain point, was phenomenal, leading many people in the industry to believe that while they might lose a job with one company, they would never "lose all the jobs" in the industry. To many working in the Internet industry before the crash, work in the technology field wasn't risky, but rather seemed a sure thing. The case of the Internet industry exemplifies the extremes of risk taking by employees, with the industry's rapid rise and fall along and with a particularly wide range of outcomes, from long-term unemployment to stock-option riches over a relatively short amount of time. This is a clear case of the attraction to and the effects of risk taking at work, and this clarity helps to reveal the social forces that shape those risks.

Risks Are Welcomed

How did employees come to see taking risks as vital to their financial well-being, their continued job prospects, or their reputation within a field? As a group, workers in the Internet industry were considered the heroes of the new economy because of their enviable high-end professional services and technical jobs created by innovation and ingenuity. They talked about their choices, though, with regret and bravado, naïveté and cold calculation, passion and detachment. For me, what makes their stories so compelling is not that they represent an unusual entrepreneurial drive, but rather the opposite. People working in the Internet industry built the foundation for a new industry and a new medium with their relatively ordinary, everyday economic choices. And those choices and the rhetoric of risk that justifies them have come to provide symbolic and ideological support for uncertain work.

Risk created a sense of choice, oftentimes false, that pervaded tech workers' narratives about their careers. For people who worked in Internet start-up companies, the risks they took represented, in their own words, their hopes and dreams and "only the upside" in the words of the software engineer. But these attitudes and rhetoric about being one's own boss and having control over one's company did not emerge by chance or in a vacuum. The social context for this frenzy and the rush to boldly take risks occurred in the midst of major structural change from an economy in which 30 percent of the workforce was unionized to a workforce widely accepting of at-will employment. The attitudes toward risk that we saw during the dot-com boom happened in the context of the shift from regular, full-time employment toward a growing percentage of the American workforce in "nonstandard" jobs, many lacking health insurance, pensions, and training. Risk presented a choice when jobs were shifting from the security of regular employment to people flexibly hired to meet demand only when times were good.

For example, almost a third of the American workforce now works outside the standard, full-time employment arrangement and that includes both low-paid, part-time workers and high-skilled independent contractors. As a group, nonstandard workers are less likely to have health insurance or a retirement plan and more likely to be poor. What these workers also have in common, despite their differences in skill and pay, is that they bear more fully the brunt of economic insecurity faced by companies. Company flexibility is gained at the expense of employment security for workers in nonstandard arrangements and in volatile industries and sectors like technology.

The lure of risk becomes a powerful mechanism pulling people to think of themselves—not their companies, not their industries, and not their economies—as solely responsible for their employment. This attitude shifts social uncertainty and insecurity to individual calculable risk—risk with the potential for enormous payout according to the myths of the new economy. The lure of risk, like a siren's song, traps workers on the island of uncertainty and weakens their social safety net.

Risks Are Values

Within the Internet industry, economic risks and personal hopes were so often intertwined that risk taking was a passionate, not calculated exercise. To take risks was to believe in dreams, dreams within reach, dreams attainable through work. This was easy to contemplate when the Internet stock prices were at their dizzying heights and risks within the new economy seemed close to sure things. What struck me in interviews was not so much how people talked of their work as potentially making them rich, but rather how risky work was personally challenging. In the new economy, a person could talk about risks in the same breath as hopes and dreams—not the language of danger or impurity that risk connotes when thinking about health risks or environmental risks and certainly not the calculative measures one associates with financial accounting.

One company founder who had just closed his company described risks as values, echoing what several other respondents told me:

On a personal level, the risk is not to lose a job. Finding a job is not hard. . . . You could put those people into any environment and they would thrive. So, I don't think the risk is from job security standpoint. I think the risk is emotional. You invest a ton of emotion into a venture, into the people, into the product, into the future that when it doesn't happen you risk being emotionally crushed. To me, that is the bigger risk.

Even people who lost their jobs with start-up firms insist in interviews that they, in the words of one producer, "will not go back to nine-to-five." Being in work environments without standardized rules and regulations leads to a feeling of "making the company" and of being "listened to" as well as to a "freedom from all the b.s. bureaucracy." Part of the attraction of this work is that, through taking a risk with their companies, workers feel that they are deeply invested in them.

These cultural values of risk should be embraced by those who try to organize collective approaches for addressing economic insecurity. This cathexis that professional employees now have to their companies, their industries, and the risks associated with both presents a serious challenge for organizers trapped in the old industrial mind-set of workers versus management.

Risks Are Managed

People seek to manage their risks and think that they are capable of doing so. Job hopping, outside consulting and professional work, and risk taking are all part of the strategies high-tech workers use to guard against the uncertainty of their industry. Some people I interviewed defined the risks they took in terms of creativity—that working in the Internet industry meant that they faced "risks that they would make crappy products." Although they did not use financial terms in talking about risk, they did connect these creative risks to their chances of getting good jobs in the future. Kanter calls this a move from employment security to employability security and argues that the high-tech industries provide an unfortunate model of this practice for the rest of the economy: "Instead of counting on long-term employment with a single firm, they increasingly depend on their employability by many firms. The shift from employment security to employability security implies a fundamental change in what people should expect from their employers—and how employers should think about their interests and obligations" (Kanter 1995).

Managing risks also keeps the focus on individual blame, deflecting anger directed at companies. One unemployed junior producer dismissed his former colleagues who had bought into the new economy dream:

> So, I feel no sympathy whatsoever for people who lost however much money in stock options because that was their own naïveté to be blind to that and to really think that it [stock option wealth] was going to be a salary.

For him, even believing in the potential of stock options was naive.

EMPLOYEE RISK IS AN INVESTMENT IN COMPANIES

Risk also creates mechanisms and language for employees to buy into the goals of their companies. Long gone are the days where there was a disconnect between the interests of stockholders and the interests of employees. The discourse of risk gives potent rhetorical power to the tight alliance of employees' interests with owners' interests. Risk becomes a way that entrepreneurial values replace job security, and risk links employees' desires with the company's directions. Many of those I interviewed articulated to some degree a personal sense of "owner-ship" in their employing companies and in the projects they complete for them. Being in companies with less middle management and administrative support gives them a feeling of more autonomy in their work and, ironically, greater sense of attachment to the very companies that have eliminated loyalty within the organizational culture.

People invest in their companies in many different ways. They spend time marketing the firm in their off-hours, promoting products and services as a way to support firms' goals and generate new demand. Workers invest social capital through the connections they make at after-hours business networking events, creating links to people in the field who may provide critical resources for their compa-nies. Employee retirement funds may be invested in company stock, and in new companies there are often tacit or explicit agreements to defer some or all compensation in exchange for potentially lucrative options to buy company stock in the future.

Flexible, short-term, project-based workplaces put more of the responsibility for getting and keeping work on employees themselves. Added to even quicker turnaround times on the development of computer applications, this means that employees are expected, in the words of one programmer, to "hit the ground running" with continually updated skills, including new programming languages and familiarity with new technologies. Heightened job insecurity means workers are increasingly exposed to cyclical economic risk, and flexible workplaces have placed more managerial responsibility onto employees. As one cofounder of a news Web site put it, "I don't want someone who's going to ask, 'What's my job?' I need someone who's going to figure out that on their own." This "individualization of the labor process," as Manuel Castells (1996) termed it, aims at "decentralizing management, individualizing work, and customizing markets, thereby segmenting work and fragmenting societies."

More than 40 percent of those employed by New York Internet companies in 1999 got some form of stock options or deferred income as part of their compensation package (see Batt et al., 2001). While to some extent workers have always been exposed to the vagaries of the market, pay tied directly to stock performance is a relatively recent trend that began with shareholders' trying to hold CEOs of larger companies responsible for shareholder value. Now, with technology companies, this trend is trickling down the company ladder. What began as a movement toward economic incentives for CEOs to keep share prices high has been used by companies as partial compensation for workers who have little direct effect on share price, and there is evidence that cash-strapped start-ups used stock options in lieu of at least part of workers' salaries.

Nonstandard work arrangements also place cyclical economic pressures more squarely on the contractors, temporary employees, and freelancers who do projects for a company. These nonstandard work arrangements allow firms to hire at a higher hourly base salary in times of tight labor markets without permanently raising salary levels for the rest of their employees and without providing for the stability of longer-term employment. Without being paid for full-time work, employees must provide for the costs of their own training and spend the time and costs associated with looking for new work. Workers in the New York new media industry spent on average almost twenty hours/week in just "staying alive" through unpaid time for education and looking for new work (Batt et al., 2001). Additional pressures of off-hours socializing and networking for job prospects, business development contacts, and company marketing mean that workers within the industry are faced with work-related tasks that are unpaid.

One way that people invest in their companies is through the routine ways that they carve a path through their careers. Consider the years of industry-specific knowledge and experience gathered over the course of a career. The more specific the preparation for a job, the more closely that skill set is tied to the economic performance of a particular company or industry. Some fields, especially creative industries, require years of unpaid training and internships or work "on spec" before payment can begin. The less likely this experience translates outside the company or industry, the less fungible an employee's investment is. Those who worked in the Internet industry saw demand dry up for their specialized skills, from programming to project management. They often acquired on their own the skills that the industry needed and figured out how to retool those skills once they were no longer in great demand. Socializing at after-hours networking events—such as parties to launch new Web sites or promote companies—built the dense networks that are critical to companies in an innovative industry, as Saxenian (1994) has shown (see also Neff, 2005). After the dot-com crash, however, many people within the industry found their investment of hundreds of hours of time in building those social networks useless for helping them get a job.

Rather than producing dot-com millionaires, the New York industry in 1999 had a median salary of $42,600, which was less than the median in magazine or book publishing. What is striking is the percentage of nonstandard work arrangements in the industry. At its height in early 2000, the New York City new media industry had more than 138,000 jobs—more than the area television, magazine, and book publishing industries combined, and just under the number of workers in brokerage and trading firms in New York (NYNMA, 1997; NYNMA and PriceWaterhouseCoopers, 2000). Yet, over a quarter of those jobs (33,600) were part-time or temporary, and even through the most rapid period of growth for the industry, part-time and freelance jobs were growing more rapidly than full-time employment, even for highly skilled workers at the height of an economic boom. This does not bode well for the U.S. economy's ability to produce good, stable jobs.

THE NEW ENTREPRENEURIAL LABOR

I argue that the fundamental shift in the relationship between firms and employees in the United States gave rise to the entrepreneurial spirit of the dot-com era. Workers' rush to join in the dot-com boom was born, in part, out of a growing necessity to shoulder uncertainty. The very forces that reduced workers' job security encouraged them to align even more closely with their companies through seeking out profit-sharing plans and identifying with the products and services being produced. The cultural changes accompanying larger economic trends made risk seem manageable and even desirable at times, as attested by the attitudes of most of my respondents.

While workers in other sectors of the U.S. labor force may not embrace the high degree of entrepreneurial behavior as dot-commers did, they will come to accept uncertainty within the economy if high-tech workers expectations are any guide. Vicki Smith argues that this is already starting to occur as "uncertainty and unpredictability have diffused into a broad range of postindustrial workplaces, service and production alike" (2001, 7). The widespread acceptance of economic uncertainty—and the lure of risk for workers—poses a challenge for the labor movement and progressives to counter. Companies and workers at the top of the pyramid may indeed be able to convert uncertainty into opportunities for wealth and advancement; the increasing numbers of workers in low-end service jobs and temporary positions without the security of benefits or continued employment will not be as lucky. As income inequality increases, entrepreneurialism will continue to be a contributing factor in maintaining this inequality. Annette Bernhardt and her coauthors (2001) found that for most workers, including college graduates, wages have remained stagnant or have fallen compared with those of a generation prior, and most workers suffer loss of wages from flexible work and job turnover.

Entrepreneurialism among professional workers further erodes the labor movement's ability to cast structural problems in collective rather than individual terms. The glories of taking risk now ideologically supports increased uncertainty, just as rags-to-riches stories and the belief in educational meritocracy have bolstered stratification in other economic eras. If the labor movement fails to respond to the change in the attraction of risk taking, then workers will continue to adapt to and expect worsening job conditions. For less highly skilled workers, this outcome means an ever-greater exposure to the cyclical pressures of the economy and less political support for collective solutions.

What is historically significant in this case is that workers with bargaining power exchanged security for risk. Workers who by dint of their skills and the demand for those skills should have been able to secure long-term, stable employment instead *sought* risky work. The lure of risk foisted them into a situation of continuing uncertainty. But, unfortunately, employees now understand and accept a lack of job security as their own choice, and continued employability as their own responsibility.

Simple dismissals of high-tech workers as libertarian and anti-union do not consider these massive social and cultural transformations. Attempts to build collective solutions for a better economy must take into account the ideological attraction of risk. Those looking to organize in the new economy should think about the ways that autonomy, creativity and values could be maintained alongside increased job security. This is more than just developing the right lingo—it is about tapping into the needs and approaches that will work within high-tech culture, and, increasingly, among the U.S. labor force. Are there ways that increased security can support entrepreneurial behavior? Could an organization provide for benefits while explicitly encouraging contracting and supporting freelancing work? How can the blurred line between management and employee be addressed? Answers to these questions will be crucial for organizing new collective approaches to uncertainty.

3

The New Economy as History

Simon Head

What exactly is "new" about the contemporary American economy, and why do American workers at almost all levels have to be concerned about surviving this newness, whatever it might be? In this chapter I want to argue that what is both new and alarming about the U.S. economy is something which in a sense is not new at all, but is deeply embedded in the economic and business history of the United States, stretching back to the middle of the nineteen century and even beyond. Strictly speaking this continuity with the past embraces two parallel phenomena, closely entwined. The first of these is mass production, the manufacture of goods in very large quantities and at very high speeds that, in Henry Ford's famous words, focuses upon the manufacturing process: "power, speed, accuracy, economy, system, continuity and speed."[1]

The second is scientific management, the practice pioneered a century ago by Frederick Winslow Taylor, which governs the role of labor in mass production and brings to the work regimes of the factory floor the speed and standardization characteristic of the manufacturing process itself. The relationship between mass production and scientific management found concrete expression in the relationship between the machine shop and the assembly line in Henry Ford's early Detroit plants, where the techniques of advanced mass production were first developed from 1913 onward. In the machine shop fully automatic machines turned out the components of the Model T Ford according to strict hourly quotas and with the machines executing an identical sequence of movements to produce each part. On the assembly line workers put together these components according to equally strict hourly quotas and following a sequence of bodily movements equally repetitive and controlled.

Mass production and scientific management have therefore been around for a long time, but what is new—and alarmingly new—is how the information technology (IT) revolution of the past decade or so has renewed both practices, strengthening their hold on manufacturing industries where they have been established for a century, but also extending their grasp to leading sectors of the service economy where their hold, until now, has been tenuous. This reindustrialization of the U.S. economy is what the American workers must be concerned about surviving because it devalues their skills, erodes their job security, and undermines their bargaining power in the workplace. As a result their real wages have been stagnant for the past fifteen years, and a huge gap has opened up between the efficiency of American workers, measured by the growth of labor productivity, and their rewards, measured by the growth of real wages.

In arguing my thesis I don't want to embark upon a history of American business in the twentieth century, tracing decade by decade the continuities between these century-old practices and practices dominant in today's economy. What I would rather do is to concentrate on the business history of the 1980s and 1990s, and by doing so show how the IT revolution, which really got going in the mid-1990s, was preceded by two major developments that renewed this American industrialism and ensured that its practices were dominant in shaping the work practices of the new, IT-intensive economy that began to emerge right at the end of the twentieth century.

The first of these developments was the introduction in the United States in the early 1980s of the advanced manufacturing methods pioneered by the Japanese automobile industry, and particularly by its leading producer, Toyota. These methods gave the Japanese auto manufacturers a commanding lead in productivity over the Detroit Big Three of GM, Ford, and Chrysler (now DaimlerChrysler), and contributed to the trio's spectacular loss of U.S. market share in the early 1980s. In its 1993 study "Manufacturing Productivity," the McKinsey Global Institute wrote that "all of the characteristics of the Japanese management system . . . are epitomized by Toyota, which serves as a model of labor productivity both inside and outside Japan, for the automotive as well as other industries" (McKinsey Global Institute, 1993, 8).

Among American economists, business consultants, and business academics, it was widely assumed that the Toyota system represented a definitive break with the past American practices of mass production and scientific management. In 1989 the MIT Commission on Industrial Productivity wrote of "new factors of workplace organization" pioneered by the Japanese, which "were different in almost every feature from Detroit's mass production system" and required "the creation of a highly skilled work force." In 1990 another influential commission on U.S. manufacturing, headed by Bill Clinton's future health care czar, Ira Magaziner, wrote of how this new high performance workplace would give "front line workers more responsibility" as "management layers disappear" and workers "assume responsibility for many of the tasks" hitherto performed by management (Dertouzos et al., 1989:48; National Center on Education and the Economy, 1990, 2).

But when these analyses are set alongside the record of what really happened, I am reminded of the title of Barry Bluestone's and the late Bennett Harrison's important and influential book *The Great U-Turn* (1988), one of the first to describe the consequences of corporate restructuring, downsizing, and outsourcing for working Americans. In 2003 I wrote a book along the same lines and I thought of calling it *The Great Wrong Turn*, not only as a tribute to Bluestone and Harrison, but also as a way of drawing attention to the spectacular errors in the prevailing view of the Toyota system. These errors not only gave rise to a false view of what happened to U.S. manufacturing in the 1980s, but also laid the groundwork for an equally spectacular misinterpretation of what happened to the U.S. service economy when the digital revolution really got going in the mid-1990s.

As far as my book was concerned, my publisher persuaded me to settle for *The New Ruthless Economy* (2003), but the Great Wrong Turn lives on, and to get just a preliminary sense of the damage it has caused we need to go back to its original misinterpretation of the Toyota system. When I began looking at Japanese automobile plants in the early 1990s, what I saw seemed to be a cleaner and no doubt less noisy version of the scene that the journalist Horace Arnold had described eighty years before when he visited Ford's Highland Park plant.

Workers crowded around the cars as they moved along the line. They performed the same simple tasks over and over again, and there was a palpable sense of stress as they struggled to get their tasks done within the amount of time it took for the vehicle to pass through their segment of the line. The old alliance of mass production and scientific management seemed to be alive and well, and proof that this was indeed so came from an unlikely source, the memoirs of one of the chief architects of the Toyota system, the Japanese engineer Shigeo Shingo.

Shingo includes a brief description of his career in *A Revolution in Manufacturing*, his book on the Toyota system and his role in its creation. Shingo refers to the moment in 1931 when he read Frederick

Winslow Taylor's *Principles of Scientific Management* and "decided to make the study and practice of scientific management his life's work" (Shingo, 1985, 343). These are mere words but it becomes clear from the very first page of *A Revolution in Manufacturing* that Shingo, who died in 1990, was a true disciple of Taylor and who made sure that the Toyota system fully embodied the principles of scientific management.

Shingo's *A Revolution in Manufacturing* is particularly damaging to the MIT thesis because the book addresses what had always been thought of as among the most complex and skill-intensive tasks performed in automobile manufacturing, the reconfiguration of machine tools so that a single machine could be used to turn out components of varying sizes that belong to a variety of car models. In his book Shingo also deals with a wide variety of setup operations involving every kind of machine and devoted to every kind of product—cameras and televisions as well as automobiles. Shingo begins his discussion of machine setup by observing that "it is generally and erroneously believed that the most effective policies for dealing with set-ups address the problems in terms of skill." Few companies, Shingo continues, "have implemented strategies that lower the skill level required by the set-up itself" (Shingo, 1985, 14). To achieve this de-skilling, managers had to conduct a "detailed analysis of each elemental operation."

In words that could have been taken directly from Taylor's *Principles of Scientific Management*, Shingo describes how managers must reduce work to its most basic elements "for example, clamping, centering, dimensioning, expelling, grasping and maintaining loads." Once managers have worked out the most efficient way to perform each subjob, these jobs must then be joined so that every worker would henceforth perform the whole job exactly as prescribed by management. In Shingo's words, "operating conditions are fully regulated in advance" so that there is no longer any place for the exercise of employee judgment and skill, and even "unskilled workers" can do the job "since the operations are simple ones" (Shingo, 1985, 42, 53–55, 116).

I have described the Taylorist ancestry of the Toyota system in some detail not only because it gives chapter and verse for the errors of the Great Wrong Turn, but also because it provides compelling evidence of the resilience of mass production and scientific management. Here are practices dating from the Gilded Age that are still going strong in the digital economy of the new millennium. The coming to America of these renewed versions of mass production and scientific management have had a profound influence on the U.S. automobile industry where the Detroit Big Three have adopted these methods wholesale and have narrowed, though never entirely closed, the productivity gap sepa-rating them from their Japanese competitors.

There have also been American manufacturers outside the auto industry who have successful adapted the Toyota system to their own industry, notably Dell in computers and GE in the manufacture of household goods such as refrigerators and washing machines. In taking advantage of Japanese methods, most American companies enjoy an advantage denied to their European competitors. Since the Toyota system itself is of American origin, the operating methods of leading American manufacturers such as Ford and GM are already close cousins of their Japanese competitors. The task facing the American manufacturers therefore has been to adapt and improve systems they already had and not rebuild their systems from scratch.

* * *

The Toyota system may have brought about a revolution in U.S. manufacturing, but over 80 percent of Americans now work in service industries, and the great IT explosion of the 1990s was concen-trated overwhelmingly in the service economy. One reason why economists have been so ready to amputate the contemporary U.S. economy from its industrial past is because they have assumed that the practices of the old manufacturing economy have no place in the more genteel, white-collar world of the office, and particularly in those offices digitally wired from top to bottom. But this gentrification of the service economy overlooks the existence within services of huge, commanding sectors such as retail, wholesale, and distribution whose operations are highly susceptible to the methods of mass production and scientific management, and where increases in productivity take place much as they do on the factory floor.

I call these *industrialized services*, and they are the sectors where Wal-Mart reigns supreme. According to the McKinsey Global Institute's 2001 productivity study, between 1995 and 2000 half of the productivity growth of the entire U.S. economy took place in two sec-tors, wholesale and retail, where Wal-Mart "caused the bulk of the pro-ductivity acceleration through ongoing managerial innovation that in-creased competition intensity and drove the diffusion of best practice."[2] Wal-Mart's superior efficiency is reflected in the productivity lead it has enjoyed over its direct competitors in the category of "general mer-chandise": a lead of 44 percent in 1987, 48 percent in 1995, and still 41

percent in 1999, even as competitors began to copy Wal-Mart's strategies.[3]

The great majority of Wal-Mart's 1.2 million U.S. employees
have ceased to be service employees in any meaningful sense, and
instead represent a perverse triumph of industrialization. They are
workers on a retail assembly line who, like their counterparts on the
factory floor, are under constant pressure to work faster and speed up
the movement of goods from the unloading dock to the checkout
counter. Wal-Mart's "associates" are therefore under relentless pressure
to unload the merchandise faster at the dock, move that merchandise
faster from dock to shop floor, place it on the shelves more quickly,
and process the customer faster through the checkout counter. As on
any assembly line, mangers can exploit IT's prodigious powers of
monitoring and control to ensure that employees are meeting their
production targets, and managers can then raise these targets so that
employees have to work even faster.

* * *

Taken together, the Toyota revolution in manufacturing and
the Wal-Mart revolution in retail and distribution brought about a dramatic renewal of American industrialism at a time when, at least in
manufacturing, the home-grown version was showing its age. Equally
important was the timing of this renaissance. It happened in the 1980s
and early 1990s and so set the scene for the great explosion of IT
investment of the mid- and late-1990s. Economists have measured this
explosion by looking at the statistics for U.S. growth, productivity, and
employment, which, from the mid-1990s onward, did begin to perform
significantly better than they had for the preceding twenty-five years.

But there is another way of viewing the digital revolution, and
this requires us to look beyond the conventional criteria of economic
performance and to bring in a social, psychological, and also ethical
analysis. Once we have done this, we can then bring together the two
kinds of evidence and show how the noneconomic data can also illumi-
nate aspects of the economic data as well. So far I have only discussed
those service industries especially susceptible to industrialization, but
there is a whole other world of services, including health care and
customer service, where there is an irreducible human element linking
producers and consumers, and which resists industrialization in the
form of automated, expert systems. I'll call these *core services*.

It is a measure of how strongly this industrial tide was running in the early 1990s that, for the rest of the decade, executives, consultants, and software engineers embarked upon a hugely ambitious project to apply the practices of mass production and scientific management to core services. But there are two fundamental differences between this variant of industrialization and the industrialization of the Wal-Mart economy. In wholesale, retail, and distribution, executives and reengineers were mostly intent on controlling the bodily movements of workers, just as a century ago Ford and Taylor controlled the bodily movements of workers on the line at Ford's Detroit plants.

But with the industrialization of core services, today's scientific managers are trying to control the minds, and not just the bodies, of their white-collar employees, and it is this qualitative escalation of control that brings the social and ethical dimension to the fore. Moreover, with these attempts to manipulate and control the minds of employees, the practice of scientific management reaches beyond the proletarian ghetto of Wal-Mart "associates" and Ford assemblyline workers, and invades the gated, professional world of middle managers, administrators, and, most notoriously, physicians. Nowhere has the conflict between the managerial and the social been more acute than in the fraught relationship of physicians and managers within "Managed Care."

Managed Care came to dominate U.S. health care in the mid- to late-1980s when large employers such as GM started looking for ways to reverse the double-digit increases in health care costs that had been gathering pace since the mid-1960s. Managed care promised to achieve this by introducing the speed and efficiency of the assembly line to the treatment of sick patients—promising faster medical output with lower costs, lower prices per unit of output, and higher profits earned on increased market share and high volumes of sales. This language of mass production dominates the textbooks of managed care.

In its *Changing Health Care*, Andersen Consulting (now Accenture) speaks of "processes, reengineered to reflect the longitudinal maintenance of health—physical, mental, and spiritual" and of the "step by step performance measures that [trace] the process from the time the consumer placed the initial call to the checkout"—when the checkout in question is from a hospital, not a supermarket (Anderson, 1997, 55, 127). Ernst and Young (1996, 44) write of "the reengineering of existing [health care] processes" as a "multi-step effort" that involves "building a business case, documenting existing processes with cycle times and volumes, [and] identifying opportunities for improvement."

What do mass production and scientific management look like in a medical context? Surprisingly similar to how they look on the factory floor. Donald Berwick and Chuck Kilo, noted experts in health care efficiency and pioneers of ID-COP, or the Idealized Design of Clinical Office Practice, even cite the Toyota system as a model for hospitals and clinics to follow. According to Berwick, "Tenets of lean production that emanated from Toyota are central to the ID-COP design." Berwick lauds Taiichi Ohno, with Shigeo Shingo, one of the founders of the Toyota system, as a "ferocious foe of wasted human effort" (Anon., 1999, 66).

In an ID-COP clinic, patients must be processed along the line as fast as possible. In Kilo's words, "We strive to create offices that function at unprecedented levels of ambulatory performance." Limiting the amount of time patients actually spend with physicians is therefore central to the practice of medical speedup. In his seminal work on medical education, *Time to Heal*, Dr Kenneth Ludmerer cites some of the leading statistics of U.S. "clinical productivity." In the late 1980s many physicians felt that seeing thirty patients a day was "pushing the limit," but by the mid-1990s it was common for physicians to see twenty-five to thirty patients a day, and there were stories about "primary care physicians treating as many as [seventy] patients a day" (Ludmerer, 1999, 384).

Medical reengineers have spent a lot of time trying to figure out how best to measure the length of "doctor-patient interactions" so that the reengineers can then set about speeding them up. In her book *Strategies for Integrated Health Care*, the managed care consultant Jane Metzger writes how "capturing the start and end times of the clinical interaction is critical to managing the patient flow." In Metzger's view the most natural way to capture information on "clinician-patient interaction time" is as a "by-product of the provider (i.e., doctor) signing on to, and then signing off from a patient care system in the exam room." By "patient care system" Metzger means a computer terminal (Drazen and Metzger, 1999, 92).

Also central to this medical speedup has been the standardization of treatment, so that the expensive and time-consuming procedure of shaping treatment to the special needs of particular patients can be dispensed with. The physician who has given one of the clearest accounts of this standardized medicine is Edward Wagner of the MacColl Institute for Healthcare Innovation in Seattle, Washington. Wagner distinguishes between what he calls "usual" and planned" medicine. The physicians of usual medicine are taught that "patients are unique, their problems are idiosyncratic, and good care is highly individualized." "Planned medicine" by contrast requires "an intellectual leap for the doctor from constantly thinking and worrying about specific patients, to considering all patients with specific clinical features or needs and how these needs might be met." The task of establishing how patients with "specific clinical features" should be treated is not performed by physicians but by information systems. Managed care companies such as Aetna, Oxford, and Humana maintain vast patient databases, and Wagner explains how these can assume more and more of the responsibility for medical decision making (see Voelker, 1994).

The larger the company's patient database, the more elaborate the segmentation of the patient population that can be worked out by software systems attached to the data. With the establishment of these patient groupings, computer algorithms are used to identify a "special set of services" or protocols that distinguish the "clinically significant subgroups" and that each subgroup must receive. "Usual medical care," Wagner comments, "generally does not operate by protocol," and "many practitioners resent the notion that care should be homogenized" (quoted in Voelker, 1994).

Wagner clearly regards these "usual practitioners" as medical Luddites, and we can see why he believes that physicians practicing planned medicine should "stop worrying about specific patients" and start considering patients with specific clinical features. Wagner's philosophy reaches deep into the territory of scientific management, and for the physicians of managed care, as for Shingo's machine shop workers at Toyota, "operating conditions" are as much as possible "regulated in advance" so that the scope for the exercise of judgment and skill is narrowed (quoted in Voelker, 1994).

Once the physician has slotted the patient into a particular sub-group, he has already made his most important decision, because the patient's further treatment has already been decided upon. The physician then becomes a link in the chain of medical process. Medical reengineers welcome this industrialization of medicine:

> There is no more physician/patient relationship, at least not in the one-on-one sense. Patient care is now a team concept in which a simple sore throat can involve a dozen people. . . . The art of administering this process and ensuring that the patient has a positive experience is almost as delicate as providing patient care (Schumacher, 1999, 80).

The predicament of the physician under "managed care" reveals how practices that have been embedded in manufacturing for over a century have not only crossed over and colonized a core service industry such as health care, but have reached far up the occupation hierarchy to embrace the work of its most esteemed and highly skilled professional, the physician. This white-collar industrialization is made possible by automated management systems know collectively as Enterprise Resource Planning, or ERP. A strong case can be made that the products of the world leader in ERP, the German software maker SAP, have had a greater impact on the lives of working Americans than those of any other information technology company, Microsoft, Intel, and IBM included. Yet outside the highly specialized world of corporate computing, SAP is almost totally unknown, as indeed is the whole phenomenon of ERP.

The most elaborate ERP systems embody the principle that business processes at all levels, from the hiring of salesmen to the execution of strategic plans, all can be made to work with the efficiency of the mass production plant. ERP systems therefore extend the disciplines of industrialization well beyond the shop floor to the whole strata of professional, white-collar work including, as we have seen, the work of the physician. At the heart of these systems is the scientific manager's mania for quantification and control, which subjects lower-level managers as well as frontline workers to a degree of monitoring that erodes their freedom of action, and turns them into the oversupervised cogs of an administrative machine.

The contemporary scientific manager's search for quantification can border on the absurd. At one hospital that had installed an ERP system, management proposed that the reputation of the doctors attached to the hospital should be measured by calculating the average distance patients were prepared to travel to consult with the doctor in question. The doctor's reputation would then be ranked according to whether the average distance traveled by patients measured up to a target distance set by management.[4] The doctors were able to beat back this particularly folly, but SAP's product manuals are full of examples of quantification run wild.

In the proliferation of what it calls "Key Performance Indicators," or KPIs, SAP relies heavily on a methodology known as the Balanced Scorecard. SAP concedes the essentially authoritarian, top-down character of the Balanced Scorecard regime: It is the "linchpin between change initiated by a small number of people at the top and executed by a large number of people at the bottom."[5] A central feature of the Balanced Scorecard is that it goes beyond such conventional indicators of business performance as sales, cash flow, and profitability, and tries to quantify the business behavior of employees by setting numbered targets for its improvement.

Employees must meet with their supervisors and submit to a Personal Development Plan, which will then set out the quantitative targets the employees must attain of they are to pass muster as communicators, delegators, forward thinkers, risk and initiative takers, and more generally as "generators of results." An employee proves that he or she is an "initiative taker" by identifying "new approaches" that will increase the company's market share by 8 percent. To qualify as a "risk taker," he or she must "grow sales by 14 [percent] instead of a target 8 [percent]"; and to be a "generator of results," he or she must "work with Manager to set more realistic goals and meet 100 [percent] of them."[6]

Once the Key Performance Indicators are up and running, senior managers can check on the performance of employees as often as they want. The information-gathering powers of ERP systems allow "corporate strategists [to] monitor performance continuously using feedback from the business execution systems."[7] SAP's "Management Cockpit" is the supreme embodiment of this drive for executive omniscience. The cockpit can take the form of a conference room whose four walls are covered with illuminated charts showing every conceivable aspect of corporate performance. Each wall contains six rectangles, with each rectangle containing six charts, making a total of 36 charts per wall, and 144 for the whole cockpit.

Alternatively, the charts can be downloaded to the CEO's personal computer so that he can take the cockpit with him wherever he goes. Whether in Cairo, Illinois, or Cairo, Egypt, the CEO can monitor the minute-by-minute activities of plants, offices, machines, assembly lines, managers, groups of employees, and even single employees. He can examine the key performance indicators for the whole business and then "drill down" to monitor the performance of even the remotest outposts of his corporate empire. With the coming of these Orwellian systems, we need to reach beyond the language of economics and business and find a vocabulary equal to the task of describing what is going on.

In his book *Discipline and Punish: The Birth of the Prison* (1979), the great French historian, sociologist, and philosopher Michel Foucault develops the concept of "panoptic power," and its embodiment in an institution, the panopticon. As the title of Foucault's book suggests, the archetypal panopticon is a prison, and Foucault's definition of panoptic power is shot through with the vocabulary of punishment. As originally conceived by the nineteenth-century philosopher of utilitarianism, Jeremy Bentham, the panoptic prison was to be a "twelve sided polygon formed in iron and sheathed in glass" in order to create the effect of what Bentham called "universal transparency" (quoted in Zuboff, 1988, 320).

In the panoptic prison a central tower with wide windows "opened onto the inner wall of the surrounding polygonal structure, which itself was divided into narrow cells extending across the width of the building." Each cell had a "window on both the inner and outer walls," allowing light to cross the cell, thus illuminating "all the inhabitants to an observer in the central tower, while the observer could not be seen from any one of the cells." The major effect of the panopticon, Foucault writes, is to "induce on the inmate a state of conscious and permanent visibility that assured the automatic functioning of power" (quoted in Zuboff, 1988, 321).

For power to be exercised in this automatic way, the inmate does not have to believe that he is under constant observation, but only that the possibility of his being under observation is constantly present. In her seminal work *In The Age of the Smart Machine* (1988), Shoshana Zuboff shows how Foucault's analysis and language can easily be transferred to the nonpenal setting of the business enterprise. The attainment of panoptic power has been a goal of scientific managers ever since Frederick Winslow Taylor set up his bureaucracy of "functional foremen" at the end of the nineteenth century.

But it is only with the coming of ERP systems and their embodiment in networks of computers that panoptic power has become a real and overwhelming presence in the service economy, as it has long been in manufacturing. The empowered computer that confronts the office employee at the beginning of every working day is nothing less than Foucault's "tall outline of the central tower from which he"— the employee—"is being spied upon." Once the computer is up and running, so too is the possibility of managerial monitoring and control, though at any given moment the employee cannot know whether this power is actually being exercised. Foucault provides an acute analysis of the state of mind of those who are the objects of panoptic power:

> He who is subjected to a field of visibility, and who knows it, assumes responsibilities for the constraints of power; he makes them play spontaneously upon himself; he inscribes in himself the power relation in which he simultaneously plays both roles; he becomes the principle of his own subjection.

For those in power this is "a perpetual victory that avoids any physical confrontation and which is always decided in advance" (quoted in Zuboff, 1988, 321).

The whole concept of "de-skilling" needs to be expanded to account for the presence of panoptic power in the workplace. ERP systems de-skill the work of even highly trained professionals by embedding their analytical and diagnostic skills in the operations of automated, expert systems. But the crushing intrusiveness of ERP systems also constitute a form of de-skilling because they drastically narrow the freedom of employees to organize their own work as they see fit, forcing them to follow the rhythms and routines dictated by the system's "work-flow software."

Employees who are subject to this double de-skilling are not well placed to press their employer for a raise. We see the consequences of this in economy-wide statistics revealing the huge gap that has opened up between the productivity of American workers, as measured in the annual growth of output per head, and their rewards, as measured in the growth of their real wages. It is in the context of this wages-productivity gap that Wal-Mart casts such a long shadow over the entire U.S. economy. Wal-Mart has demonstrated the effectiveness of a service sector industrialism that combines an intensive use of information technology, a very rapid growth of employee productivity, and a harsh and highly regimented workplace regime that keeps the wages of most employees at or near poverty levels.

The danger is that the Wal-Mart model will exert a growing influence not only over its competitors in the wholesale and retail trade, but throughout the corporate world. The macroeconomic statistics suggest that the Wal-Martization of the U.S. economy is in fact already well advanced. From the first quarter of 1995 to the first quarter of 2005, the productivity of U.S. labor grew by 45 percent but the real hourly wages of U.S. workers grew by 14 percent, with the growth of productivity therefore exceeding the growth of real wages by 321 percent. From the first quarter of 2001 to the first quarter of 2005, the years of George W. Bush's first term, the productivity of U.S. labor grew by 14 percent, while its real hourly wages grew by a mere 1.3 percent. So during the Bush years, the wages-productivity gap has widened alarmingly to 1,000 percent.[8]

This widening gap is a measure of the unfairness that now permeates the U.S. economy and does so at the expense of most working Americans. But for corporate profits, the wages-productivity gap is a windfall. When the productivity of labor rises and its compensation stagnates, then, other things being equal, the cost of labor per unit of output will fall. At the same time profit margins and overall corporate profits will rise, and so will the stock price of any corporation that can impress Wall Street with its own particular version of this rosy scenario. CEOs and senior corporate executives can join the party as they cash in their stock options and add millions of dollars to already inflated salaries and bonuses.

The rampant unfairness of the "new economy" makes the case for the labor movement as strong as it has been at any time since the coming of the New Deal. Unions are needed for the same reasons that they were needed at Ford and GM in the 1930s—to prevent the mistreatment of employees and to obtain for them a fair, living wage. The detailed agenda for labor movement is equally clear: to reform the National Labor Relations Act so that the rights of employees to organize are properly protected and so that ruthless, union-busting corporations like Wal-Mart can no longer flout the law with impunity.

Yet labor's political influence is at a low ebb. In part this is an inevitable consequence of the Republican Right's control of both the Congress and the White House. But the labor movement can no longer count on the Democrats to push its agenda. As a member of Senator Kerry's Advisory Panel on the Economy during the 2004 campaign, I saw how easy it was for Kerry, after paying lip service to labor's agenda during the primaries, to ignore that agenda during the campaign. He listened instead to such pro-Wall Street Democrats as former Secretary of the Treasury Robert Rubin and former Deputy Secretary Roger Altman.

In October 1996, I attended a "Teach-In for Labor" at Columbia University in New York City that was designed to strengthen ties between the labor movement and the surviving elements of the old anti-war coalition of feminists, civil rights activists, and political progressives. This coalition-building got nowhere, in part because the then leader of the AFL-CIO John J. Sweeney, who attended the teach-in, could not find a language that would appeal to this broader constituency.

With the destruction of New Orleans revealing the depth of social and governmental decay in the United States, the time is now surely ripe to relaunch this coalition and to widen it to include the progressive wing of the Democratic Party that, post-Katrina, may now be emboldened to take on the party's pro-Wall Street center. But for the coalition to take off, the AFL-CIO itself needs to speak with a clearer and more radical voice than it has done in the recent past. However painful and damaging the labor movement's present internal power struggle may now be, it may turn out to be a blessing in disguise if it can bring about a leadership renewal that is long overdue.

NOTES

1. *Encyclopedia Britannica*, 14th ed. (1929). Henry Ford, "Mass Production."
2. U.S. Productivity Growth, 1995–2000, Section VI; Retail Trade. A Report by the McKinsey Global Institute, October 2001. Available at http://www.mckinsey.com/mgi/publications/us/, accessed February 6, 2006.
3. Ibid.
4. Patrick M. Georges, "How Management Cockpits Facilitate Managerial Work." Available at http://www.patrick-georges.net/en/download_22.php, accessed February 6, 2006.
5. SAP Strategic Enterprise Management, "Translating Strategy into Action" Available at www.juergendaum.com/news/sap_sem_wp_bsc.pdf, accessed February 9, 2006, 20.
6. Ibid., 24.
7. Ibid., 38.
8. U.S. Department of Labor, Bureau of Labor Statistics. Data for employee real wages: "Average Hourly Earnings, 1982 Dollars, Production and Non Supervisory Workers, 1995–2005." Data for employee productivity: "Major Sector Productivity and Costs Index: Output, All Persons, 1995–2000." Both tables available online at http://www.bls.gov.

4

No Deal or New Deal? Knowledge Workers in the Information Economy

Seán Ó Riain

FROM SILICON VALLEY TO THE CELTIC TIGER

In the 1990s, Ireland attracted huge amounts of foreign investment and underwent an economic boom that helped it leapfrog toward the top of the European income league. The industrial heart of the "Celtic Tiger" was its connection to the global information economy and the growth and boom in the Information and Communications Technology (ICT) industries in the 1980s and 1990s, respectively. There is much more in the Irish case, however, than a simple story of neoliberal globalization. Foreign investment remained central to Irish industry but indigenous industry, supported by the state, also became increasingly sophisticated and internationally competitive. Furthermore, while public sector employment expanded significantly, local demand was critical to growth. All of this was managed through an increasingly dense network of institutions of "social partnership" extending across almost all spheres of the political economy and integrating local actors, state agencies, and European Union programs. In fact, the Irish formula for translating economic globalization into national development has depended upon a whole set of interventionist measures to coordinate the economy—significant initial spending on social and regional infrastructures; social pacts that coordinated wages, taxation and employment; an interventionist industrial policy where state agencies

worked closely with firms to develop them; and public subsidies for
social services (Ó Riain, 2004).

In the 1990s, and particularly in the later years of the Celtic
Tiger boom, professional employment expanded and scientific and
technical occupations grew particularly quickly (Table 4.1). Software
was a surprising industrial success story and employment grew particularly rapidly among software workers—although clearly dominated by
men, the numbers of women also grew. This chapter draws on partici-
pant observation and interview research with software developers in the
Republic of Ireland during the Celtic Tiger boom from 1997 to 2002.
The chapter draws heavily on research conducted in a software team I
worked on for twelve weeks in 1997. The team was part of the Dublin
subsidiary of a Silicon Valley information technology company that I
call USTech, which was producing a software product under contract to
a different U.S. company (Ó Riain, 2000).

For Robert Reich (1991), these software workers would be
examples of an emerging global class of "symbolic analysts." The
symbolic analyst possesses the conceptual knowledge and the ability to
analyze and solve a variety of technical, social, and business problems
through the manipulation of symbols, concepts, and meanings—skills
that are in high demand in the new global economy. Premium
economic returns no longer go to the mass production of large volumes
of standardized goods, they go instead to the best designs and most
appropriately customized versions of products. Such high-value
products require the skills of symbolic analysts to distinguish them
from the crowd.

Table 4.1: Growth in Professional Employment in Ireland, 1991–2002

Occupation	Percentage of Total Employment 1991	Percentage of Total Employment 2002	Percentage Change 1996–2002
All Professionals	12.8	16.1	37.2
Men	11.7	13.1	34.0
Women	14.7	14.6	41.4
Scientific/ Technical	1.9	3.0	49.5
Men	2.3	4.0	47.6
Women	1.0	1.5	57.2
Software	1.0	2.1	170.6
Men	0.9	2.5	240.8
Women	1.4	1.6	83.7

Source: Census of Population, Republic of Ireland, 1991, 1996, 2002.

According to Reich, new information and communication technologies make it possible and even necessary to reorganize firms into "virtual" corporations and employees into global telecommuters. To facilitate open communication and innovative problem solving, corporations have transformed themselves into global web-shifting networks of firms and divisions within firms that have open lines of communication between employees, decentralize authority to those employees, and replace a fixed hierarchical structure with a shifting, flat organizational structure. For Reich the global workplace is essentially a "virtual place" where the constraints of space, social organization, and local institutional arrangements have been overcome. The politics of the workplace is replaced by a virtual space of knowledge sharing and creation. As one of the USTech managers noted in a thank-you e-mail message he sent to a contract graphic design firm in California with which we had been working:

> Our project team was truly an international virtual-team, with up to 8 hours of time-zone difference among the different team members. We expected you to work at such a hectic pace, yet, we also demanded extreme flexibility from you in all respects. It is very rare that anybody of your caliber would be able to excel on both these fronts.

However, there was clearly a politics in the workplace where I spent my time as a (less-than-expert) technical writer. Tensions emerged between software developers over levels of commitment and competence. Teasing, status competition, and light-hearted banter intermingled in the everyday life of the software workplace—punctuating the long periods of silence as we worked at our PCs and chuckled quietly at the jokes our friends were e-mailing us from elsewhere. Local managers colluded with local workers to handle international managers' knowledge and expectations of local performance. Disputes raged over deadlines and the demands of local and international managers for new features.

AUTONOMY UNDER PRESSURE: INSIDE THE SOFTWARE WORKPLACE

There is a "deal" being struck beneath this apparent seamless connection of workers, employers, and markets that Reich observes. In their research on almost 200 San Francisco Bay Area high-tech start-ups, James Baron, Diane Burton, and Michael Hannan found that these firms most often used an "engineering model" in dealing with technology workers. Firms choose workers based on the technical task, lure them with "cool technology," and use peer pressure to ensure their performance. Companies are least likely to use the classic factory model, where workers exchange effort and independence for money but little else. Having long tried and failed to impose factory-style arrangements on high-tech workers, many firms had to adapt to the unique demands of technical communities. Forced to compete for workers, firms attracted developers with interesting work, relaxed supervision, and for the elite developers, a share of the bounty. Workers selected, based on their skills, were controlled at work by, in many cases, the supervision of their peers.

This tells us little, however, about how this deal plays out in practice. Chris Benner (2002) points out a crucial tension in the organization of work in Silicon Valley and beyond. While work has become more socialized with the rise of teamwork, careers have become more individualized, with growing use of individualized performance pay within firms and job insecurity and job hopping across firms. Teams are assembled from a mobile labor force to put together the right mix of skills. However, there is a deep tension here—the bonds that make for good teamwork are consistently bruised and broken by the arrival and departure of new co-workers. For the Irish workers whom I studied, this tension was just as much a reality as for the Silicon Valley workers in the "engineering model" of employment. With high turnover, individualized human resource management strategies, and nonunion approaches to workers dominating, Irish high tech looked a great deal like Silicon Valley for workers—perhaps not surprisingly given the massive influence of U.S. and Silicon Valley companies such as HP and Intel in the Irish ICT industry. Few of the workers I interviewed expected to stay with USTech for more than a couple of years, and all expected that their career development could well take them to a different firm. When I called the company four years after my fieldwork, only six of the twenty-four people I had interviewed in 1997 remained.

The high-mobility career pattern with little attachment to the employer (or to the employee by the firm) became a reality for these particular software developers in the 1990s—even in the apparently "semiperipheral" region of Ireland. The careers of such software developers converged significantly with those of their counterparts in the leading high-technology regions such as Silicon Valley or global cities such as New York and London (Saxenian, 1994; Girard and Stark, 2002). The limited structured internal labor markets in such "flat organizations" encourage interfirm mobility as employees can drive up their salary and get more interesting work by moving rather than staying within the firm.

Connections to co-workers were in sharp contrast to the constant awareness that the members of the team might be dispersed at short notice. This can happen either by corporate decision (the team beside us was disbanded overnight when USTech in Silicon Valley halted development of the product on which they were working) or through the decision of individuals to leave the team. Mobility then is a mixed blessing—the advantage to employees of being able to leave with few repercussions is balanced against the lack of constraints on companies, changing employees' responsibilities and even getting rid of them (within the bounds of the law). These advantages and dangers are even more significant for contractors who live and die by this double-edged sword (Kunda, Barley, and Evans, 2002).

While software developers may move quite regularly from job to job, they have an intense relationship with each other once in a particular job. In informational and design work, teams work closely together on specific projects. The project team schedule at USTech had three main phases, a middle period of "normal work," a hectic period before releasing the product at the deadline, and a beginning period of rest and negotiation after the deadline and the release have passed. In the weeks before the team's next major deadline, life in the team cubicle becomes busier and busier. The team works longer hours and becomes more and more isolated from the life of the company around it. Internally, the team becomes more cohesive, communication becomes more urgent, technical arguments take on an edge they didn't have before, and any delay or instruction from outside is met with a barrage of criticism. As the deadline approaches the hours worked by the team begin to build, putting a great deal of stress on the increasingly dissatisfied software developers. The combination of the high level of autonomy the software workers have in how they carry out their work and organize their day with a concrete sense of pressure to get the work done was striking. Decent pay, conditions, and autonomy at work are not in and of themselves a protection against pressures to work long hours.

The long hours are reinforced by the job insecurity of the industry, according to a study of a Boston software firm by Leslie Perlow (1997). Workers dedicate themselves intensely to one project so that they will be asked to participate in the next, in what Perlow calls a "vicious work-time cycle." Those who fall off the fast track find it increasingly difficult to clamber back on. Individual heroics to meet unrealistic deadlines are rewarded, rather than sustained progress on long-term issues. The system encourages engineers to do whatever it takes to solve an immediate crisis while ignoring any costs imposed by interruptions or failures of coordination and long-term planning.

Ofer Sharone's (2004) study of a Silicon Valley software team shows that the pressure to work long hours and to commit to work above all else is reinforced by individualized pay structures. Software developers are ranked in relation to one another, so that their "performance pay" becomes what is in essence "competition pay," driving a competitive pressure to work longer and display a greater commitment than their colleagues. These pressures seemed less extreme in Ireland— the hours worked appear somewhat fewer than in the United States (although good data are hard to find), and research by Aileen O'Carroll (2002) shows that in many Irish firms workers were able to impose a set of time norms of their own, which included a more reasonable set of expectations around working to meet deadlines and restricting longer hours.

But the pressures certainly remain, driving hours up at USTech as the deadline approached. While not as long as the hours worked by some other software development firms in Ireland the work hours crept up toward 60 hours/week. The team leader worked constantly often late into the evening and the night. Weeks earlier, one developer told me:

> I've a feeling this is the calm before the storm. My attitude when its calm is get out of here at 4:00 or 5:00 'cos when it gets busy . . . you have to draw the line yourself as far as hours go; you have to say once in a while, "Sorry, I have something on tonight; I can't stay." You have to keep your standard hours around 39/40. If you let your standard hours go up to 45, then they'll still come to you and ask you to do a few extra hours that evening; they won't think about that extra 6 hours you're doing as part of your standard. It's up to yourself to draw the line.

As the deadline nears, however, he ends up staying late and coming in two weekends in a row. These hours are largely accepted as the norm.

ORGANIZATIONAL, SOCIAL, AND POLITICAL ECONOMIC CONDITIONS OF THE SOFTWARE DEAL

Many observers, and indeed many software developers, see the pressures of work in the high-tech workplace as simply "natural," an inevitable consequence of the market pressures that companies face or of the level of interest that software developers have in their work. But there was little shortage of complaining about work hours and pressures among the software developers with whom I worked, and there is evidence in all the major observational studies of software work that developers try to control their hours and set limits around the demands that companies can place upon them—even if they love the work itself. This suggests that we need to look deeper to uncover the organizational, social, and political conditions that make possible the software workplace pressure cooker—despite the resources available to software workers to resist this pressure.

ORGANIZATIONAL STRUCTURE: PROJECTS, TEAMS, AND DEADLINES

The core of the typical software organization workplace—and perhaps of the knowledge economy itself—is the autonomous project team. The mechanism for controlling the design project team is the project deadline. As the final requirements are usually somewhat vague and the actual work done by the team cannot be directly supervised by management, the deadline becomes the focus of management control and team efforts. "Do what needs to be done to get this specification working by the deadline" is the broad task of the team. The deadline is the mechanism by which management brings the intensification of time into the heart of the team. The mobility of staff in and out of project teams, controlled through deadlines, is the basic organizational process that surrounds the work of software developers and that becomes the building block of software firms.

Part of the design of project teams is oriented toward the rapid incorporation of workers with diverse sets of knowledge and in the course of my time at USTech a number of contractors were brought into the team to carry particular tasks or to work on particular modularized elements of the product. The combination of the relatively short amount of time required to join the team and the relatively high degree of transferable skills among the software developers meant that loyalty to the employer was never likely to be a motivating force for workers. Software developers, even if they ended up spending a long time working for USTech, never *expected* to stay long.

After the team deadline is met the team goes into temporary collapse with the work pace slowing dramatically. After the product release, individual team members begin to negotiate their roles in the next phase of product development. The team begins to fragment as the focus of the team shifts from getting the work done to building a career and as the team members look outward to their future opportunities within and beyond the team. The mobility of team members through various learning paths within the team and outside it is negotiated in this phase, laying the foundation for the next prerelease phase in three to four months time. This is clearly a volatile and risky time— ultimately, some of this development work was brought back to Silicon Valley. Some months after I left the team Jim and Paul, two contractors, went on to positions elsewhere in the global industry when their contracts were not renewed. There is a clear tension between the desire of the company to build up experience with the firm's products among employees and the efforts of the software developers themselves to avoid reliance on such firm-specific human capital and to develop the skills that they can translate into rewards on the open labor market.

Ultimately, the nature of the firm itself is challenged. Underneath the conventional organizational diagrams, we often find a very different set of organizational dynamics—as teams become "profit centers" within the company, they gain autonomy but lose supports and infrastructure, creating pressures around training and other collective goods. The market is not only the context within which firms compete, but the market is brought within the firm itself—shaping the experience of work through pressures on the team, career through individualized performance pay, and management through the weakening of many traditional central supports for management and production. Workers in project teams are much more likely to experience the pressures of the market directly as the buffers of the firm are punctured.

SOCIAL STRUCTURES: NETWORKS AND TECHNICAL COMMUNITIES

How do workers handle these pressures? There are strategies that they pursue within the workplace—in my research the control of the flow of information to managers about technical problems, progress on development tasks, the feasibility of adding new features, and so on was a crucial resource for the software developers. But software workers, and many other knowledge workers, have also developed technical communities that are in many ways serving as substitutes, albeit often partial, for the role once played by the large industrial firms.

New forms of technical communities have emerged where workers in the same technical occupations swap stories and tips, build contacts leading to their next jobs, and protect themselves from the global corporations that hire them. Large corporations typically try to create a technical community within the firm, but the technical communities spill out. Employees create firm-crossing networks of workers who share interests, contacts, and information. Their relations conform to common technical interests rather than a common employer (Ó Riain, 2002).

The team members maintained contact with their own networks within the industry—at times contacting friends for technical advice and regularly sending bad jokes around e-mail lists of friends. The short-term contract staff who flitted in and out of the team put a significant amount of work into maintaining their networks, constantly talking on their mobile phones about technology, upcoming jobs, and people in the industry. For all the team members, but particularly for the contractors, social networks replaced many of the functions of the firm (Nardi, Whittaker, and Schwarz, 2000).

The technical community is not without its own problems—these social networks are often heavily dependent on personal ties and the ability to fit into industry culture. Often the culture is heavily masculine—in both its confrontational and interactional style of constant competitive argument and in its patterns of socializing, often around sports or the pub. In its more extreme moments, "techie culture" can become a force for elitism. "The young guys in the industry—they are young and stupid; they're out to prove themselves," says an engineering manager in his Silicon Valley office. "When you're like that you feel immortal; you work hard and play hard. You are the exalted, you feel . . . like you are a god. Think of a hot young designer—he understands at the molecular level how the world works. No one else has any hope of understanding what they do. Think of the power."

Nonetheless, technical communities challenge transnational corporations even as they remain dependent on them. Even mighty Microsoft has worried about the emergence of Linux, a new operating system designed through a decentralized network of developers and distributed freely and globally. Linux is only the most visible tip of a broad movement for open-source software, software that is designed collaboratively through widespread technical communities and that cannot be held as private intellectual property. Although these products often originate in government and university research and investment, the technical communities that sustain and push forward the development of technologies such as Linux have a power of their own. These technical communities are all the more difficult for major companies to control since they are organized through decentralized, semiformal social ties, connecting people across multiple organizations and countries.

POLITICAL STRUCTURES: GOVERNING THE HIGH-TECH REGION

As market mechanisms fragment the firm, the technical community, the region, and, ultimately, the state are drawn ever more into resolving the problems of capital—and occasionally even those of workers—in the new high-tech deal. The firm externalizes many of the roles it played in sustaining longer-term investments in learning and in staff through training, basic R & D, and other functions. In this context, the region became a critical space where many of these problems become evident as firms reduce the security they offer employees and externalize the costs of social reproduction as much as possible.

Although it is true that the work can be done anywhere on the globe as long as one has·a modem, talking face-to-face is still important for picking up information, working together, and keeping on top of the job. In fact, the demands of the global economy for increased flexibility and specialized learning actually make keeping up both local and worldwide ties even more critical. Electronic relationships are poor substitutes for shared cubicle space. Even when I worked as an untrained technical writer on a software team in Dublin, I contributed informally to the testing, debugging, and screen design of the educational software program we were creating. Meanwhile, my counterpart in Silicon Valley was barely able to elicit any cooperation from the Dublin developers in her attempts to write the program manual. The ease of communication between the programmers and me and the trust built on daily face-to-face relationships made it possible for me, the much less trained of the two technical writers working on the program, to make a greater contribution to the final product.

As internal labor markets become less reliable as the basis of careers, networks outside the firm become critical. Careers are built using mobility between firms to bargain for improved wages and access to technical learning and these mobile careers only increase the importance of close interactions and strong local cooperation while working on any particular project. The emergence of "the region" as a critical space for innovation also facilitates mobility as employees find it relatively easy to job hop within the region and others to migrate to the region, attracted by the concentration of high-technology jobs (Saxenian, 1994).

Firms, too, rely on the region. Public investment in education, concentrated for a time on the supply of scientific and technical graduates, played an enormous part in sustaining firms such as USTech. Furthermore, since the 1980s, a network of semipublic institutions had emerged—funded and sponsored by the Irish state and the European Union (EU) and often linked to the universities—that supported innovation and research. Innovation centers, programs in advanced technology, technology centers, and other institutions were an important collective set of supports for individual technologists and business people. These state-supported institutions helped to build interfirm networks, while the middle classes of the technical communities benefited handsomely from the Irish two-tier welfare state. The region and the state picked up at least some of the slack that had been created by the retreat of the institutions of the firm.

When high-tech workers build global ties, they typically do it off-line through migration, contacts between companies, and meetings of technical standards organizations. Saxenian and Hsu (2001) have documented the rise of such connections: Hsinchu Science Park in Taiwan and Silicon Valley are closely tied through alliances between firms, emigration to Silicon Valley followed by return migration to Taiwan, and perhaps most of all by a group of "astronauts," so called because they spend as much time in the air traveling back and forth as on the ground in either place. The rise of the virtual economy has brought with it an explosion in international business travel designed to build the face-to-face relationships necessary to make the virtual world work.

In the face of the "cultural crisis of the firm" (Schoenberger, 1997) software workers were exposed more directly to both markets and politics. These workers were, on the one hand, more nakedly capitalist than under bureaucratic employment systems as the cash nexus and the marketized renegotiation of labor contracts figured more regularly in their work lives. On the other hand, they were more exposed to the vagaries of economic growth and its social consequences—in this sense they were more open to political mobilization around issues of collective social reproduction and were more embedded in the politics of the regions that were increasingly important to the class relations in their workplaces.

PROBLEMS AND OPPORTUNITIES
OF THE SOFTWARE WORKPLACE

The deal that is being struck in an informal level in software work-places, which is supported by these organizational, social, and political institutions, has significant costs. The pressures imposed by the dead-line create the conditions that lead to employee burnout—manifested in the exhaustion of the team members up to and after the deadline and also in the decision made by the senior manager of the project to resign due to overwork. This is most obvious in the work-family nexus where work demands come to dominate family life, leaving very little space for workers to negotiate alternative work and family time arrange-ments. This can only contribute to the situation where, despite its image as "modern" and "cosmopolitan," the software industry contains significant gender inequality, an inequality that worsens at every stage as women move through the educational, hiring, and career development phases.

Time pressures that are both unpredictable and demanding create problems not only within firms but also beyond the company walls. Research shows that long and unpredictable work schedules put increasing stresses on family life and undercut broader patterns of civic and political engagement. In a Silicon Valley study, Marianne Cooper (2000) found that software developers who were fathers were reluctant to even mention their family responsibilities as they might be seen as impinging on their claims to be the go-to guy. Such pressures reinforce the underrepresentation of women in science and engineering. Further-more, much research suggests that the engineering culture obstructs women's advancement. A project team up against a deadline draws on typically male idioms such as war and sports in the drive to get the job done. Perlow and Bailyn (1997) argue that women's working styles rely more heavily on personal interaction than on individual heroics and thus are systematically devalued by the engineering culture. Tech-nical communities provide more community for some workers than for others.

Software workplaces also create a great deal of volatility and insecurity in the labor market so that employees lack strong employ-ment guarantees. Even in the tight labor market of the late 1990s, "employment security" gave way to "employability security." However, when career gains are based on the threat of mobility, this seems to inevitably lead to increased labor market inequality as the threat to leave is only effective when replacing the employee is diffi-cult. As it is inherently based on scarcity, mobility as a career strategy can only work for some. But once again, this is a problem for companies as well as for workers. Every team within USTech is responsible for turning a profit and has its own set of customers, but, as the managing director of USTech notes, "This can make it difficult to get someone to pay for key investments in training and research." Other problems arise in the internal fragmentation within the firm as teams working on related problems communicate more intensively with their customers than with the other teams within the firm. There is an "organizational integration deficit" as firms abdicate many of their previous functions as providers of the collective goods necessary to socially reproduce their labor force, its skills, and commitment.

There are problems within the software deal for software workers—if pay and conditions are better than most, there are pressures of time and commitment and the boundaries between work and family and social life are ever-more difficult to maintain. Even the best-paid workers do not expect to spend their careers with one firm, whether they jump or are pushed (and often they are not sure which will happen first). While pay and conditions are still central, there are relatively new issues here for professional workers of time pressure, uncertainty, and the boundaries of working life. These are issues that lead these workers directly to a concern with broader issues of social reproduction—the social investments and institutions that support any labor force, and particularly the skilled workers of a knowledge economy. Where large firms have reduced their commitments to individual workers, this creates enormous pressures on workers but also opportunities for creative political movements. There are new issues for workers in knowledge workplaces and new bases for connecting those workplace concerns to broader community, regional, and national political struggles around social investment and welfare supports.

In her book *Regional Advantage*, Anna Lee Saxenian (1994) characterizes the Silicon Valley social world as a combination of competition and community; indeed, these technical communities combine individualism and collectivism in a variety of ironic ways. Workers who rely on one another to solve technical problems also nevertheless explain their success or failure as a result of individual skill, and they pursue their careers through individual job hopping rather than collective bargaining or moving up the firm's ladder. Self-interest and group interest are in profound tension with each other within these communities, and members have few common solutions to shared problems such as insecurity and the work-time cycle.

However, even the apparently individualist software industry is rooted firmly in the social life of technical communities and public investments and supports of education, the welfare state, and an activist industrial policy. If such collective institutions ensuring security of income and long-term learning can be strengthened, technical communities could emerge as an important alternative model of economic organization to increasing corporate dominance of the workplace. Celebrations of the arrival of "boundaryless careers" within "portfolio capitalism" ring hollow in the wake of the dot-com collapse and the subsequent economic malaise (Stiglitz, 2001).

Nonetheless, it is easier to visualize software developers pursuing a sectional agenda, making common cause with employers in return for concessions, rather than combining their resources into an alliance with other workers as part of a broader movement. In the industrial era, it was craft workers—and particularly those who maintained the machinery of production or occupied particularly crucial roles in production—who occupied this ambiguous position between worker solidarity and employer co-optation. Where these craft workers participated in cross-class alliances, such as in the UK and generally in Europe, labor movements were much stronger than in countries where they did not, such as in the United States (Voss, 1993).

As we enter an informational economy, it is "knowledge workers" who appear as the contemporary era's labor aristocracy—as the information economy comes to value knowledge, skills, and control over intellectual property, it is the workers who most directly create, and partly control, this knowledge who have the most bargaining power in dealing with their employers. While all workers bring their knowledge to bear in the workplace, recent decades have seen a growing international class of knowledge workers who are valued almost entirely for their ability to apply or create new bodies of knowledge. The Silicon Valley software developer is perhaps the iconic figure of these new workers—but there are many others, from financial advisors to marketing managers and from educational consultants to electronic engineers.

Will these workers become valuable figures in a broader movement for fair, egalitarian knowledge workplaces, or will they become individualized "knowledge capitalists" in their own right? The answer to this question rests in large part on political mobilization and its challenges. A crucial starting point then is the issues that face knowledge workers in the contemporary economy—while pay and conditions still matter, in jobs where pay is often good and offices comfortable, the key issues may well be security, autonomy, and setting boundaries around the demands of the workplace. To attract these workers into unions, organizing will need to move far beyond job control and pay rates to broader issues and new kinds of workplace issues. Unions will need to convince these knowledge workers that they can help them set limits to employer demands on their time and social lives, that they can provide security without the straitjacket of corporate loyalty, and that they can offer a lifetime of learning that will be properly rewarded. Existing strategies will also be challenged as unions are pushed to organize through unconventional channels outside the boundaries of the firm—networks, technical communities, and technical user and interest groups. This is a challenging terrain, but not an impossible one.

5

The Second Adolescence of the New Economy: China's Engineers at Work

Andrew Ross

In 2001, toward the end of my field research for *No-Collar* (my book about new economy workplaces) (Ross, 2003), I interviewed an employee in an Internet service firm based in downtown Manhattan. The firm was shedding its workforce rapidly, and she fully expected to be let go in the near future. In moments of distraction, she told me that she pried old sewing needles from between the floorboards beneath her. These were leftovers from the garment workers whose toil had directly preceded hers in that same Soho loft space. What, she mused, would her company leave behind? And would her industry follow the garment trade's fate in being dispersed from its New York base? At that time, even after the worst of the dot-com crash, she said that it seemed indulgent for her, as a Web designer, to speculate in this way. After all, her trade had no more than a few years of history behind it.

Such musings were viewed with more gravitas by the technologists among her colleagues. They were fully aware of how supply had caught up with demand for their skills, and how their work was being priced down and sent overseas as a result. Craft know-how had secured bargaining leverage for its initiates for only so long. "Everything that can be commoditized, will be," joked one of them, alluding to the company's mantra "Everything that can be digital, will be," which had been adopted by the Internet service industry as a whole. Java work that had been billed at $175 an hour by the firm could now be done for a fraction of the cost in Hyderabad. It was only a matter of time, he assured me: "We will soon be in the same boat as the garment industry."

In downtown New York, where Internet start-ups once co-existed, cheek by jowl, with garment shops, a standard vein of sick humor about "high-tech sweatshops" had flourished among employees working 80-hour weeks. But the more flattering comparison was with nineteenth-century craft workers who enjoyed bargaining power through their monopoly of skills. According to this loose analogy, Net workers were often described as "digital artisans." Indeed, they had been a true labor aristocracy in the new economy, enjoying workplace benefits and incomes that were unprecedented. But the days of secret craft societies were long over. Artisanal skills could no longer be hoarded the way they used to be, either through freemasonry or through control of the labor supply on the part of exclusive craft unions. Technical knowledge was much too easily transferred, and there were not functional IT unions to regulate supply and protect members. In a profession that favored the young and in a technological field where knowledge was openly shared on an increasingly global basis, almost every component of a job was destined to migrate.

Even though they were acutely aware of these factors affecting their livelihood, the technologists I interviewed were still shocked by the rate of dispersion of IT jobs in the years to follow. Indeed, by 2004, it was clear that the postrecession experience of millions of IT employees had refashioned the original company mantra into "Everything that can be outsourced, will be." The reasons for this outflow were at least threefold. First, the rapid liberalization of trade and investment in key offshore sites in East Asia, South Asia, and Eastern Europe. Second, the development of global IT networking that made it possible to chop up any white-collar service job, distribute the parts globally, and reassemble them seamlessly. Third, the global extension of the kinds of corporate reorganization that had occurred during the new economy heyday in onshore countries. Where once it stood in stark contrast to the formal work rules and rituals of a traditional organization, the fluidity of the archetypal new economy start-up, assembled—with minimal starch and maximum flex—to turn on a dime, was now being generalized into a normative corporate model.

The consequences are far from exhausted. If the unfettered global flow of work and investment succeeds in washing away all social contracts about mutual responsibilities between capital and labor, there is no guarantee that anyone will be left standing, not even in sectors that were once regarded as stable features of the professional landscape. In Shanghai, where I subsequently did research for my book *Fast Boat to China* (Ross, 2006), I heard a joke going the rounds of the business community: "Pretty soon, lawyers will be the only people left with jobs in America." Not bad as lawyers jokes go, but, given the rate at which the work of paralegals and junior associates is being sent off-shore, even this may turn out to be a generous estimate.

OUTSOURCING AS A WAY OF LIFE

Given the capacity of IT employees to garner public attention, knowledge of how deeply outsourcing had hit the profession was quite widespread. By 2003 the unemployment rate for computer scientists stood at 5.2 percent and for electrical engineers, at 6.2 percent. These were levels unthinkable during the previous two decades when such professions were lionized as the leading edge of American job creation (See Lohr and Richtel, 2004 and Lohr, 2004). In the first quarter of 2004, the Bureau of Labor Statistics showed a 9.5 percent unemployment rate among computer programmers. Demand for skilled technology employees had fallen off precipitously, and the labor market slump was affecting some of the most highly valued occupations and industries in the American economy. Between 2001 and 2004, software-producing industries lost an even larger percentage of jobs (16 percent) than manufacturing (at 15 percent).[1] By the time that the venture capital firms in Santa Clara County got back into funding technology start-ups, outsourcing was considered a requisite part of any eligible business model.

In the face of such statistics, the most popular myth propagated at the height of the New Economy of the 1990s rapidly collapsed. Low-value manufacturing, it had been claimed, would keep on flowing to developing countries, but the high-value jobs, especially those in technology industries, would stay. Sustained growth in the service sectors would continue to offer opportunities for laid-off blue-collar workers who were willing to retrain away from the old "buggy whip" industries. By the beginning of the 2004 election year, it was no longer possible to push this line of argument among manufacturing workers. Nor could the same logic of moving up be applied to those laid off in high-tech or in producer services. To put it simply, there were fewer places at the higher end of the value chain—in finance, industrial R & D, high-tech, or professional services—where employees could move up in expectation of a stable career. Moreover, many of those high-value jobs were the same ones that every other technology-saturated country, especially those in East Asia, were hotly pursuing—jobs that American, European, and Japanese employees have traditionally been assured is their birthright (Tonelson, 2000). With China leapfrogging up the production chain, it will very soon be in a position to compete for the top-end slots at the same time as it absorbs jobs lower down the chain. No industrializing country has been able to compete so comprehensively and with such rapidity.

While some business sectors were hard hit by the recession, the generous savings and handsome profits reaped from outsourcing more than compensated. Between 1990 and 2003, overall corporate profits rose 128 percent, CEO pay rose 313 percent, while average worker pay rose only by 49 percent.[2] In the three years following the recession's end, corporate profits showed the fastest growth rate since World War II, increasing at an annual rate of 14.5 percent after inflation (see Krugman, 2005). By contrast, labor compensation recorded its lowest share of national growth for any recovery in the postwar period. As for the CEOs, who were rewarded for creating "shareholder value" by ordering the layoffs and transfers, they finally broke the barrier of the 300 to 1 ratio between their average pay and that of the average worker in 2003 (Sum et al. 2004). Average CEO compensation at the fifty firms outsourcing the most service jobs increased by 46 percent in 2003, compared to a 9 percent average increase for all CEOs (Anderson et al. 2004).

But it wasn't just in paychecks that domestic workers got the short end of the stick. Productivity rose by over 4 percent annually from 2002 through 2004, prompting business commentators to suggest that U.S. workers (who already worked much longer and harder than those in any other developed nation) could easily absorb the extra burden of job tasks inherited from their laid-off brethren.

Without doubt there are short-term winners in this game, but there is absolutely no empirical basis to the free-trader belief that the communities losing the jobs and investment will see benefits in the long term. Moreover, it is not in the actual tally of jobs or dollars lost, but rather in downward wage pressure and the establishment of a permanent climate of job insecurity that we are likely to see the most sustained impact of offshore flight. Outsourcing is not a temporary economic trend. It is fast becoming a way of life, regarded more and more as a social, as well as an economic, norm. Inevitably, it is altering our perception of what a job is, transforming the customs and conventions through which we earn our livelihoods. In a postindustrial society, where uncertainty and risk have increasingly become burdens for individuals—rather than for employers or the state—to shoulder, work is less and less standardized, and a job no longer defines what a person is (Beck, 2000).[3] As the pace of outsourcing hastens these changes, the definition of a job is mutating into something closer to its etymological origin—a discrete "lump" or "piece" of work that exists only for the duration of its fulfillment.

The predominant tendency among onshore IT professionals has been to respond to this economic insecurity in the same spirit of existential challenge that was the neocorporate trademark of the new economy years. "Career management" is the name of the game, and it is perceived as a professional test as much as an occupational hazard. The aim is to keep moving and to keep reinvesting your skill set so as to stay ahead of the curve of commoditization (see Chet, 2006, for an ethnography of postbust IT employees in Austin, Texas). Even so, their ranks have not been immune to the antiforeign sentiment that has suffused the less-tolerant sector of public debate about offshore outsourcing. For some displaced workers, it has been simply easier to blame the faceless foreigner for "taking" their job than to hold companies accountable for paying Third World wages and asking First World prices.

While this kind of chauvinism is unfortunate, much of it derives from a lack of information about the conditions facing overseas employees who are the presumed beneficiaries of job transfers. In China where I went to do fieldwork at the other end of the job traffic, there have been tens of millions of jobs lost in the last decade. Chinese job loss is just as much the result of corporate globalization and neoliberal privatization as is U.S. job loss. Indeed, the flow of hot money into the country depends on the creation and maintenance of an economic climate tilted toward privatization. The precariousness of those holding down jobs in the coastal economy is reinforced by the job hunger of underemployed populations in the inland provinces and in the far west, already earmarked as the next frontier for buccaneer foreign investors to move to. The bread and butter of U.S. employees is now umbilically linked to the job insecurity of these workers on the other side of the planet.

This is not just the case with labor-intensive manufacturing. Recent foreign investment has been higher and higher up the value chain in technology-driven manufacturing, high tech, process and product design, and a whole range of professional services. Hardly a month goes by without the opening of a new foreign-invested R & D center in one of Shanghai's or Beijing's high-tech parks. Virtually every scaremongering, Yellow Peril-esque newspaper story about outsourcing mentions the 300,000 engineering graduates being turned out of China's universities annually. How can honest Americans compete, the stories imply, with this colossal industrial army of skilled workers?

The answer, as I discovered in my research, was by no means straight-forward.

Chinese employees inducted into these high-skill sectors are participating in the second adolescence of the new economy. Their workplaces are not financed to the same degree as the dot-com work-places of the late 1990s; they do not draw on the same legacies of free-style bohemianism or techno-libertarianism; and they do not consider themselves self-styled creators of an alternative form of capitalism. But the pressures they face in the workplace, in the balance between work and life, and in the labor market (now subject to "global arbitrage") are cognate in many respects. Not only that, their ability and willingness to conform to managerial demands will affect the livelihoods of onshore survivors of the new economy.

Though they are heirs to a much-lionized work culture—"the great Chinese engineer"—their exposure to Western business practice and to the novel ethos of self-direction makes them a relatively new breed—urbane, aspiring, and none too patient. However inexperienced, they are not absolute beginners. As I discovered, the attitudes they bring to the workplace have already been molded by several factors including the socialist-era career experience of their parents and grand-parents, expectations about their role as minor-league pioneers of the nation's high-tech future, folklore and business literature about market capitalism, and the steady pressure to forge their own way in a world without guarantees. Though their bosses would prefer it, they are not unformed, raw material, waiting to be processed into ideal corporate citizens.

WORKING ON THE VALUE CHAIN GANG

As the core of my research, I spent the best part of a year interviewing skilled Chinese employees and their managers in foreign-invested companies in Shanghai and the Yangtze Delta. Most of the firms I visited were located in the industrial corridor that runs from Shanghai's shiny new urban center of Pudong on the east coast to the ancient upriver cities of Suzhou and Wuxi (See Ross, 2006).[4] For technology-driven companies where I did most of my interviewing, the supply chain in this corridor is almost complete. The Lower Yangtze region is rapidly replacing the Pearl River Delta as the country's primary economic engine, and the lion's share of its foreign direct investment is flowing into higher-value production than into the predominantly labor-intensive factories of the south. Indeed, the Yangtze Delta economy is increasingly the high-tech core of China's claim to be the "world's factory." Shanghai's own booming service sector is spearheading China's less plausible aspiration to challenge India in also becoming the "world's office."

Because all of this growth is based on comparative advantage in Asia as a whole, my research also took me to India, Taiwan, and the west of China to see how companies played workers off against each other in regions with a lesser cost differential than in the United States. In the IT-enabled Services (ITeS) sector, for example, low-wage competition between India and China—the world's two largest countries— is already shaping how and where white-collar jobs are finding their way to Asia. I found that the going rate for engineers in the big Indian cities was lower than that of their counterparts in east China. This was not a widely known fact, and the international business press, accustomed to seeing China in general as the lowest wage floor, regularly reported the opposite.[5] Even in the ITeS industry, knowledge about such wage comparisons was spread unevenly. One thing was clear, however. India's trained workforce was not growing fast enough to keep up with demand for all the back-office, call-center, and ITeS work brought to the subcontinent by the Business Process Outsourcing (BPO) boom.[6] As a result, the major software companies in India (TCS, Satyam, NIIT, Mphasis, Infosys, Wipro) had all established offshore offices and development centers in Shanghai or Dalian or both to backup their Indian operations, to service their large Asian clients, or to grab a large portion of the massive growth forecasts for Chinese IT.[7] The sector, heavily backed as a "pillar" industry by Beijing, had already attracted U.S. multinationals like IBM, HP, EDS, and Bearing Point.

What pressure did this put on their respective workforces? In India, employees were told they must work harder or they will lose their jobs, like everyone else, to China. In Indian IT companies operating in Shanghai, I found that employees were told they must work harder because their Indian counterparts were paid less. "Every so often, my manager reminds me that the company pays me more than it pays a programmer in Mumbai," reported one of the Shanghai employees. "I am sure he thinks it will make me work harder. And, to be honest, it probably does." Employers had long used such intimidation to speed up the work rate or win concessions in labor-intensive industries. Now, these threats were being applied in white-collar services that were split between different locations.

The contact zone between managers and employees was sharply defined by cross-cultural factors. Mainland employees were all too often stereotyped by foreign managers (from the United States, Europe, India, Japan, and other East Asian countries) who arrived with expectations of a compliant workforce and a fast profit. Consequently, managers tended to attribute most workplace conflict to cultural differences. In their mind, the Chinese had not yet become "modern individuals" and were still locked into a collective mind-set, shaped by centuries of authoritarian discipline. In other words, their potential to become ideal corporate material is handicapped by local cultural traits.

There surely were such differences; yet I found that the conflict often had more to do with the unpredictability of a new industrial environment where the rules of work were not yet settled. What managers expected and what employees were willing to give was by no means a settled matter. Nor was the outcome a matter of purely local concern, relevant only to those with an interest in the regional labor market. China's pivotal position in the global economy meant that the result of this informal bargaining potentially affects us all.

The India-China comparison, richly layered for all sorts of historical reasons, was a case in point. I interviewed Prasanna Lahoti, a regional director at Tata Infotech, on a trip to scout out a Shanghai location for his firm. He had consulted some of his expat friends in Shanghai about the likelihood of finding the right kind of workers. The Chinese, they had reported, were "a very industrious, process-oriented community. . . . Once their training is established, then the job gets done." But wasn't his technology industry supposed to be based on generating creative ideas? "Creative people," he responded, "often come with a lacuna of being process oriented. In any case, you only really need 10–20 percent creative people who are conceptualizing the solution. Converting that into an application is a process-oriented activity."

This view of Chinese employees as process-driven and lacking in creativity was as firmly shared among Indian managers as among American and European business expats (see Kobayashi-Hillary, 2004, 219–229). Prakash Menon, president of the Shanghai-Indian Business Association and kingpin of the city's Indian community, offered his own detailed account of this consensus:

> What we find is that the Chinese mind is outstanding when it comes to the problem-solution approach in methodology. The minute you get into concept application, there are issues. The Chinese mind is finding it exceptionally more difficult to take the concept and apply it to ten different places. Because what is required of an IT engineer— when it comes to application programming—is to solve problems. As the problem comes to him, he needs to see from his realm of knowl-

edge, he needs to put it all together, synthesize, and therefore then be able to come to the solution. How do you do things that you don't know anything about? We find that to be an issue. Once a process is defined, the Chinese mind is an outstanding execution, top class. But if you want the guy to tell you what the specs for the program are, then you've got a problem. Therefore, the educational system must bridge that.

Menon's firm, NIIT, which had come to Shanghai as early as 1998, was making up for what he believed the Chinese educational system lacked. The company's regional 125 educational centers, offering a three- or four-year training in IT skills, were placed in twenty-six provinces and served as many as 30,000 students. Catering to those who had not gone to college or who wanted a career change, the courses were designed to introduce the kind of training that was required for networking and programming. Many local authorities were asking for the programs to be embedded in public educational curricula. In addition, the Shanghai center had initiated a program for training project managers and specialists in information architecture and product design. It was this kind of training, in Menon's opinion, that spoke to the difference between what he called the "Chinese mind" and the "Indian mind":

If you handhold the Indian to attempt to solve a problem, you won't get the solution. The Indian will expect you to keep holding his hand. The trick to the Indian mind is not to hold his hand, but to get him to explore and cross that wall. If you give him help once, then he keeps coming back to you. If you tell him nothing, then he flies, from the first problem onwards, and he doesn't need you at all. He knows. If you take the Chinese mind, and try to adopt this, you will completely and wholly fail, because the Chinese mind works exactly the other way around. You have to hold his hand. If you don't, he's just going to sit tight. He will not want to explore. The reasons are unknown to me. We don't know if it's an old cultural thing of saving face, but the guy just doesn't move. You have to hold his hand, get him to cross the wall, give him that opportunity to fly on his own, and then he does.

By acknowledging his bewilderment at the ultimate cause of Chinese self-discipline, Menon was admitting that the "Chinese mind" might be unknowable to him. But his comparison was aimed at a foreign manager's understanding of how employees respond to demands in the workplace. More bluntly, it was based on an assessment of the specific skills required in the IT service industry, some of them routine in nature, others more attuned to problem solving and conceptual development. Since "the Chinese mind is a lot more disciplined than the Indian mind," its strength, according to Menon's comparison, lay in the execution of instructions and orders, while "the Indian is extremely weak in execution." But, for the higher-end tasks, what is most "valued in software is a very undisciplined mind—I'm using the word *undisciplined* in a positive way—to be able to explore possibilities, and probabilities."

Michael Mi, a Chinese manager at TCS, agreed that "the Chinese people are traditionally more used to doing what they're told to do . . . which may actually be an advantage for the BPO, because you are told to do something. The most primary objective of outsourcing to somebody else is that first you want to make sure that things get done the way you want, strictly following the original instructions." Employees who followed orders were exactly what IT outsourcing required, given the need to operate at a long distance from clients. That was also one of the reasons why manufacturers had flocked to China. For all the tech-industry talk about valuing ideas and smart solutions, the art of blindly following orders was the more mundane reality in most software service jobs. According to Allen Qian, Mphasis general manager at its Shanghai center, "In the software development area, we don't need too much creativity. Although they call this high tech, it's not actually a very complex or difficult business. Actually, people only want us to do the kinds of things they want a computer to do. They already know how to do it, so it doesn't require much creativity."

Contrary to the policy of Mphasis in India of seeking out experienced engineers, Qian focused on recruiting fresh graduates. "Their minds are so fresh I can educate them," he reasoned, and, besides, "they are also willing to do any kind of job." Above all, however, the newly graduated were "willing to compromise on salary." Qian, a native Shanghainese, bristled at the suggestion that Chinese employees did not stack up. "Compared to the Indian engineer," he insisted, "they are superior. The Chinese are always thinking of clever ways to reach a goal or solution." With the United States, however, there was no comparison. American engineers controlled all "the most advanced resources in software," in his opinion, and "are encouraged to do their own thinking." "All the other countries," he observed, were "just following U.S. technology. We are not inventing anything."

In this game of comparing national expertise, Indians and Chinese were inevitably played off against each other. At another Indian IT company, for example, I interviewed two managers back-to-back. The first, an Indian, delivered the customary bromide about his industry's worship of ideas and creativity. "That's what we are all about. We have to have outspoken employees, young people with free-flowing information and ideas." In India, he pointed out, "we have that kind of democratic, open environment." Stopping himself from pronouncing that Chinese engineers lacked this kind of initiative, he observed that "they merely followed instructions, and never stopped presentations, for example, to ask questions." The second manager, a Shanghainese with international experience, said exactly the opposite. "It's the Indian engineers who are almost entirely process driven. They understand what code you want them to develop and they never deviate from this or that kind of module."

Obviously, national pride influenced comments like these, but there was a lot hanging on such perceptions. Chinese and Indian skilled workers were about to be assigned new roles in the international division of labor. These roles had not yet been fixed; yet managers' perceptions about the respective strengths and weaknesses of the "Indian mind" and the "Chinese mind" were already feeding into decisions about when and where operations and tasks would be assigned. Given the expectation of easy mobility, short-term factors could make all the difference in such decisions. For example, this particular Indian manager's low opinion of his Chinese employees had not blinded him to one feature that all technology managers could surely appreciate: "The Chinese engineer," he observed, "hasn't yet learned how to hoard information. Techies everywhere else do some hoarding to boost their individual advantage, but as yet the Chinese are too naive; they give it all up when asked to do so." Until they learned how to use their knowledge as a bargaining tool, their naïveté, from this manager's perspective, would make them invaluable in an industry prone to job hopping and wage inflation.

They may have been naive in some respects, but the fresh recruits whom I interviewed were fully aware of how their performance could make certain segments of an industry more locally attractive to investors. If the results favored them in the short term, they were also aware that the wind could change quite rapidly. They knew that employers and investors would always be looking elsewhere for a better return, that their offshore managers had to squeeze harder, and that their own skills and proficiencies were only a temporary match for their jobs. Johnny Lu, who worked under the Indian manager quoted above, described how this came across: "Chinese have little experience with foreign managers, and we just can't always understand what they want. Sometimes my manager wants me to follow the manual, and sometimes he wants a new problem fixed and then asks me how, but there are other times when I can't be sure. I like to learn new things, but I also like to be logical, and have the same approach to my work. He won't be my manager forever."

Alice Luo, a colleague on Lu's project team under the same manager, put it another way. "He doesn't know how to react to some of the new contracts, so we are affected by his confusion, and sometimes we joke about it to ourselves." Luo was also clear about the relative value of her skills. "I will never speak English very fluently, and so Indians will always have an advantage over me. But there are other areas where our training and our culture can deliver more value. An Indian company in China can get both, and so ideally this should be a good job for me for a long time. But the industry changes and technology changes very fast. I am young, and I need to anticipate the changes for myself, or I will be left behind." Asked about the implications for the national economy, she smiled as she responded: "I don't think China will be left behind again."

Lu and Luo's savvy estimates of their manager, the IT service industry, its international scope, and the need to protect the future of their own livelihoods were reminders that any workplace-based generalizations about the "Chinese mind" were likely to be crude and inadequate. Nor were they going to sit still long enough for managers to adjust these stereotypical perceptions. Though they both worked for an industry giant, strategically positioned in several countries to ensure its continued share of a growing global market, Lu and Luo were lukewarm about their own commitment to their employer. Each confirmed that they would be moving on, as soon as they had acquired enough training from the company, adding to the growing army of job hoppers in the industry. Lu asked if I had heard of the expression "roadkill on the information superhighway," which was originally from an AT&T ad. "I want to avoid being in that situation," he concluded.

THE RIGHT PRICE

For global corporations, the chief barrier to accomplishing "knowledge transfer," the favored euphemism for skilled outsourcing, was not the widely acknowledged concern about theft of intellectual property. The real obstacle, as I found out, had more to do with the difficulty of finding an adequate labor supply at the right price. From the moment I began to mingle with Shanghai's foreign businesspeople, I heard managers' complaints about the high cost of local wages, and the scarcity or disloyalty of technically skilled workers and professionals with the requisite work mentality and experience. I found that wage inflation, high turnover, and rampant self-interest among these employees were impeding the pace of value-added outsourcing. Prone to jump ship with some regularity, their paper-thin loyalty to employers was generating disquiet among investors.

As the world's largest recipient of foreign investment (having overtaken the United States in 2003 and netting more than $60 billion in 2004), China is often seen as a primary beneficiary of corporate-led globalization. Yet the flightiness of multinational capital is no longer a secret, not even to the ordinary Chinese who watch the multimillion dollar investments pour into their cities by the month. They have formed their own expectations from watching how corporations come and go in other countries. Many of the employees I interviewed saw little reason for loyalty toward managers they believed were unlikely to be their bosses for very long. Soaring turnover in the private sector—I found rates of up to 40 percent in some high-skill precincts—is perhaps the most obvious indication of this attitude. In their ceaseless pursuit of the cheapest and most dispensable employees, multinational firms have made it clear they will not honor any kind of job security. At times, it looks as if workers in China's transitional economy might be returning the disrespect. In stark contrast to their weak ties to employers, loyalty to China itself and to the grander goal of growing the nation out of its technological dependence on foreign expertise is a much more common cause of the allegiance of the skilled workers whom I interviewed.

Without a functional union to represent them, workers without skills had very few collective means to improve their conditions on site. The few official ACFTU unions (or All-China Federation of Trade Unions) that I came across in the foreign-invested firms were given names like "staff club" or "welfare committee" to appease managerial fears. Even so, the volume of worker protests and wildcat strikes has risen "like a violent wind" in the description of the Ministry of Public Security, since mass layoffs in the state sector began in 1997 (Solinger, 2005; Lee, 2000). After the spring festival holiday of 2004, significant local instances of unskilled labor shortages began to appear, resulting in a shortfall of almost two million workers in South China (Weifeng, 2004; Yuan, 2004; Ren, 2004; Johnson, 2004; Anon., 2004). *BusinessWeek* dutifully asked, "Is China Running Out of Workers?" (Roberts, 2004. See also Yardley and Barboza, 2005 and Fuller, 2005).

How could this be in a country with such a bottomless supply of workers, and with so many unemployed and "floating" in search of work? While some demographers cite the declining birthrate as a possible explanation (Yang, 2005), the most immediate reason is that foreign investors in the labor-intensive export sector only want to hire teenage girls (*dagongmei*)—the cheapest, most pliable, and most expendable members of the workforce. So, too, in higher-skilled jobs, only those who are freshly graduated or who have some experience with international business and work practices need apply. The millions of workers who are skilled but who have worked for a state-owned enterprise are considered damaged goods, incapable of being retrained for the more punishing discipline of a capitalist work ethic. The labor shortage, then, is shaped by managerial requirements that are set by bias, and tailored to the maximum exploitation of the young and vulnerable. But even within the bounds of the labor pool considered acceptable, even among the ranks of workers who meet these selective standards, corporate managers are confronted with employee shiftiness rather than the "flexibility" they would have preferred to see.

On the other side, local and central government cadres are pulling every power lever they have to ease the bottleneck and provide foreign investors with what they want—an abundance of skilled labor at a discount price. This is the latest in a long list of favors that officials in developing countries have had to offer as part of what is misnamed as "free trade." Investors have come to expect a never-ending welcome parade of tax holidays and exemptions, acres of virtually free land, state-of-the-art infrastructure and telecommunications, discounts on utilities and other operating costs, and soft guarantees that labor laws and environmental regulations will never be seriously implemented. If the state's massive human resources recruitment effort succeeds—if a surplus pool of talent materializes, and the current wage inflation is brought under control—then the way will be clear for corporations to transfer more and more high-skill operations and ever-greater quantities of high-value investment capital into China. The much lamented U.S. job loss and capital flight of the last few years may well be seen as a trickle in comparison with the mass migration to come.

For the time being, skilled workers with a few years of experience had adopted their ability to job hop as their most powerful bargaining tool. Gao Fenzhen was a machine tool operator, without a university degree, who had trained at the Vocational Technology Institute in Suzhou, the Yangtze Delta city with the highest volume of foreign direct investment (FDI) in China. Promoted to technical lead after only eighteen months at an American electronics company, he had a clear sense of that power. "I know I can get a better offer by signing with [a new semiconductor plant that was currently hiring down the road], and I am almost sure my boss will offer me more to keep me here." His confidence was magnified in Daniel Chou, a college-trained engineer in the same company, who had put in his two years and wanted to work with higher technology: "My career comes first, and I can tell my manager this. The response is up to him, but I don't think I will lose. Chinese like me have to put ourselves first. We don't have the advantage of time." Chou acknowledged that his hard-nosed attitude was shaped, in large part, by the faithless conduct of employers. "Foreigners will leave when they find a cheaper environment," he observed, matter-of-factly. "Right now, we are where Singapore was ten years ago, and they will leave as soon as we get to be too expensive."

While the bargaining power of employees like Gao and Chou was always experienced individually, it was felt collectively as wage inflation by the HR managers of companies. For some firms, it had become a factor in whether they would stay put for very long. For most of the others, it affected the decision about when they would decide to move higher-end operations to the region. This put employees like Chou at the center of an industry-wide dilemma. His desire to work with higher technology could only be met by a company that was transferring advanced operations from a more expensive location, either from the United States, Europe, or East Asia. Yet corporate executives would only transfer these units when Chinese skill sets were high enough to meet the challenges of management and innovation, when the labor costs could be contained, and when they felt their intellectual property would be secure from theft. Until those three conditions were met, overseas employees might be able to hold onto some of the jobs destined for transfer to Asia.

In the fully measured environment in which the Suzhou engineers operated, every task was subject to a cost-benefit analysis, weighed against its equivalent in several other locations around the world. Daniel Chou knew that what he could do and what he got paid were decisive pressure points in a global industrial chain. Neither the quality of his work nor the size of his pay packet were exceptional in and of themselves. He just happened to be in the right place at the right time. His parents were also engineers, in a factory that had produced the first tractors in China, making way for the mechanization of the rural communes. But, for all the local fame attached to the company's name, their own salaries and skills had no significance beyond the boundaries of their Henan township.

Given how closely they followed their employers' methods of pricing skills and locations, it was no surprise that Chou and many others were already dreaming of starting their own companies. In a few years time, he imagined himself and his friends pooling resources and heading to the western provinces, where Beijing had been enticing investors with its Go West policy. Who knows, they might even steal a march on their current employers. "We would like to do something for ourselves," he shrugged. "In Suzhou, all the big decisions have already been made, by people far away."

While they displayed no special trust toward their employers or their government either, most of my interviewees were motivated by a sharp sense of national pride. One of Jacky Wu's primary tasks, as a process engineer, was to ensure that production lines were transferred smoothly from his company's plants in Penang and Bangkok. His job entailed visits to these sites, and close working relationships with engineers whose knowledge was also being transferred. "It's not very high technology," he explained, "but we still have to prove that Chinese engineers are as good as Thai or Malaysian or Singaporean ones. If China wants to go further and actually create technology, our engineers have to be better, and maybe one day we can be as good as the Americans and Japanese. Then I can work with the really high-tech stuff." If you took his reasoning at face value, then Wu's motivation on the job was driven, in part, by national pride. He knew, of course, that the jobs of the Thai and Malaysian engineers would be lost as a result. "I think they will have some problems," he noted soberly, "but China has also many people without jobs."

Wu's attitude was common among engineers who worked close to assembly and testing operations. They tended to measure themselves against their counterparts in Asian countries that had hosted the first offshore sites for technology companies ten or twenty years before. For product engineers, the comparison was with locations in Japan, Europe, and the United States and it was more complicated by far. "Right now, it looks as if we are still twenty years behind," estimated Li Xiao Lin, who oversaw a design division at an American electronics firm, "but Chinese learn very fast and if we have good access to American knowledge, maybe my country can do it much more quickly. Right now, in my company, I think that Corporate would give us more control over design, but they are worried . . . not about China, but about whether we can retain our talent."

When engineers like Li made comments like this, it was not always clear whether they were identifying with the interests of their employer or those of their nation. Company loyalty was very thin on the ground, but since most wanted to work with higher technology, they were motivated to help their companies move offshore as much as was technically possible. To that degree, their personal ambition coincided with the company's goals of further transfers. In fact, their morale would probably drop if the company failed to do so. Ultimately, however, they tended to view the greatest benefit as falling to China itself.

THE REAL CHINA CHALLENGE

In the short term, foreign investors could profit from the nationalist sentiments of their Chinese employees. After all, the zeal of engineers for bringing technical knowledge to China coincided with the corporate need for a workforce that was enthusiastic about moving up the industrial value chain. If, in the minds of employees, their ultimate aim was to grow China out of its technological dependence on foreign expertise, the immediate impact was in complete harmony with the foreigners' local goal of harvesting offshore profits, before moving on to cheaper locations. Deng Xiaoping's famous dictum "It makes no difference whether the cat is black or white, as long as it catches the mouse" worked just as well (indeed, exactly as it was intended) for the foreign capitalist as for their patriotic employees.

Many of my interviewees noted the irony, but saw no contradiction. "I am in favor of this direction," commented Li Xiao Lin, "and our government is doing the right things to keep us on this path. Things may change in ten years, but so far it is a win-win for both China and the West." In fact, it was almost always described as a win-win situation. But surely there must be some losers? "In some other countries, yes, I have heard things are not so good; they are losing their industries, and they sometimes blame China." He added, "But China has had so many troubles, all of our families have suffered so much, and we have too many of our own people to take care of."

Pressed on this issue, Li acknowledged that he had personally witnessed some of the international friction generated by offshore transfers. At his company, where operations were about to be transferred from Singapore and the United States, some of his colleagues had noted that their counterparts in these overseas sites had stopped responding to their queries about technical applications. "Maybe they are not happy about losing their jobs," one of them mused diplomatically, "and they don't want to help us anymore; I can understand this behavior, maybe I will feel the same way," she added, in anticipation of what she assumed was a likely occurrence. A Singaporean manager at an American disk drive company, responsible for transferring production lines from Singapore, told me that his engineer colleagues over there had pleaded with him to go slowly so that they could hold on to their jobs for a little longer. The "system," he explained to them, would not permit it. Those who had been assigned to come over to teach mainland engineers how to do their jobs were not at all happy. "But they are professionals," he observed, "and they know how to be responsible in their positions."

Earlier that day, I had interviewed a Chinese engineer at Lilly, whose previous job at Trane required him to be sent to La Crosse, Wisconsin, to learn the ropes as part of a planned production shift to China. "The American workers were very angry," he recalled, "and demanded that the managers send all the Chinese home. I would probably have felt the same way." But there was no personal animus, he added. "Outside of the workplace in the bars, they were very friendly to us. We had to go instead to the Denver plant for our training, and then, for one reason or another, the production line was not moved to China." The difference in response between the militant American workers who resisted the plant transfer and the Singaporean engineers who aided the transfer because of their "professionalism" wasn't just a difference of class. Regional location was a big factor. Singaporeans had come to accept their lot as a way station in the global production chain. Twenty years ago they had seen the jobs come, and so they were more stoic about seeing them go. By contrast, the workers in Wisconsin had not yet gotten the message—resistance is futile—that employers wanted to send.

But their resistance would not amount to much in the long run if they could not communicate effectively and meaningfully with their counterparts in Singapore and Suzhou. Acting together on the combined knowledge might help to establish some control over their mutually shared livelihoods. It might even prove more useful to them than shoring up the job know-how that their employers were trying to shift from one workforce to another. In the period of national industrialization, workers in many countries had been able to forge this kind of common solidarity. As a result, they were able to push for strong labor unions, progressive taxation, and a sheltering raft of employee benefits that are the prerequisite for a relatively equal and humane society. Workers in the new corporate free-trade economy, where employers are able to operate runaway shops on a global scale, are having to start all over again, building up the international connections and mutual trust that will bring justice for all.

This time around, skilled workers and professionals subject to "knowledge transfer," are in much the same boat as the unskilled. Moving business assets from one place to another is no longer a matter of transplanting factories or offices. Increasingly, it means extracting thinking skills and processes from the heads of decently paid employees and moving these faculties to a human resource, to use another corporate euphemism, in a much cheaper part of the world. This is a more complex and fraught logistic than shipping out plant machinery on the next boat. It is also a much more insidious process, especially for employees who are expected to collude in the effort to upload the contents of their brain by actively training their likely replacements.

It is the chilling task of science fiction to imagine what kinds of future technologies will be developed to make this extraction all the more efficient. And yet, the basic steps are already considered routine in most multinational companies, and the race is on to formalize the more advanced ones. Nor is knowledge transfer a recent innovation. The de-professionalization that knowledge workers are currently experiencing is really only an updated version of the de-skilling undergone by the craft artisans of the nineteenth century when industrialists used new factory technologies and other administrative measures to undermine the artisans' control over their own work rhythms and schedules. Knowledge of their trade had to be extracted from them, too.

Today the human and economic drama of these transfers is being played out with a cast of millions in countries like China and India. Yet the outcome is far from guaranteed. The rules of free trade have been written to facilitate the technical and legal capacity of corporations to transfer their physical and fiscal assets with the minimum friction. But these rules have been challenged, and it is widely acknowledged that more innovative alternatives to the corporate vision of global free trade now exist. They are equally global in scope; they are based on the principles of fair trade, sustainable economics, and socially conscious investment, rather than on short-term profit and plunder; and they take their cue from the human rights and environmental standards that are habitually left out of free-trade agreements, whether brokered bilaterally or through the World Trade Organization (WTO). The push to recognize these standards has come from trade unions, nongovernmental organizations, and the myriad of activist groups that belong to the alternative globalization movement (See Nader et al., 1993; Ross, 2004). But the will to see them realized can only come from a deeper fraternity of workers and employees sharing knowledge, tactics, and goals across national borders. This will only happen if workers are able to communicate with the same ease, trust, and conviction that their employers do. In this respect, China remains our biggest challenge. Not because it poses an economic or military threat, but because it is the biggest and weakest link in the communication network aimed at combating the trade in what economists euphemistically refer to as "global labor arbitrage," and what contrarians call "the race to the bottom."

NOTES

1. Economic Policy Institute, "Offshoring Issue Guide," http://www.epinet.org/content.cfm/issueguide_offshoring. A University of Illinois report showed that the IT industry still had a larger impact from outsourcing job loss than other industrial sectors. See Srivastada and Theodore, 2004.

2. The figures are culled from *BusinessWeek*'s annual survey of CEO pay for 2003. See the analysis by United for a Fair Economy at http://www.faireconomy.org/press/2004/CEOPayRatio_pr.html. Accessed September 14, 2006.

3. Beck describes this pattern well, arguing that the working life to come will resemble women's experience more than men's—a combination of part-time work and occasional stints at full-time employment.

4. The firms I visited ranged, in size and scale, from Chinese start-ups to top brand multinationals. I interviewed employees at global corporations like GM, GE, Lucent, Lilly, IBM, DuPont, Nokia, Phillips, Maxtor, Hewitt, Bearing Point, AMD, Cadence, Motorola, Fluor, Kulicke & Soffa, National Semiconductor, and Fairchild, as well as at smaller companies, both local and foreign, in the private sector. The three main sites for my interviews were the Yangtze Delta region were Shanghai Pudong Software Park, Zhangjiang High-Tech Park, and Suzhou Industrial Park, the biggest magnet for foreign investment in all of China. For more on these and other research sites see Ross, 2006.

5. Some organs, like the business-oriented *Shanghai Daily*, had a local incentive to promote this factoid. Thus, a September 20, 2003, story reported that companies paid $3,000 to $4,000 for an Indian engineer, and only $2,000 to $3,000 for the Chinese counterpart.

6. From 2002 onward, the rise in BPO demand was so sharp that analysts almost immediately forecast a labor shortage down the road. With outsourcing growing at an annual rate of 50 percent or above, India simply could not produce the necessary supply of English-speaking employees with basic computer literacy. A NASSCOM-McKinsey study in the summer of 2004 showed a shortage of as many as 200,000 IT and ITeS employees. The deficit was estimated to grow to 3.6 million in the next eight years. See Magee, 2004.

7. A 2003 research report from the respected Gartner consultancy estimated that China would outstrip India's global lead in software development and ITeS by 2006, pulling in up to $27 billion in business. The forecast proved altogether premature. A January 2005 McKinsey report showed China's revenues from IT services were barely half of India's $12.7 billion a year, and their growth was being driven by domestic demand from small and midsized companies. Nonetheless, the original report, reinforced by research by NASSCOM, the institutional voice of the Indian IT, triggered an Indian invasion.

6

Globalization and Labor Resistance to Restructuring in Information Technology

Immanuel Ness

As the Internet is used more and more as a medium of communication in the United States, we are entering a new era of collective action in the form of what I call *micro-organizing*. These new organizing forms are typically spontaneous actions. Information technology (IT) and new media workers have used micro-organizing to defend their job stability and challenge the prevailing wisdom that the U.S. technology workforce is somehow inferior to that in other countries. Micro-organizing forms of resistance have emerged using the Internet as an organizing tool, as a means to mobilize supporters, and as a method to influence public policy. Skilled information technology workers, the very people who once were expected to benefit the most from the Internet and the new economy, are using these technologies for their campaigns for better working conditions. In the wake of the dot-com collapse, companies have used political and economic forces to erode the working conditions for information technology workers in the United States. In response, there has been a steady rise in micro-organizing in the United States by information technology workers outside of unions from 2000 to the present.

Indeed, the very concepts of the workplace as a *place* and of employment as involving an *employer* are becoming outdated. As a result, the economic clout of IT workers has eroded significantly. One consequence of this transformation is that it is necessary to rethink the nature of employment laws and the enforcement of regulations at a fundamental level. Further, it is not only the regulatory regime that is out of alignment—private organizations, public institutions, social programs, and activist strategies that have constituted progressive politics in the social welfare state also need to be rethought in light of the changes of globalization.

The economic turmoil now embracing the IT industry reflects recent recognition of the economic limitations of IT work that appeared with the collapse of the dot-com bubble; the growth of nonstandard work and its distinctive appearance in the IT industry; and the growth of skilled and professional nonimmigrant workers in the high-technology sector, with the use of foreign-owned labor contractors as intermediaries between migrants and U.S. firms. Foreign IT workers are recruited to work in U.S. firms on the assumption that no American citizens can be found to fill the job tasks.

The reality is that IT work does not create quick wealth for everyone working in the industry. Some IT programmers earn high wages and steady incomes at large firms where high-technology is core to operations, but most do not become millionaires or even break into middle-class jobs that can provide long-term employment stability. Among U.S. workers, this trade-off is represented as hard work now in exchange for a promise of rich compensation or stock ownership later. Foreign nonimmigrant visa holders working in the United States are given a similar bargain: that short-term contract employment in the United States will bring long-term wealth and income stability. But the reality is that U.S. firms are exploiting foreign workers and domestic workers alike. As we will see in the examples below, IT workers are struggling to simultaneously analyze global employment changes and to organize themselves in such a way that protects good jobs. However, corporate propaganda frequently leads workers to demonize foreign workers while government policies permit transnationals to extract further surplus labor from exploited migrant laborers. This chapter approaches labor outsourcing with a fundamental warning that all forms of xenophobic and nativist responses to the globalization of work must be resisted.

PLAYING THE INDIA CARD

A growing number of academics, pundits, and journalists are now using India as the scapegoat for moving IT jobs abroad and replacing U.S. workers with lower-paid workers. They argue that if U.S. workers do not gain competitive skills and work for lower wages, jobs will go off-shore. The literature on labor training is dominated by business school professors preaching that if the United States is to compete in the global economy, the country must promote education and training to catch up with foreign workers that have one way or another left Americans in the dust (Friedman, 2005; Levy and Murnane, 2004; National Research Council, 2000; Papademetriou and Yale-Loehr, 1996).

Thomas Friedman, a columnist for the *New York Times,* is one of the most recognized figures to put forward the argument that new technology has allowed skilled foreigners to replace U.S. workers. He equates the challenge the United States faces from India and other countries "practicing extreme capitalism" with the challenge at the height of the Cold War in the late 1950s. Friedman's bestseller *The World is Flat* is based on a recent visit to Infosys, a leading IT corporation in Bangalore, the high-technology center in India. Friedman tells us that India has gained a technological and manufacturing edge to compete and surpass the United States. The book does not consider the fact that while India's IT sector may be growing, the rest of its economy is in shambles, although Friedman admits to being escorted throughout the country without wandering too far from the modern five-star hotels and lavished by corporate officials at leading IT complexes.

He posits that with India's focus on education and rapid technological advances the United States has lost its competitive edge as Internet technology has facilitated the instantaneous capacity to perform functions anywhere in the world. It is this so-called convergence of technology that Friedman sees as "flattening" the world's economy. Friedman does little more than popularize what most corporations already know—that labor cost savings can be achieved through shifting technology and manufacturing abroad. The rolling out of telecommunications in India is not new to most observers of the global economy—but Friedman admits he was too busy covering the U.S. war in Iraq to divert attention to economic globalization.

Indian IT workers are primed by leading multinational firms—Intel, Microsoft, IBM, Siemens, and others—to travel to the West as guest workers in the IT sector. Most migrant laborers are confined to workplaces and housing complexes controlled by contractors—the equivalent of a modern-day indentured servitude. Upon returning from the United States, Indian IT workers recall disturbing stories of lives that revolve around work and the promise for a better life. After a three-year stint in the United States, most Indian IT workers consider living and working in India to be liberating, according to interviews that I conducted in 2005. One IT worker I interviewed had returned to India from the United States after paying most of his salary to a contractor who had promised him a green card. In effect, workers like these are paying contractors for the privilege of working and the chance at a job in the United States in the future.

For the economically privileged graduates of the Indian Institute of Technology, a large university system with locations in seven cities, the opportunity to obtain a visa to work in the United States seemed almost like a guarantee of a lifetime of wealth and prosperity.[1] Just as U.S. high-tech workers were thought to be willing to risk losing traditional jobs for the potential of riches, Indians and other workers on nonimmigrant visas are also risk takers. The possibility of making long-term connections with leading American corporations through working for contractors 12–16 hours/day and six days/week inspires many young Indian technology workers to work in the United States. Upon completion of their stay in the United States, most know that they can return to India and live comfortably working for Indian IT companies and subsidiaries of multinational corporations.

NONSTANDARD WORK IN INFORMATION TECHNOLOGY

When IT companies were doing well, industry advocates argued that the shortage of skilled IT workers necessitated a large increase in the number of visas for foreigners to fill the labor shortage. Once the industry recession hit in 2000, thousands of workers were laid off. Companies introduced nonstandard work arrangements in reaction to the intense competition created by slow growth. The term *nonstandard work* emerged in the mid-1990s to define the new flexible structure of the U.S. labor force that, according to a study by the Economic Policy Institute (EPI), encompasses all forms of alternative employment. Nonstandard workers include part-timers, independent contractors, contract workers, temporary workers, on-call workers, day laborers, and self-employed workers. By 1997 the nonstandard workforce encompassed an estimated 30 percent of all workers in the United States. That same year, the EPI study found that approximately 13.7 percent of the total American workforce was employed in part-time subcontract work, encompassing 47 percent of all nonstandard workers (Kalleberg et al., 1997).

The transformation of employment from traditional employment to nonstandard work arrangements has permitted businesses to hire U.S.-born workers and migrants as contractors. In the IT sector, nonstandard work manifests in different and particular ways not widely seen in other labor markets. The general trend in the U.S. high-tech workplace is the growth of temporary help and outsourcing through staffing firms to replace permanent full-time positions that once paid decent wages and provided health benefits. In many instances, nonstandard workers are contracted for a short time and discharged when the job is completed. When IT professionals find themselves without a contract job, they do not receive benefits, pensions, health care, and severance fees that would have accompanied such a position in the past.

The drastic changes in the U.S. IT industry shifted jobs from full-time permanent positions to the outsourcing of labor, creating millions of nonstandard jobs. This nonstandard work provides few, if any, of the benefits of the traditional job. Under the traditional arrangement, wages paid to workers must be sufficient to pay for basic survival needs. Under the new, restructured work arrangement this tacit bargain in high technology is undermined as every worker may potentially become an owner through hard work and greater risk taking, a way of life that has been promoted by the Bush administration through its ownership society rhetoric. In short the IT workforce owns all the responsibility of meeting their basic needs like health insurance, but control none of the resources or wealth within the industry.

To invent nonstandard jobs where workers engage in *risk taking* while corporations are *guaranteed* profits, employers offer the possibility of riches that are almost never realized by workers. More importantly, the nonstandard job reduces employer commitment to the worker. This arrangement is now the dominant trend in high-technology industries. The ownership option of employees' owning stock in their employer, even if realized, offers limited upward mobility for workers, as they are even more closely bound to the employer than in traditional jobs.

Data from the Bureau of Labor Statistics show the failure of the IT industry to recover from the dot-com collapse and the lack of job growth in the industry. For the first time since the emergence of the IT industry, a large segment of the labor force remains unemployed. Evidence of the permanent loss of jobs in IT is demonstrated in Table 6.1, which shows a sustained rise in unemployment in the industry. The annual unemployment rate in information technology more than doubled from 3.2 percent in 2000 to 6.8 percent in 2003.

While mass layoffs within the economy gradually declined from 2001 to 2003, layoff statistics in the computer and electronic products industries show, in absolute terms, that there are far fewer IT jobs than in the late-1990 boom years. Table 6.2 shows that the absolute number of mass layoffs in the computer and electronic products

Table 6.1: Annual Unemployment Rate in the U.S. Information Industry

Year	Unemployment Rate
2000	3.2%
2001	4.9%
2002	6.9%
2003	6.8%
2004	5.7%
2005	5.0%

Source: U.S. Bureau of Labor Statistics, Current Population Survey, 2005.

industry is still nearly three times as high as that of 1997. After hitting a peak of 131,487 in 2001, layoffs have declined to 42,370 in 2003. The implications of the statistics are that while mass layoffs may have declined, the industry has yet to recover fully. Moreover, given the high rate of unemployment, both service and production workers in information technology have permanently lost jobs. The expansion of the guest worker program in the U.S. information technology sector will almost certainly create further job instability.

Table 6.2: Extended Mass Layoffs in the Computer and Electronics Industry

Year	Number of Layoffs
1996	23,268
1997	15,593
1998	44,575
1999	30,085
2000	22,227
2001	131,487
2002	81,410
2003	42,370

Source: U.S. Bureau of Labor Statistics, 2004, Extended Mass Layoffs

According to Rob Sanchez of Zazona.com, workers employed at large established companies in Silicon Valley or Washington State expect to stay for their entire careers. However, younger workers at start-up companies in the new media industry frequently consider the jobs as a way station to a better job or career. A growing number of workers in the IT industry continue to sacrifice wages today for potential earnings as owners in the future. While many take this risk, only a few will be lucky enough to become independent owners   or to gain enough wealth that they no longer have to work. As unemployment grew in the IT industry to unprecedented levels, many more workers found themselves involuntarily out of work, rather than retiring rich at a young age. Thus, despite the rhetoric of success and the confidence that so many in the industry espouse, many will end up as life-long employees or marginal nonstandard workers who perform perfunctory tasks. If this were not the case, the employment relationship that gives power to a few over the many would be rendered meaningless. The great deception in contemporary neoliberal society rhetoric is that each person is an independent agent, responsible only for his or her own life.

OUTSOURCING AND OFFSHORING

In the IT industry, *outsourcing* is commonly used to refer to a cost-cutting measure in which work is contracted out to an independent firm that hires its own workers to perform tasks. Often these workers hold H-1B nonimmigrant visas. From February 2000 to February 2004, Congress permitted 165,000 H-1B visas. During the 2004 campaign, the high levels of unemployment in the IT industry made the program a hot-button issue. Thus, no new visas were issued until Congress enacted a new program several weeks after Bush was reelected in 2004. Over 2005, the number of new H-1B nonimmigrant visas has climbed to nearly 125,000. In addition, many workers are now performing the same tasks for contractors to U.S. firms while in their home countries; hence the emergence of the term *offshoring*.

Outsourcing and offshoring are typically not conducted by small businesses seeking to lower costs through hiring foreigners at low wages. The leading U.S. clients for outsourcing firms are multinational technology corporations that seek to lower costs by strategically shifting labor on a global scale. According to neoliberal trade theory, reducing barriers to the movement of temporary service providers is vital to advancing global economic growth, particularly in developing countries. Aaditya Mattoo, an economist at the World Bank, asserts:

> Indeed, there is good reason to believe that reduced barriers to the temporary movement of service providers will produce substantial global benefits. Significant gains already are being realized, for example, in the software industry—some 60 [percent] of India's burgeoning exports are provided through the movement of software engineers to the site of the consumer. And with greater liberalization of barriers to the movement of people, many more developing countries could "export" at least the significant labor component of

services such as construction, distribution, environmental services, and transport. Furthermore, a major benefit of the fact that such movement is temporary is the presumption that both the host country and the home country would gain (Mattoo and Carzaniga, 2003). The writers ignore the crucial issue of working conditions for migrant and U.S.-born workers, which are typically undermined as corporations search for lower wages and higher profits in new regions.

ON-THE-JOB RESISTANCE

Resistance to globalization has taken a spontaneous form, as U.S. information technology workers take direct action against their employers through on-the-job resistance. Typically, this type of spontaneous militant activism or micro-organizing never gains organizational traction, since workers are quickly dismissed from their jobs before they can organize themselves into associations. Evidence of worker militancy both within their companies and through Internet organizing indicates that direct experience being victimized by employers produces worker resistance. The terms *militant* or *radical* are not conventionally proffered by IT industry leaders to describe the common programmer or skilled specialist. Why, then, are high-technology workers suddenly becoming a *cause célèbre* through their increased militancy in the face of globalization?

Frequently, H-1B replacement workers depend on U.S. workers to train and coach them. To smooth the transition, retaining experienced workers diminishes the possibility of major mistakes and, according to one human resources recruiter, "establishes a sense of continuity." In countless cases, however, experienced high-technology workers have resisted the outsourcing of their jobs. Resistance to the outsourcing of high-technology work has taken many forms, from campaigns against individual companies or government representatives, to the formation of organizations to promote job growth. For the most part, resentment is directed against corporations that engage in outsourcing and offshoring and the government policies that sanction them. However, the anger sometimes takes the form of an anti-immigrant nativism.

THE PREVAILING WAGE SHAM?

A leading advocate against nonimmigrant visas is Rob Sanchez, a software engineer from Arizona. Sanchez, who lost his job at age 45, claims he was too old to compete with low-wage nonimmigrant visa holders. "This whole thing hit me in the face," he said. "I worked in software for more than twelve years until my career crashed and took a downward spiral. For most companies, the ideal age is under 30 years and the traditional cutoff point is 40. Once you hit 50, you are in the graveyard."

Subsequently, Sanchez began an Internet campaign aimed at raising public awareness of unemployment resulting from foreign competition for skilled work. As a member of the "anti-H-1B movement," Sanchez advocates the restriction of nonimmigrant visas. In 2002 Sanchez launched Zazona.com, an Internet Web site that provides information on the impact of nonimmigrant visa programs on high-skilled workers in the United States. Two years later, Sanchez regularly sends 1,000 newsletters to more than 1,000 recipients.

The Zazona site includes a guest worker data base that contains information about thousands of U.S. companies that hire foreign workers to replace U.S. workers, including job categories, locations, and salaries of foreign workers. The data base, obtained from official U.S. government immigration records, provides documentation on high-technology companies including Cisco Systems, Intel, and Motorola. Documents from the U.S. Department of Labor released to Zazona.com through a freedom of information request demonstrated that many positions offered by contractors and independent firms were open only to foreign H-1B holders, even when U.S. citizens were seeking jobs in the industry. Zazona.com has also exposed a growing number of companies taking advantage of immigration laws in order to pay lower wages. The Department of Labor, which is responsible for overseeing the H-1B process, has not monitored information technology firms for such violations.

One of the primary reasons high-technology corporations hire foreign workers is to reduce prevailing wage rates in the industry, even though the U.S. government forbids the use of nonimmigrant visa holders to lower wage costs. As Sanchez explains, "The law says the H-1B worker can be paid as much as 10 percent below the prevailing salary in the industry. If year after year, foreign skilled workers are paid 10 percent less, wages for everybody in the industry, both citizens and immigrant, will get lower and lower." Hiring nonimmigrant visa holders has the allure for corporations of reducing prevailing wages for U.S. workers. U.S. middle-aged workers earning higher salaries tend to be replaced by new, younger workers entering the industry, further eroding wage rates. Many workers like Sanchez say that the IT industry is in a constant state of churning, searching for younger workers and forcing older workers out, and Sanchez asserts that the vast majority of IT workers in the U.S. seek permanent full-time work that provides job security. "For a long time workers felt secure, feeling that their employers needed them, only to find out that they have been replaced by foreigners holding nonimmigrant visas who make a fraction of their wage." Nevertheless, while some IT workers are "a little worried about their job security," Sanchez explains, "most usually think they are immune to the outsourcing of their own work." Then, "when they do lose their job to a foreigner, they then start to complain, contact political officials, or join high-technology and labor organizations that oppose U.S. guest worker policy."

Business groups such as the Arizona Chamber of Commerce and national groups like the Information Technology Association of America (ITAA) and the National Association of Software and Service Companies (NASSCOM) complain that there is a shortage of every kind of worker. Many U.S. activists seeking to reduce outsourcing of work to nonimmigrant foreign visitors think that the purported shortage of skilled labor is largely a fiction to cover the loss of domestic jobs and the exploitation of foreign workers. Sanchez and other proponents of limiting nonimmigrant visas argue that foreign subcontractors should be restricted because they encourage U.S. employers to dismiss high-wage, skilled U.S. workers and provide ready and willing replacements to work as contractors. Moreover, foreign labor contractors like Infosys, Tata, and Wipro benefit from a system that restricts foreign workers from moving to higher-wage jobs, driving down the labor standards among U.S. and foreign workers.

HIGH-TECH BODY SHOPS

One of the earliest and best publicized disputes concerning unfair job competition between foreign nonimmigrant and U.S. high-technology workers is the Sona Shah legal dispute, which continues to influence debates on immigrant workers. Shah, an American citizen of Indian descent, lost her programming job at the investment bank Goldman Sachs when the firm decided to subcontract the entire department to ADP Wilco, a London-based global outsourcing firm. ADP Wilco casts itself as a cost-efficient way to reduce labor costs by replacing higher-paid permanent staff with lower-paid temporary workers:

> Users of ADP Wilco's outsourcing solutions can benefit from lower operating costs. Processing expenses become a variable cost based on

transactional volumes, rather than a fixed overhead requiring a significant up-front investment. This results in a more predictable profit stream and a fast-track return on investment.[2]

In 1998 Shah found herself working in New York City's financial district alongside foreign programmers whom Goldman Sachs had outsourced through ADP Wilco. Most of the workers were earning a fraction of the going wages for programmers, $200–$250 per hour. Still, Shah told me that ADP Wilco billed Goldman Sachs $275 per hour.

Working conditions differed as well. Shah said in an interview that H-1B workers typically worked 70 hours a week, significantly more hours than full-time Goldman Sachs employees, who also received health benefits and pensions. "Wilco workers from around the world barely made enough to make ends meet and certainly not enough to save," she added. Even some normally complacent H-1B workers began to complain about their working and living conditions. Most of the H-1B holders lived with co-workers across the Hudson River in New Jersey in ramshackle housing obtained through ADP Wilco.

ADP Wilco, according to Shah, is a body shop, a word that conjures images of indentured servants permitted in the United States to maximize corporate profits, only to be sent home upon completion of the job. Most, though, believe they stand a chance at permanent employment. Shah noted in an interview that "H-1Bs are told to work diligently without complaining in return for the possibility of getting a job in their home country or coming back to the United States on L-1 visas as essential company employees."[3] While some H-1B workers may earn enough to establish a business back home, Shah contends that most are essentially part of the global trade in workers. Subcontracting company executives, however, say that not all nonimmigrant high-technology workers end up working at low wages under poor conditions. But most body shops are smaller firms that mislead workers by promising that they will make it big in the United States, only to subject workers to living precariously and not paying them at all. Workers who complain can always be fired, subjecting them to deportation by government authorities. This is exactly what happened at ADP Wilco, say Shah and other visa holders who worked for the company and whom I interviewed.

When H-1B workers at Goldman Sachs discovered the disparity in salary and benefits, a large number wanted greater parity. In 1998, Shah and H-1B employees who complained about their conditions were dismissed. Shah claims she was dismissed because she was a regular employee and had pursued a long legal and political battle against ADP Wilco and the practice of outsourcing in general. Federal law stipulates that U.S. workers are not to be displaced by foreigners if they have equivalent skills, and Shah claims she is a victim of illegal outsourcing by ADP Wilco. For Shah, the lawsuit has metamorphosed into a crusade against outsourcing. Claiming that she cannot find work elsewhere in the industry, Shah has publicized her plight and has initiated a campaign to change the law by advocating directly to members of Congress.

This campaign supports a bill (HR 2702) sponsored by Connecticut Democratic Rosa DeLauro, which would place restrictions on outsourcing through subcontractors and impose limits on both H-1B and L-1 visas. Among the growing number of bills directed at outsourcing, DeLauro's proposed legislation is seen as the toughest and most serious in curbing the abuse of H-1B and L-1 visas by foreign subcontractors operating in the United States. Among several bills initiated by Republicans, HR 2154, sponsored by Representative John Mica of Florida, is viewed by activists as a sham. Shah supports the DeLauro bill because it caps L-1 visas, which currently have no limit, at 35,000 per year.[4] The bill also requires companies to pay comparable wages to U.S. workers and nonimmigrant visa holders, and bars businesses from laying off U.S. workers for 100 days before L-1 workers are hired.

Shah has put together a packet of information that high-technology workers can use to lobby their representatives to support HR 2702, which is gaining momentum in Congress. Shah pressed Democratic Representative Bill Pascrell of New Jersey to sign on to DeLauro's bill. In January 2004, after two meetings with local IT workers, Pascrell came out in support of the proposed legislation.[5] Shah has traveled to regional meetings of IT workers to promote DeLauro's bill and is active in the Programmers Guild, an organization founded in the late 1990s by New Jersey IT workers with a reach throughout the metropolitan area. The group has successfully lobbied the New Jersey state legislature to pass a law that prohibits the outsourcing of state jobs. Currently the guild is active in pressing members of Congress to support the DeLauro bill. Shah is emphatic in her support for both U.S. workers displaced by nonimmigrant workers and foreign workers who are exploited by corporations and outsourcing firms that pay them a fraction of what domestic workers earn and that treat them like indentured servants.

DIRECT ACTION ON THE INTERNET

One of the best recognized worker struggles in the IT industry was between Siemens Information and Communication Networks (ICN), a unit of the giant German multinational Siemens AG, and Mike Emmons, a high-technology contract worker at the firm's Lake Mary facility, several miles north of Orlando, Florida. Siemens is a multi-billion-dollar conglomerate with nearly 420,000 employees worldwide, working in businesses ranging from electrical engineering, lighting, and power to transportation, medical equipment, financing, and real estate.

In May of 2000, Emmons and twenty other workers in Siemens ICN's Lake Mary IT department were laid off. Twelve workers in the department were employed by Siemens ICN and eight, including Emmons, were working under contract. The contract workers at Siemens had worked continually for extended periods of time, and Emmons had been working at the facility for six years. Along with the others in the department, Emmons was offered severance pay in exchange for staying on for three months to train replacement workers. As steady, full-time work was hard to come by in the industry, all but one of the workers accepted Siemens' offer, including Emmons.

In June, about twenty replacement workers were subcontracted to Siemens by Tata Consulting Service, an Indian-based company that recruits high-skilled workers in India to work on nonimmigrant visas in the United States. Siemens saved substantially through outsourcing the department. Emmons was told by an Indian national holding a green card that the foreign workers at the Lake Mary operation were paid $1,000 per month in foreign currency plus $2,000 per month in expenses, replacing an equal number of American workers paid an average of $60,000 per year. Tata brought in twenty replacement workers to start training for programming jobs that, Emmons claims, "they were not qualified or prepared for."

In July, after giving a PowerPoint presentation showing the Tata employees how to do his work, Emmons decided to quit. Before quitting, however, Emmons and several other workers initiated a campaign to challenge the outsourcing—slowing down the work process, downloading information indicating that the Tata workers were in the United States on the wrong visas, and playing the Johnny Paycheck song "Take This Job and Shove It" on their computers.

The workers discovered that the replacements were not even holding H-1B visas, which require immigrants to have special skills that American workers do not possess, in this case, programming skills. The Tata replacement workers were in fact on L-1B visas, which require workers to have both special skills and specialized knowledge of the company. Emmons said that he and others found "a management training document that described what we had to teach them," ostensibly for the replacements to qualify for L-1Bs. Employees in the IT department appealed to U.S. Representative John Mica, Republican representative representing the Lake Mary area.

Before the November 2002 election, the workers received a letter from Representative Mica's office saying that he would write a bill to protect them. By Thanksgiving, the workers were still awaiting legislative action, so Emmons and others leafleted in Mica's neighborhood. Emmons launched what he calls an "e-mail bombing campaign" against Mica and others in Congress who paid lip service to the problem of outsourcing by introducing bills they knew would not pass.

Before leaving the company, Emmons sent workers e-mail disparaging Siemens labor practices that replaced skilled U.S. workers with skilled foreign H-1B and L-1 workers. Many workers feared losing their jobs if they complained, so most workers supported the e-mail campaign in unconventional ways. Emmons recalls that "when the e-mail hit, all the Siemens workers were cheering on the shop floor. I received so much mail that my Web server was filled with responses of support from the workers." After reading Emmons's e-mail, one thousand workers at the Lake Mary plant shouted their approval. Months after leaving the company, Emmons then sent a report to Siemens ICN workers based on a news story aired on the local CBS affiliate in Orlando, and Emmons continues to send out updates.

The controversy over Siemens's dismissal of twenty workers continues. Emmons and the unemployed Siemens workers learned through the Federal Election Commission that Representative Mica had received campaign donations from Siemens and the high-technology industry. After Emmons complained again to his representative, Mica responded with an e-mail saying, "I will not be your representative anymore," even though he was still in office, and suggested that Emmons should "contact the two Democratic Senators should he have any further questions regarding the issue."

In May 2003, Mica introduced legislation (HR 2154) that would block third-party contractors from issuing L-1 visas, but the bill never passed. Frustrated by the inaction, Emmons ran for Mica's House seat. Running as a Democrat, Emmons called for national health care, saying, "I believe that we should not depend on corporations for our health care and if the government ran it, it would be more efficient." Following his dismissal from Siemens, Emmons' own health care premiums rose from $804 to $1,472 per month, a serious issue since his daughter requires ongoing medical care. Emmons abandoned his bid for Congress in April 2004, unable to collect enough signatures before the deadline.

Emmons continues to run the OutsourceCongress.org Web site, which monitors actions taken by members of Congress on issues of outsourcing and offshoring of high-technology jobs. The Web site is a hodgepodge of articles, congressional testimony, and angry criticism that includes commentary from the Federation for American Immigration Reform (FAIR), an anti-immigrant organization, as well as supporting testimony by the AFL-CIO's Department of Professional Employees. Emmons stresses that he's "no expert on U.S. policy," and is not against immigrants per se, but that he opposes the replacement of U.S. workers by foreign nonimmigrant contract workers.

The Emmons' case demonstrates that radicalization of high-skilled workers may occur when an employer informs employees that they are to be replaced by foreign nonimmigrant workers and the opportunities this presents for micro-organizing. The standard procedure for replacing high-wage U.S. IT workers with low-wage Indian H-1B visa holders is for the company to offer to retain certain employees for a period of six to ten weeks to train the replacement workers. Keeping workers slated for unemployment is at odds with standard human resources practice, which cautions that displaced employees could become disgruntled and become a source of potential conflict and dissention. Given this departure from standard practice, the informational discharge meeting is an essential part of the process of replacing U.S. workers with foreigners contracted through third-party firms. IT workers are often warned that if they do not comply with the procedure and train their replacements, they may be fired straightaway and risk losing severance pay, if any is offered at all. Employers count on the fact that if they place outsourced U.S. workers in jeopardy of losing their wages and benefits, they can impose discipline that will contribute to compliance with the plan.

Nearly all workers scheduled for replacement agree to such terms, since they need the wages, look forward to the severance pay, or are in desperate need of the health insurance. Moreover, if the U.S. worker does not accept the terms of dismissal, he or she could potentially lose eligibility for unemployment benefits, since rejecting the terms is tantamount to quitting. Nevertheless, corporations that require U.S. workers to train H-1B replacements establish a new employer-employee dynamic ripe for on-the-job conflict, disruption, and potential chaos.

BROKE ON THE GOLD COAST

Connecticut typically ranks first in the United States for average annual pay, a distinction the state has held for the past several decades. Apart from significant pockets of poverty in the major cities such as Bridgeport, Hartford, New Britain, and New Haven, Connecticut residents have enjoyed relative stability, even during the postindustrial shift to services. The state is home to leading multinational corporations including General Electric and United Technologies. The state's huge military-industrial complex has softened the blow to industrial workers. Electric Boat, a unit of General Dynamics based in Groton, is the leading producer of submarines; Hartford-based United Technologies is parent to Pratt & Whitney and Sikorsky, two leading producers of jet engines and military helicopters. Additionally, the state economy depends on robust finance, real estate, and insurance sectors, which sustain high-wage jobs and a high standard of living. Renowned for its skilled workforce, Connecticut is one of the last states where one would expect workers to be scarce. The robust high-technology sector has given workers a confident sense of stability and constancy.

From 2000 to 2002, however, thousands of IT workers in Connecticut lost their jobs as the recession intensified and caps on foreign worker visas increased. The majority of those losing their jobs to foreign guest workers were older workers who had been in the industry for over ten years. Of particular concern to displaced IT workers was that large corporations in the state were using foreign contractors to find replacement workers from India and elsewhere.

John Bauman, a 56-year-old high-tech worker from Meriden, Connecticut, was one of the thousands of IT workers in the state who lost their jobs. Unable to find work, Bauman called a meeting among colleagues in the industry to discuss the problem of the growing use of foreign nonimmigrant visa holders as replacements for permanent workers. To his surprise, fifty IT workers showed up at the first meeting, and nearly 100 workers in the region came to a meeting in November 2002.

In March 2003, the workers formally constituted themselves as the Organization for the Rights of American Workers (TORAW), a worker advocacy group demanding that companies stop replacing U.S. IT workers with foreign nonimmigrant visa holders. TORAW called on the government to take steps to deter both outsourcing and offshoring of jobs. Within a year, John Bauman, then the president of TORAW, said that the organization had 200 members across the country. It remains to be seen if TORAW will become a guild or a union representing the interests of high-tech workers, but the organization is eager to work with unions to build a broader coalition. The AFL-CIO's Department of Professional Employees supports limitations on nonimmigrant visas and is working with TORAW on bills to curb and monitor outsourcing and the importation of foreign workers.

TORAW has worked with Representative Rosa DeLauro on legislation that she introduced to address these issues (HR 2702; see the earlier discussion). TORAW has also helped push Connecticut Democratic Senator Christopher Dodd and Republican Representative Nancy Johnson to introduce the *USA Jobs Protection Act of 2003*, companion bills in the Senate (S 1452) and House (HR 2849) that would place tighter restrictions on H-1B and L-1 visas.

FIGHTING NATIVISM AND XENOPHOBIA

Nativism and xenophobia have long been deep-seated facets of the United States. Virtually every new wave of immigrants has endured prejudice and victimization. TORAW claims to have steered away from any form of xenophobia in its public statements and disassociates itself from individuals or organizations that seek to limit immigration. Still, the organization gave CNN anchorman Lou Dobbs its Man of the Year award in 2004 to recognize his opposition to foreigners. Dobbs—a leading neoliberal advocate—promulgates a nativist perspective in his book *Exporting America* that is misleading working-class Americans to think foreign workers and footloose corporations are moving jobs around the globe, leading to greater unemployment in the United States. While Dobbs has become a cheerleader for the nativist American concept of closing the borders and returning to an isolationist past, he works for Time-Warner, a company that benefits from the growing movement and capital and concomitant growing global labor migration, and his own cultural products, Dobbs' broadcasts, are seen all over the world.

Beyond just outsourcing, TORAW and a growing number of organizations support the global justice movement's opposition to the expansion of neoliberal trade policies that allow international corporations to shift production and service jobs overseas. But this position is not shared by Indian workers who feel that de-investment will hurt their economy. Indeed they are correct: Global justice for many Indians requires advocating fair wages and decent working conditions.

WORKERS ORGANIZING WORKERS

Sona Shah and TORAW have set up models for lobbying federal officials to place restrictions on nonimmigrant visas that displace U.S. IT workers. The campaigns have had some success. In 2004, outsourcing became a ubiquitous word in most middle-class households, and Congress could not agree on the number of worker visas to be issued. Another sign of the campaign's effectiveness is that a bill that extended H-1B visas to 195,000 foreign workers expired in 2004. When the legislation was not renewed, the limits reverted to the pre-2000 level of 65,000, despite enormous political pressure from high-powered industry lobbyists. However, after the 2004 elections, intense pressure from the IT industry raised the number of H-1B visas to the levels before the expiration of the law. The attempt to counter this reflects the work of activists such as Shah, Rob Sanchez, Mike Emmons, and John Bauman, as well as the emergence of grass-roots lobbying groups ready to pounce on any bill that fails to protect U.S. workers.

While no law has passed yet, the issue of outsourcing and offshoring is used by some members of Congress as a means to demonize immigrants and to exploit xenophobic and nativist sentiment. Guest worker programs that serve as models for a new immigration policy evoke the essence of bad nonstandard jobs: low-wage labor; social isolation from the general workforce; indentured servitude; and upon completion of the job, forced deportation to one's home country. Campaigns of U.S. IT workers—supported by strong unions—could provide leadership in helping to bring about global justice in labor, rather than blaming even more powerless workers.

The Internet has emerged as the primary means of unifying skilled electrical engineers, programmers, and new media workers to share common experiences and relay important information on vital legislation and labor market trends. In addition, high-technology workers also make use of face-to-face gatherings and meetings to avail themselves of networks to locate employers and contractors needing work. Some groups, without constituting themselves as formal organizations, meet regularly for dinner to chat with friends and get up-to-date on the latest news in the industry. As steady jobs become harder to find and IT workers are increasingly channeled into contract work with definite beginning and ending dates, this organizing is gaining momentum throughout the country.

IT workers are also engaged in autonomous organizing against their employers and former employers. In early 2002, emerging high-tech organizing gathered steam, with IT workers forming organizations across the country, especially in regions with large high-technology workforces. As the campaigns that I have discussed in this chapter show, to date, almost all of this organizing has occurred independent of labor unions. The portrait of micro-organizing in this chapter is that of workers organizing themselves, even if their political analyses and strategies seem at times unconventional or even politically conservative. Still, it remains to be seen if workers will be successful in preserving good jobs, as the structure of high-tech work increasingly shifts toward nonstandard work arrangements like contracting. More likely, in the near future work in the United States will begin to resemble work in India, where jobs are doled out on a piecemeal basis when they become available. In India a new movement has emerged that presses corporations to guarantee a set of annual hours. A similar effort may be effective in the United States as well.

NOTES

1. Established in Delhi in 1961, the Indian Institute of Technology maintains regional campuses in Kanpur, Kharagpur, Madras, Bombay, Guwahati, and Roorkee.
2. Available at http://www.adpwilco.com/outsourcing/out-over.htm, accessed February 13, 2006.
3. L-1 visas are intended for employees transferred from a foreign company or branch to a U.S. affiliate of the same company. L-1A visas are for executives and managers, while L-1B visas are for employees with specialized knowledge. L-1 visa holders may extend their stay for up to seven years and may apply for permanent residency in the United States
4. From 1999 to 2002, the number of L-1 visas issued per year rose almost 40 percent, from 41,739 to 57,700. See Hafner and Preysman, 2003.
5. Paul Brubaker, "Pascrell to support work visa reform: Resident urged congressman to act." *Montclair Times*, January 2, 2004. Available online at http://www.montclairtimes.com/page.php?page=6757, accessed Feb. 13, 2006.

7

Boom and Bust: Lessons from the Information Technology Workforce

Danielle van Jaarsveld

A common theme emerging from previous chapters is that employment relationships that feature "new economy" characteristics, such as increased job mobility, and shorter job tenure, may still have needs that can be addressed by collective representation, even though the characteristics or their employment relationships in new media typically challenge traditional union strategies. The information technology or IT workforce is an appropriate focus for this study because it is a paradigmatic case for the characteristics associated with "new economy" jobs, such as nonstandard employment relationships, increased job mobility, and shorter job tenure. These characteristics typically challenge traditional union strategies and are an increasingly common feature in employment relationships. Yet, that does not necessarily mean that this workforce is uninterested in collective representation.

The dramatic change in labor market conditions that occurred between the dot-com boom (1995–2000) and the dot-com bust (2000–) affected the IT workforce directly. During the heady days of the dot-com boom, popular media accounts of the workforce experience in these employment relationships were primarily positive; empirical research analyzing the experience of workers in these employment relationships revealed that the reality of these employment relationships is much more complex (Kunda et al., 2002, 248–255).

Studies undertaken during the dot-com boom showed that many high-skilled contingent workers relied for the most part on non-union, nonprofit labor market intermediaries (LMIs) to address many needs traditionally provided by internal labor markets and unions (van Jaarsveld, 2004, 368; Batt et al., 2001; Benner, 2002). Similarly, the response by firms to the dot-com bust with downsizing confirms that new economy workers are still vulnerable to the same forces as "old economy" workers.

The insights from the chapters within this book confirm that the IT workforce is heterogeneous with respect to working conditions, employment status, and the willingness to participate in collective action (van Jaarsveld, 2004). This heterogeneity is, in part, an outcome of the broad scope of the IT occupational subcategory itself. Information technology is "the study, design, development, implementation, or management, of computer-based information systems" and includes production and applications of hardware and software.[1] These jobs are spread across industries and are unlikely to be confined to the IT sector (Hilton, 2001). This diversity also extends to employment arrangements: IT workers find themselves in a variety of employment arrangements, and may even be full-timers and independent contractors simultaneously.

For unions, the IT workforce represents challenges on several levels. First, IT workers are more likely to be in contingent employment relationships that may complicate access to formal collective bargaining. Second, as a result of their increased mobility between employers, the concerns of this workforce can change as a function of their employment classification and employer. Third, IT workers are generally perceived as having good working conditions and little need for unionization, although the recent trend toward IT outsourcing and the waves of downsizing that accompanied the dot-com bust may alter those perceptions. Fourth, the IT workforce is assumed to be anti-union (Robinson and McIlwee, 1989; Hossfeld, 1995; Milton, 2003; Hyde, 2003). Therefore, this chapter contributes to the understanding about viable forms of representation by examining the options for representation and advocacy available to this workforce, and by offering important insights about this workforce and the organizations that advocated upon their behalf.

Lessons from two efforts to represent suboccupations within the IT workforce are examined in this chapter in order to analyze what types of representative forms are suitable for a workforce that is mobile, highly skilled, and traditionally nonunion. The industrial relations literature assumes that the various characteristics of high-tech workers—a high degree of individualism, increased levels of mobility, and significant economic power—reduce the likelihood that traditional unionism will take hold (Robinson and McIlwee, 1989; Hossfeld, 1995; Milton, 2003).

Despite these challenges, some efforts to provide both full-time and contingent IT workers with representation have gained some traction. Organizations such as WashTech/CWA, Alliance@IBM, IAPE 1096, and Working Today challenge these assumptions. WashTech/CWA has evolved to represent workers beyond Microsoft, both contingent and full-time. These organizations offer many services traditionally associated with unions such as advocacy and mutual aid, yet formal collective bargaining is not as much of a focus, moving away from a traditional model of unionism (Webb and Webb, 1920). Working Today, meanwhile, is a nonprofit, labor market intermediary that provides members with access to benefits. IAPE 1096, in contrast, represents IT workers employed by Dow Jones and is a national local that participates in traditional collective bargaining functions (i.e., negotiating contracts and files grievances). These four efforts can be classified into two separate categories, union (i.e., IAPE 1096) and moving toward a union form (i.e., Working Today, WashTech/CWA, and Alliance@IBM).[2]

Some of these efforts reside within the jurisdiction of the Communication Workers of America, or CWA, specifically IAPE 1096, WashTech/CWA, and Alliance@IBM. Considering that the CWA's traditional constituency of media and telecommunications workers have experienced directly the emergence of the Internet, the CWA recognized that although new economy workers are a challenge to organize the occupational growth in information technology areas cannot be ignored. Entertainment unions have also embraced new economy workers, and their efforts are well documented by John Amman and Tris Carpenter in their chapters in this collection.

To build on the emerging themes from previous chapters, two questions are addressed in this chapter: 1) What level of representation is appropriate for this workforce, and 2) What kind of organizational structure suits this workforce? Evidence from two case studies that focus on the Independent Association of Publishing Employees (IAPE 1096) and the Washington Alliance of Technology Workers (WashTech/CWA) inform this chapter.

PREVIOUS RESEARCH

Studies undertaken during the dot-com boom have shown that some IT workers, particularly those in contingent employment relationships, relied on nonunion, nonprofit labor market intermediaries, a form of collective representation to gain some employment stability (Batt et al., 2001; Benner, 2002; van Jaarsveld, 2004). A labor market intermediary is generally described as an organization that matches workers with jobs (Kazis, 1998). In part, because the influence of unions has declined in recent years, workers are increasingly turning to labor market intermediaries to address many of the needs that, historically, unions have fulfilled (Osterman, 1999). More recent studies suggest that the services offered by many labor market intermediaries have expanded well beyond the scope of this definition (Benner, 2002; Hyde, 2003). Chris Benner (2002), who has studied labor market intermediaries in Silicon Valley, classifies labor market intermediaries into two categories, for-profit, and nonprofit. These labor market intermediaries provide a range of services including access to training, benefits, and job advancement opportunities.

Ichniowski and Zax (1990) offer another perspective on the situation by recognizing the prominent role that associations could assume in the workplace. Although their article was published in 1990, it is prescient given the emergence of noncollective bargaining entities such as Working Today, WashTech/CWA, and Alliance@IBM. They found that traditional union organizing strategies held little appeal among workers (Ichniowski and Zax, 1990). Yet, the demand for the benefits unions provide remained (Ichniowski and Zax, 1990; Freeman and Rogers, 1999). While private sector unions tend to view associations as a threat to "traditional unionism," Ichniowski and Zax (1990) suggest that these associations could evolve into bargaining entities mirroring their counterparts in the public sector.

In many ways, these associations are more attractive to white-collar workers, including IT workers, because they are devoid of characteristics that may discourage them from joining unions. Unions that represent white-collar workers engage in a distinct set of activities because of the unique characteristics of white-collar workers. These activities may include negotiating minimum wage levels, and negotiating outside of formal collective bargaining through labor-management committees formed to address specific issues. In addition, they tend to emphasize publicity and lobbying, as opposed to resorting to the strike weapon (Heckscher, 1996).

Several theoretical models for representing workers with new economy characteristics have been developed. The first model, "occupational unionism," developed by Dorothy Sue Cobble (1991), builds on the craft model applying it to low-wage, low-skilled workers as opposed to elite tradesmen. The second model, "associational unionism," developed by Charles Heckscher, encourages the organizing of workers across several dimensions such as race, gender, geography, and occupation (Heckscher, 1996). The third model, "geographical/occupational organizing," developed by Howard Wial (1993), proposes concentrating organizing efforts on workers in a specific region with common occupational interests. The fourth model, "citizenship unionism," devised by Katherine Stone (2004), builds on aspects of the previous three models. Citizenship unions would negotiate working conditions with groups of employers in a specific geographic region, thereby addressing the increasing mobility among workers. Citizenship unions would not only represent workers' concerns, but also represent the interests of these workers as citizens in the community (Stone, 2004). The main idea behind citizenship unionism is that workers' interests could gain broader support by transforming them into citizens' concerns (Stone, 2004).

While each of these theoretical models addresses some aspect of the experience of a highly skilled workforce in employment relationships with new economy characteristics such as nonstandard employment relationships, increased job mobility, and shorter job tenure, insights from the efforts of two organizations to represent IT workers reveal the demands and the type of representation these workers are seeking to address these demands. Both IAPE 1096 and WashTech/CWA represent IT workers, albeit with very different skill sets, and are affiliated with the CWA.[3]

THE CASE OF IAPE 1096

Initially formed in 1937 as an independent union to discourage the Newspaper Guild (TNG) from organizing its employees, the Independent Association of Publishing Employees (IAPE) represents a diverse white-collar workforce including employees in news, advertising, sales, information technology, production, and administration employed by a single employer, Dow Jones. Of these 1,600 union members, the two largest occupational groups are information technology and news (van Jaarsveld, 2004).[4] In 1997, IAPE affiliated with the Communications Workers of America, becoming IAPE 1096. The scope of the bargaining unit is national and includes 61 locations across the United States and Canada (McClendon et al., 1995; van Jaarsveld, 2004).

IAPE 1096's experiences in representing highly skilled workers at Dow Jones offer lessons regarding the relevance of collective bargaining in an environment that features a high level of flexibility, and technological change. IAPE 1096 has grappled with several issues, such as understanding the demands of its growing IT constituency and developing strategies to balance Dow Jones' need for flexibility with the needs of its membership. These experiences offer valuable insights for the labor movement about both the information technology workforce and, more generally, the white-collar workforce. Illustrating the importance of IAPE 1096's experiences in representing an IT workforce (van Jaarsveld, 2004), WashTech contacted the IAPE 1096 leadership to discuss its experiences with the Newspaper Guild, prior to WashTech's affiliation with the CWA. The membership of IAPE 1096 itself has undergone a transformation in response to technological advances within Dow Jones, with the IT membership growing into the largest segment of IAPE 1096's membership.[5] IAPE 1096's leadership, therefore, needed to address this growing constituency that harbored little in the way of natural union support. One IAPE 1096 member, and an information technology professional, explained that when he first arrived at Dow Jones, "I believed that unions were for factory workers and blue-collar workers and I never thought that IT would be represented by a union." He soon came to recognize the benefits of a union when Dow Jones started downsizing its workforce: "We would have fewer people, less pay, and less OT. It is a lot better being in the union."

IAPE 1096 responded to Dow Jones' actions with a number of strategies to protect its members. Because it represents journalists, its ability to engage in political action is limited because journalists are prohibited from engaging in political activities. Moreover, with its origins as an independent union that represents workers employed by one company, its organizing efforts are also limited. Therefore, IAPE 1096 depends on formal collective bargaining and mutual aid strategies to represent its workforce. In addition, it evolved from an independent union into a "real union" in 1997 in part as a response to Dow Jones' change in strategy in dealing with IAPE 1096 (van Jaarsveld, 2004).

The leadership of IAPE 1096 has overcome their obstacles through efforts on several levels. As the membership of IT workers in IAPE 1096 increased, the union has adapted its representation strategies, and the IT membership has recognized the efforts the union has made on their behalf.

During the dot-com boom, Dow Jones managers encountered difficulties retaining and recruiting IT professionals. For example, Dow Jones' own dot-com venture, WSJ.com, held less appeal for IT job applicants with the requirement to join a union and the absence of stock options.

In 1999, Dow Jones realized that it needed to address its recruitment and retention problem particularly in the IT area because it could not compete with start-ups that were offering stock options to attract IT workers. Moreover, the company needed to revise its IT job descriptions and compensation system, which were out of step with the rapid advancement in technology skills. The idea of concrete skill sets is relatively useless because IT skills are mutable. It is difficult for work practices to be developed that are flexible enough to accommodate this rate of change. For example, a skill such as Java that was in demand during the dot-com boom is now a skill that is much more common.

To address this problem, management formed a labor-management committee in 1999 to revise compensation and job descriptions for its IT workforce through a reorganization of the IT department. The committee considered each family of jobs and brought in managers and employees for each family to collect input from all the stakeholders who would be affected by any changes. Management included representatives from IAPE 1096 in this process because it needed to understand how to reorganize the IT department, and it needed to convince workers to support the transformation of IT employment practices. As a result of this process, job descriptions and compensation for 750 people were revised over the course of a year.[6] Participating in this process also increased the visibility and legitimacy of the union for many IT workers. Before the process, IAPE 1096's information technology members were skeptical about the relevance of union membership to IT workers. However, following the IT reorganization process, as the following quote reveals, they recognized the advantage of union representation: "Before the IT reorganization I did not see the value of the union. I had not been exposed to it. I have had steady raises at [Dow Jones] as a result of the union and the IT reorganization was significant. The union isn't the be-all and the end-all, but it does create a level playing field against unscrupulous management." As this quote illustrates, the involvement of the union in the process reduced suspicion about the union among its IT membership.

By protecting working conditions through formal collective bargaining, IAPE 1096 has also increased its relevance to its IT members. In August 2004, following several well-attended rallies by

IAPE 1096 members at different locations and threats made by report-ers to impose a byline strike, IAPE 1096 ratified an agreement that included annual wage increases of 2.5 percent, and 3.0 percent, particu-larly surprising considering that management imposed a wage freeze in 2003. While the union fought hard to protect the existing health plan coverage for its members, it did agree to allow management to shift the bargaining unit into a new health plan. Job security provisions were improved, and Dow Jones offered its unionized employees a $1,000 ratification bonus (Daily Labor Report, 2004).[7]

Through formal collective bargaining processes, IAPE 1096 has also limited the replacement of full-time IT workers by contingent workers. One mechanism that discourages widespread use of contin-gent workers at Dow Jones is the collective bargaining agreement, which covers agency temporary workers and part-timers. The terms of the collective bargaining agreement do not require temporary workers to pay dues, but after they have worked at Dow Jones for a year, they are converted to part-time status and are required to pay. This contract language discourages Dow Jones from relying on temporary workers for extended periods of time.

Outside of formal collective bargaining, IAPE 1096 has also had some success in advocating on behalf of its membership. In June 2001 IAPE 1096 approached Dow Jones about adding contraceptive coverage to one of its insurance plans that covers over 45 percent of its workforce. In April 2002, three Dow Jones employees filed a complaint about this issue with the Equal Employment Opportunity Commission (EEOC) against Dow Jones, and IAPE 1096 won the case in December of that year. This victory for IAPE 1096 also included two years' retro-active reimbursement for previously uncovered contraceptive expenses.

THE WASHTECH/CWA CASE

In 1998 a group of contingent workers from Microsoft formed WashTech. The organization later affiliated with the Communication Workers of America (CWA) to harness additional resources to chal-lenge Microsoft, other high-technology employers in Washington State, and the temporary employment agencies. The Newspaper Guild (TNG-CWA) was a logical partner because of similarities between content creators for newspapers and content creators for computers. WashTech became WashTech/CWA Local 37083 (TNG-CWA). In contrast to IAPE 1096, WashTech/CWA's membership includes a workforce spread across several employers. While IAPE 1096's membership consists primarily of full-time employees, WashTech/CWA's membership is more diverse from an employment contract perspective.

The features of these employment relationships complicate formal National Labor Relations Act (NLRA) representation of the workers WashTech/CWA seeks to organize, including high levels of employment mobility and relationships with temporary employment agencies and client firms. These realities influenced WashTech/CWA to adopt alternative strategies to address its membership's needs. For these workers, benefits, advocacy, job security, and access to training opportunities ranked among their highest priorities.

Similar to that of IAPE 1096, the WashTech/CWA initiative is multi-faceted. WashTech/CWA's constituency consists of a highly skilled, high-wage workforce. Their strategy for acquiring members is shaped by workforce characteristics and the employment practices of high-technology firms. As mentioned earlier, within the IT workforce a wide variety of skill levels exist. Beyond skill level, diversity also surfaces for these workers in terms of their employment classification and the identity of their employer. This flux creates a problem for an organization trying to represent workers in this situation. Their workplace concerns can change as a function of their employment classification and employer.

In contrast to IAPE 1096's membership, access to benefits is a primary concern to these workers because of their job mobility and job insecurity. To address this need, WashTech/CWA offers its members access to comprehensive medical benefits, dental benefits, and legal services through its affiliation with the CWA. WashTech/CWA has also improved the benefits of its members by pressuring employers. For example, WashTech/CWA publicized the difference in benefits offered by temporary employment agencies to Microsoft agency contractors. After WashTech/CWA publicized this information, Microsoft required temporary employment agencies to improve their benefits.

Training opportunities are also important to highly skilled contingent workers. While IAPE 1096's membership has access to employer-provided training, WashTech/CWA's membership identifies training as a priority in both interviews and through surveys. In many cases they do not have access to employer-provided training opportunities as a result of their employment status. This workforce needs to upgrade its skills frequently to remain competitive in this rapidly changing industry and to gain access to better-paying positions. This realization motivated WashTech, the CWA, and Cisco in 2001 to establish a regional training center for both members and nonmembers in the Seattle area.

Similar to IAPE 1096's experience, advocacy became an important issue when it became obvious that temporary employment agencies were silent on Microsoft's introduction of policies that negatively affected agency contractors. WashTech/CWA advocates on behalf of its membership through legislative lobbying, providing access to accurate information, and through coalition building.

At the state and federal levels, WashTech/CWA members advocate on behalf of contingent workers, broadening the organization's reach beyond the highly skilled contingent workforce and garnering widespread respect for their efforts. The introduction of the Computer Overtime Exemption to the Washington Minimum Wage Act raised fears of similar legislative restrictions, and convinced the members that lobbying at the legislative level needed to be an important element of their representative structure. In April 1999, WashTech/CWA won its first legislative victory when the Washington State Senate passed Senate Resolution 8402 (Contingent Workforce Study Bill). This bill created a task force to study Washington State's growing contingent workforce. WashTech/CWA and the Washington Labor Council worked together to generate support for the bill.

The offshoring and outsourcing trend being experienced firsthand by this workforce has raised WashTech/CWA's national profile in the United States. WashTech/CWA successfully convinced Congress to request the U.S. General Accountability Office to study the impact of offshoring on the IT workforce. On this topic, they have also contributed to the effort to regulate the offshoring of work outside of the United States through the introduction of legislative bills under consideration, not only in Washington State but also in thirty other states.

Both IAPE 1096 and WashTech/CWA maintain active Web sites. Although the highly skilled contingent workforce is described as independent and resistant to collective representation, both Web sites receive a constant stream of messages on workplace issues. While this workforce may be decentralized, these Web sites provide workers with a forum where they can exchange ideas and opinions about a variety of issues, creating in essence an electronic community for these workers who may not be in the "line of sight," but who can communicate with each other in an electronic medium.

Another aspect of both IAPE 1096 and WashTech/CWA is coalition building. Both IAPE 1096 and WashTech/CWA are affiliated with the TNG-CWA. Further, WashTech/CWA has joined a coalition of advocacy groups such as the National Alliance for Fair Employment (NAFFE), which represents a variety of contingent workers across industries in the United States to pressure state legislators to address issues related to contingent workers.

Overcoming antiunion attitudes among this workforce and a lack of experience with unions through a combination of strategies, WashTech/CWA developed an organizational structure that responds to the needs expressed by this workforce, and it shares some similarities with the strategies utilized by IAPE 1096.

LESSONS FROM IAPE 1096 AND WASHTECH/CWA FOR ORGANIZING THE HIGHLY SKILLED WORKFORCE

Webb and Webb (1920) identify collective bargaining, mutual aid, and political action as the primary functions of unions. Since then, union strategies have shifted in emphasis among these competing roles. As internal labor market practices weaken, and white-collar occupations expand, unions are struggling to revise their strategies to suit the emerging environment.

IAPE 1096's leadership has learned several lessons from representing a workforce experiencing increasingly flexible working conditions and a high degree of technological change. Consistent with the growing intensity of technology in media, the IT segment of its membership has expanded beyond other occupational groups for the first time in its history.

IAPE 1096 has responded in several ways to growing pressures for flexibility that intensified between 1991 and 2003. First, IAPE 1096 evolved in its structure from its identity as an independent union into one affiliated with the Communication Workers of America (McClendon et al., 1995). Second, IAPE 1096 has limited, widespread use of contingent workers and prevented more significant changes to pensions and other benefit plans through formal means of collective bargaining. Third, IAPE 1096 cooperated with management to address recruitment and retention problems encountered during the dot-com boom that resulted in increased compensation for the IT workers IAPE 1096 represents. Fourth, IAPE 1096 united its diverse workforce through mutual aid strategies, such as filing a lawsuit with the EEOC on behalf of its membership.

In contrast to IAPE 1096, WashTech/CWA addresses the rich diversity of this workforce by organizing along narrower occupational and geographic dimensions, although its workforce is dispersed across several workplaces. The strategy is shaped by the characteristics of the highly skilled workforce, as opposed to a single employer. Although the concerns of its members are subject to change, WashTech/CWA responds to this reality by focusing on occupational identity. Concentrating on occupational identity as opposed to employer identity also diffuses conflicts of interest that could arise between workers who have different employment contracts.

In terms of benefits, members of IAPE 1096 receive their benefits from their employer, Dow Jones. However, in the WashTech/CWA example, members are less likely to receive benefits from an employer because of their contingent employment status. Therefore, the remedies suggested by the associational unionism model and the citizenship unionism model offer some insights about how WashTech/CWA is addressing this issue. As a feature of both models, WashTech/CWA provides its members with access to medical, pension, and training benefits.

Associational unionism and citizenship unionism also have features that resemble WashTech/CWA's efforts to advocate on behalf of its constituents. Associational unionism includes advocacy on behalf of workers through the use of multiple strategies (Heckscher, 1996). In the citizenship unionism model, workers' issues are linked to citizens' issues to gain broader support (Stone, 2001).

A comparison with WashTech/CWA's strategies reveals that the organization uses some features from each of these four theoretical models. The appearance of some features suggests that while none of the theoretical models is applicable in its entirety, they do offer some lessons for representing the interests of contingent IT workers. Heckscher's associational model of unionism and Stone's citizenship model of unionism most closely resemble the strategies in use at WashTech/CWA.

From both the IAPE 1096 and WashTech/CWA case studies, I find that new economy jobs are not so different from old economy jobs the need for representation and protection in the workplace remains. The needs of both IT and contingent workers are multifaceted and, therefore, require an organizational structure that can deploy a variety of strategies to represent the demands of constituent employees. It is too early to tell whether WashTech/CWA will come to resemble IAPE 1096 as it evolves.

NOTES

1. Available online at http://www.uefoundation.org/report1.html, accessed May 23, 2002.

2. A nonunion form is discussed in Batt et al., 2001, and in Christopherson and van Jaarsveld, 2005.

3. The IAPE 1096 case study draws on over seventy-five in-depth interviews that were conducted with Dow Jones IT and human resource managers, Dow Jones general counsel, Dow Jones chief technology officer, IAPE 1096's officers, IAPE 1096's stewards, IAPE 1096's members, IAPE 1096's lawyer, and TNG-CWA national union officers between September 2002 and September 2003. Detailed notes and recordings from each interview were transcribed to facilitate analysis of common themes. Archival material including collective bargaining agreements, memoranda of understanding, and company-supplied documents pertaining to organizational structure and IT job classifications supplemented evidence from the interviews. In addition to the qualitative research, an individual-level survey instrument was administered to collect data about the union attitudes of IT workers.

The WashTech/CWA case study consists of interviews, Internet-based information, and survey data to consider strategies that are suitable for the representation of high-tech workers. First, interviews were conducted with Microsoft contractors, union organizers, academics, and lawyers. Second, information was gathered from WashTech/CWA's Web site and its "electronic bulletin board," which represents another aspect of the research strategy to develop an understanding of the issues important to this workforce. The high degree of Internet use for communication purposes among this workforce makes this source of material a very useful and appropriate one. Third, three sets of secondary survey data collected by Microsoft and WashTech/CWA were used to validate the findings drawn from interviews and Internet sources.

4. These jobs are protected by an agency shop clause.

5. For more details, see van Jaarsveld, 2005.

6. According my interview with Tracey Hogan, it had taken a year to revise one or two job classifications on previous occasions.

7. "IAPE Members Approve Dow Jones Contract Imposing Premium Payments for Health Care," *Daily Labor Report* 154: A-2, 2004. For more details on this contract, see van Jaarsveld, 2005.

8

Economic Development and the Labor Movement in the New Economy
Lessons from Silicon Valley

Chris Benner

The dramatic pace of technological change, complex restructuring of firms, and continual competitive pressures for rapid innovation that are a central component of the information economy are contributing to fundamental transformations in work and employment. As part of this transformation, production organized around smaller workplaces connected together in complex, constantly shifting networks operating at multiple spatial scales, from the local to the global, is superseding the centralization of production in large enterprises that was the dominant feature of the industrial era. For many workers, one result of this trend is greater insecurity, as they increasingly have to update their skills, change jobs, and even change careers more frequently. Some analysts have gone so far as to characterize the typical information-age worker as a "free-floating individual, connected on-line to a variety of task-performing organizations, ever-competing for resources and personal support, and assuming limited responsibilities towards limited people for a limited time" (Carnoy and Castells, 1997, 35).

If the workplace is being eroded as a basis for worker solidarity in the new economy, are traditional unions outdated? If industrial unions are less effective in the context of a constantly shifting workplace, what other alternatives are there for the labor movement and for information technology workers? One response, which I discuss in detail elsewhere (Benner, 2003) is the (re)emergence of occupational communities—groups of workers who are linked more closely by their similar skills, social bonds, and labor market experiences than by their position in their employing organization. In many information technology occupations, workers have been coming together to create occupation-based associations, frequently using a "guild" terminology with names like the System Administrators Guild, the HTML Writers' Guild, and the Silicon Valley Web Guild. Once thought to be remnants of a preindustrial social order all but wiped out by the development of mass production, new forms of guilds now seem to be reemerging, as workers come together to share knowledge, build contacts leading to their next jobs, and try to protect themselves from the insecurity and volatility of information-age labor markets.

Another area of innovation in recent years has been union efforts to improve the quality of jobs through engaging in a variety of community-based economic development strategies. In recent years, unions and central labor councils have engaged in a range of new local economic development initiatives, including living wage campaigns, subsidy accountability policies, sectoral training and other workforce development initiatives, industrial modernization programs, and a range of capital investment strategies. The AFL-CIO's Working for America Institute, for instance, documented a range of sectoral partnerships in a range of industries throughout the country that promote improved competitiveness and better job quality. The economic development efforts of the labor movement in Milwaukee, and particularly of the Wisconsin Regional Training Partnerships, have been well documented (Eimer, 2001; Parker and Rogers, 1995; Parker and Rogers, 2001). Kriesky (1998) has two case studies of central labor councils' involvement in economic development initiatives in Oregon and Iowa. Luce (2001) provides a specific examination of labor councils' involvement in the living wage movement.

This chapter addresses these questions by examining a particular case study: the economic development initiatives of the South Bay (Silicon Valley, California) Central Labor Council (SBCLC). Since the early 1990s, the SBCLC has engaged in a number of high-profile economic development initiatives that have been a critical component of a broader resurgence in union activism in Silicon Valley. In analyzing these efforts, I will argue three central points. First, the structure of Silicon Valley's regional labor markets, characterized by networked production systems and volatile employment dynamics, makes a focus on local economic development issues essential for improving working conditions of workers in the region. The lack of workplace stability and the dramatic inequality between high-tech and locally serving industries in the region severely limit the potential impact of traditional organizing strategies, thus requiring broader economic development initiatives in order to significantly improve workers' livelihoods. Second, these economic development initiatives position the labor movement as a clear advocate not simply of union members but of working families more broadly and, in the process, have helped the labor council build a broad labor-community coalition. Third, while these economic development initiatives have achieved some remarkable successes in a number of key policy areas, they have had only limited influence on the high-technology industries that dominate the region's economy. This weakness is rooted in the minimal union representation within high-tech firms and the limited leverage the labor movement has over firms in this sector of the economy. Thus, however critical the economic development initiatives are for building a broad labor-led progressive coalition, they cannot substitute for direct worker organizing. The labor movement in the region still faces the central challenge of translating the social mobilization linked with a broad economic development strategy into specific organizing efforts that can expand formal union recognition in strategic industries in Silicon Valley. In this light, these economic development initiatives can be seen as a necessary but not sufficient strategy for labor's long-term revitalization in the area.

This chapter continues by first discussing unions' role in economic development, particularly in the context of the structure and dynamics of Silicon Valley's labor markets. The following section provides some background on the recent evolution of the labor movement in the valley. The subsequent section describes specific economic development campaigns and strategies developed by the Central Labor Council. I then finish with a discussion of the lessons and implications that emerge from these experiences.

UNIONS, THE NEW ECONOMY AND SILICON VALLEY LABOR MARKETS

One of the prominent characteristics of labor markets in Silicon Valley is the relative lack of the workplace as a basis of long-term stability or solidarity for workers. Regional labor markets are characterized by rapidly changing skill requirements and volatile employment conditions. The Silicon Valley region has two times the national percentage of the workforce employed in temporary agencies, with up to 40 percent of the region's workforce involved in nonstandard employment relationships (Benner, 1996b). Rapid turnover has become the norm, even for people classified as having "permanent" employment (Carnoy et al., 1997; Gregory, 1984; Saxenian, 1996). A random survey of workers in Silicon Valley, for example, found a median job tenure of just under thirty months, with only 46 percent of respondents having had the same job for the previous three years, and 23 percent reporting having had three or more different jobs in that time (Pastor et al., 2003). Even for those staying in the same job, skill requirements change rapidly, resulting in high levels of uncertainty and insecurity (Benner, 2002).

The volatility in the region's labor markets is fundamentally tied to the nature of competition in the high-tech industries. Competitive success for firms and industries in information technology industries depends on constant innovation in both developing new products and services, and in improving production processes (Shapiro and Varian, 1998). As David Angel describes, "In an era of intensified global competition, it is the ability to anticipate and create new market opportunities, to develop new products ahead of competitors and to reconfigure production processes rapidly in response to changing production requirements that offers the best prospect for long-term profitability of firms and industries"(Angel, 1994, 4). This drive for constant innovation leads to a continual cycle of creative destruction, with new products, firms, and even entire industries replacing existing products, firms, and industries, while surviving firms are forced to restructure their operations and products. Layoffs in the midst of economic growth are not unusual, but in fact have been a common experience in Silicon Valley throughout its history. Indeed, flexible employment practices, with open labor markets and widespread circulation of skilled personnel among multiple firms, have been key to the long-term competitive success of firms and industries in the region (Saxenian, 1994).

Such labor flexibility would not be a major social concern if it resulted in widespread economic prosperity. Even during the booming 1990s, however, wages stagnated for the bottom half of the labor market and inequality increased (Benner, 1996; Benner, 2002). As the cost of housing skyrocketed in the region,[1] an estimated 55 percent of jobs in the valley in 1996 paid less than $15.72 an hour, the threshold of pay in full-time work needed to sustain a family of four without public support (Rosner and Benner, 1997). In addition, with high levels of temporary and contract employment, Silicon Valley workers are particularly vulnerable to economic downturns, as firms are able to shed workers rapidly. The unemployment rate in Santa Clara County (the heart of Silicon Valley), for instance, soared from a low of 1.3 percent in December 2000, to 7.7 percent in the space of just thirteen months, and peaked at 8.9 percent in October 2002, more than three percentage points higher than the national average at the time. By 2003, the region had lost a total of nearly 20 percent of all jobs and average pay declined by 22 percent (Sylvester, 2003). A survey of Silicon Valley workers in June 2003 found that more than a quarter of adults in the valley—a full 25.6 percent—had been laid off at least once since January 2001, and that 34.7 percent had at least one person in their household out of work for more than three months in that time (Steen, 2003, JV:SVN, 2003).

Unions have largely been invisible in the history of the high-tech industry in Silicon Valley and have certainly not been seen as important components of economic development in the new economy. This is in stark contrast to the widespread recognition of the role of unions in promoting economic prosperity during the New Deal and postwar era. By bargaining for wage and benefit gains for their members in union- ized firms and providing political support for broad Keynesian macro- economic demand-stabilization programs, unions helped solve the problem of maintaining effective demand in the economy and solved critical "collective actor" problems facing individual firms (Dunlop, 1958). Although employers benefited from this broad social compact— through both larger markets for their mass-produced goods and more predictable labor relations enabling them to take advantage of new economies of scale and productivity improvements associated with their substantial capital investments—they would not have gotten there on their own. Unionization helped stabilize labor relations and increase aggregate demand, which all firms had an interest in attaining but no single firm had the ability or interest to solve on its own.

In the "new economy," the role of worker representation in ensur- ing conditions of economic success is less clear. In our rapidly chang- ing, information-based economy, innovation and labor flexibility have become more critical in ensuring economic success than have employ- ment stability and predictable labor relations (Castells, 1996; Burton- Jones, 1999). Complex collective bargaining arrangements, which were once seen by even the Harvard Business School as contributing to improved management systems and enhanced worker loyalty (Slichter et al., 1960), are now seen more frequently as hindering innovation and firms' ability to respond to rapidly changing competition. The impor- tance of unions' role in ensuring aggregate demand has been under- mined by globalization and the increasing reliance on neoliberal finan- cial policies instead of Keynesian demand-stimulus policies to moder- ate business cycles and promote economic growth. In this context, unions face an uphill battle in defining a new role that clearly promotes economic prosperity, rather than simply defending the interests of their members and potential members.

The strategies the labor movement is pursuing to meet this challenge are still being developed, but there are two fundamental features of these new approaches worth noting. First, while maintaining effective demand remains important, the role of worker representation in the new economy is more likely to entail ensuring "effective supply," that is, improving the range of factors important for advanced production, particularly in relation to skilled workers and labor market functioning (Rogers, 1996). As a result, unions have been paying increased attention to workforce development and sectoral training programs in order to increase the supply and quality of a skilled workforce (AFL-CIO Working for America Institute, 2000). They have been experimenting with "intermediary" placement programs that can simultaneously improve cross-firm career ladders for individuals and lower employers' search costs, thus increasing the efficiency of labor market adjustments (Herzenberg et al., 1998; Benner, 2002). Increasingly, unions have also been playing a role in industrial modernization programs, attempting to increase the competitiveness of industries through training, technical assistance, and technology transfer programs.[2]

The second strategy is the union movement involvement in regional development. Contributions to economic development are likely to take place more effectively at a regional or metropolitan scale, rather than at the state or federal level.[3] The primary force driving this is the increased importance of regionalization in structuring economic activity. This may seem counterintuitive in an increasingly global economy, but the phenomenon is now well established in the economic geography literature (see, for instance, Scott, 1988; Scott, 1998; Storper, 1997; Barnes and Ledebur, 1998). The increased importance of regional economies results partly from long-term sectoral shifts in the economy, in which the share of the workforce in industries that serve only a local area (for example, retail sales, social and health services, education, and so on) has increased relative to those industries that are regional exporters (Persky and Wiewel, 1994). Even for export-oriented industries, economic regionalization is present in the increasing importance of innovation that emerges from the informal information exchange and "relational assets" rooted in the social interactions, sharing of tacit knowledge and development of conventions, informal rules, and common cultures that are built in region-specific clusters of firms (Storper, 1997; Maskell et al., 1998; Maskell and Malmberg, 1999). Furthermore, from the perspective of social mobilization, economic regions are being increasingly recognized as an important scale for public policy intervention and labor and community organizing (Pastor et al., 2000; PolicyLink, 2000; Ness and Eimer, 2001; Luria et al., 1999; Orfield, 1997).

UNIONS AND ECONOMIC DEVELOPMENT IN SILICON VALLEY

In developing a framework for engaging in economic development initiatives, the labor movement has increasingly used a "high-road/low-road" metaphor. In this framework, the goals of unions are threefold: 1) to "cut off the low road," discouraging firms from competing through price-cutting and labor-squeezing strategies by implementing labor standards and subsidy accountability systems; 2) to "pave the high road," helping firms compete through innovation and quality improvements by investing in the skills of their workforce and the quality of their production systems; and 3) to "enable workers and firms to navigate from the first to the second" by building effective training systems and modernization programs (Parker and Rogers, 2001; AFL-CIO Working for America Institute, 2000). While this is a useful metaphor and helps frame a series of useful strategies, there are at least two additional features of economic development that need to be incorporated into this framework in the Silicon Valley context.

First, it is becoming increasingly clear among economic development professionals that strategies for intervention are not limited to influencing individual firms and workers. With the increased focus on regional economies and industry clusters, innovative economic development interventions focus on new organizational approaches, creating institutions that promote interaction, knowledge transfer, skill development, and networking within industry clusters, rather than assisting individual firms (Bradshaw and Blakely, 1999; Porter, 2000). In addition to investment in physical infrastructure, investment in the social and political infrastructure that sustain factors of production, including a well-educated and healthy workforce and high levels of civic engagement, has also been shown to contribute substantially to economic competitiveness (Castilla et al., 2000; Saxenian, 1999; Saxenian, 1994). Unions are well placed to play a role in such an approach, and indeed some of the union-led sectoral-training programs could be considered as "best-practice" models in cluster promotion.

The challenge emerges, however, when the successful evolution of industry clusters involves significant "churning" of firms and jobs. This dynamic can be clearly seen in the information technology industries that dominate Silicon Valley's economy. In these industries, markets and technology change extremely rapidly and in unpredictable ways, and those firms that succeed are those that are able to innovate by developing both new products and improved production processes to shorten the time to market. Many new firms emerge and grow rapidly, taking advantage of new market opportunities. At the same time, many firms are unable to adapt effectively to these rapid changes. For example, more than half of the top one hundred public companies in Silicon Valley in 2000 were not on the list ten years earlier. Furthermore, of the one hundred largest Silicon Valley public companies in 1985, only nineteen still existed and were in the top one hundred in 2000.[4] While the regional economy has continued to thrive, many individual firms have not. In this context, union strategies could likely play a more productive role facilitating economic innovation and labor market adjustment, rather than preserving jobs in existing noncompetitive firms. While there are models of craft-based and associational unionism that reflect this possibility (Heckscher, 1996), most unions are rooted in firm-based representation systems, making such a broader approach challenging. It also makes building representation systems in nonunionized industries more difficult, requiring new models that don't depend solely on firm-based representation.

The second major challenge in promoting "high-road" economic development in the region is the substantial inequalities that exist between driving industry clusters and locally serving industries. The information technology industries that drive the regional economy have global markets, extremely high levels of productivity, and high profitability. Many locally serving industries, in contrast, are much more limited in their markets, more labor intensive, and have thinner profit margins. The result is stark inequality between regional export clusters and locally serving industries. While average payroll in the software, computer, and semiconductor industries was all over $100,000 a year in 1999, average payroll in local and visitor services, which employ 25 percent of the total workforce, was only $24,000 a year and only $39,000 a year in the government/education sector. Between 1998 and 1999, average payroll in driving industry clusters rose by 20 percent, while those in noncluster industries rose by only 1 percent (JV:SVN, 2001).

In this context, strategies to promote the high road in locally serving industries are likely to be limited by the thin profit margins in service and retail industries. These strategies may ultimately be less effective than those that focus on either helping people get work within driving industry clusters or leveraging the activities of these high-tech firms to provide more local benefits. This has been accomplished directly in cases where firms in driving industries subcontràct to locally serving firms. For example, the Service Employees International Union (SEIU) in its "Justice for Janitors" campaign targets the wealthy clients of cleaning services firms, rather than the cleaning services firms themselves. In most cases, however, the connections are not direct, and unions have to use political power to influence a range of local ordinances, zoning decisions, and investment in public-sector institutions to influence firms in the driving industry clusters. Doing this effectively, however, requires significant cross-union coordination and the development of broad labor-community alliances. Central labor councils (CLCs) are strategically placed to play a role in this type of coordination, but until recently most labor councils in the country have lacked any significant vitality or creativity. Recently, there has been a widespread revival in CLC activity, and the increasing recognition within the labor movement of the strategic importance of CLCs is encouraging (Ness and Eimer, 2001). The strategic important of CLCs is clearly evident in the case of Silicon Valley.

LABOR REVIVAL IN SILICON VALLEY

Most studies of the Silicon Valley economy pay little attention to unions, and the history of the region's development is frequently told without any mention of unions (Saxenian, 1994; Lee et al., 2000; Kenney, 2000; Winslow, 1995). With extremely low unionization levels in information technology industries, this is perhaps not surprising. Nonetheless, levels of unionization in Silicon Valley are higher than the national average, with a long history of unionization in the food processing industry in the valley and significant current densities in construction trades, the public sector, health care, certain retail sectors, and hotels (Johnston, 1994; Matthews, 2002). During the 1960s and 1970s, the labor movement played an important role in a resurgence in Democratic politics in the region, but faced declining influence amid lower unionization rates through the 1980s (Brownstein, 2000).

Labor's resurgence in the valley in the 1990s was lead by the South Bay (Silicon Valley) Central Labor Council, which represents more than 90 local unions and over 150,000 workers who are affiliated with it. The election of Amy Dean as executive officer of the labor council in 1994 marked a significant turning point. Dean had moved to the region several years earlier, after gaining experience as the political-education director of the International Lady Garment Workers

Union (ILGWU) in Chicago. She brought a new level of strategic vision, leadership, and energy to the labor council, as well as a vision for pursuing a broad social movement agenda:

> Dean recognized that for labor to advance in the New Economy, it would be necessary to understand the unprecedented changes in corporate structures and strategies and in labor market institutions and practices that were taking place. She also knew that understanding without power could accomplish little, so union-organizing efforts and involvement in electoral campaigns became priorities. Finally, for labor to succeed, other constituencies in the valley needed to find common cause with labor's initiatives, so coalition-building became a third critical emphasis. Labor's program had to expand to include a broad notion of social equity and a concern for the needs of all working families. (Brownstein, 2000)

To help further these goals, the SBCLC established a separate nonprofit policy and research institute called Working Partnerships USA. The labor council and Working Partnerships are distinct entities, with the labor council focusing on organizing efforts and political campaigns and Working Partnerships conducting research, developing policy initiatives, and providing education and training. The two organizations are closely linked, however. Over time, Dean built a committed and diverse staff, which grew from a handful in 1994, to nearly thirty people in 2001. Critically, the staff reflected the ethnic and gender diversity of the region with a majority of the staff nonwhite and with women in many key leadership positions. When Dean resigned from her post in 2004, she was succeeded by Phaedra Ellis-Lampkins, a dynamic young African American woman who has continued the tradition of a vibrant, community-oriented labor movement.

Establishing a separate nonprofit turned out to be critical for three central factors. First, it provided access to new *funds*, since as a nonprofit organization Working Partnerships is eligible for the kind of funding from major foundations and the public sector that a labor organization is not. Second, Working Partnerships helps put a new *face* on the labor movement. The research reports and training programs developed by Working Partnerships clearly represent something different from the labor movement's more traditional organizing and political activities. This new face reaches new audiences and builds alliances with people and organizations that might not be possible otherwise. Third, the new organization provides an opportunity for creating new *friends*, particularly with community and faith-based allies. Working Partnerships serves as an umbrella representing the interests of a broad coalition of progressive forces in the valley, not just labor unions. While it clearly remains primarily directed by the labor movement, the creation of a new entity has facilitated the broadening of coalitions around a variety of issues.

The economic development initiatives pursued by Working Partnerships are best understood in the context of a broader strategy that includes research and policy development, education and training, and developing new models of employee representation. The research efforts of the organization initially focused on identifying and documenting issues that working families in the area are facing, including high levels of insecure employment, growing inequality, and a declining standard of living for large sectors of the region's workforce (Benner, 1996b; Benner, 1996a; Benner et al., 1999). This research played an important role in changing public policy discussion, shifting debates away from simply celebrating the economic success of the region, toward addressing urgent social problems. The general research on social conditions paved the way for more policy-oriented reports focused on specific proposals.

Economic development initiatives have also been closely linked with the organization's education and training programs, a significant portion of which have been centered around a participatory nine-week "leadership institute" that provides participants with a deeper understanding of economic changes in the region and the political institutions that help shape the region's development. Participants, who now total over three hundred, are strategically recruited to represent five key constituencies in the region: labor leaders, community organizations, leaders of faith-based communities, public-sector staff and elected officials, and leaders from the small business community and ethnic business associations. The sharing of experiences across these constituencies in an educational context has helped create long-term collaborations, by building a common vision of social justice and a deeper mutual understanding of the problems facing different community residents. Furthermore, the education program has directly fed into economic development initiatives, as during each nine-week session students do research and policy analysis related to a current campaign.

Finally, in addition to trying to help existing unions in their organizer training, Working Partnerships has also been experimenting with new models of worker representation. These efforts (described in the next section) center on serving the needs of the rapidly growing temporary workforce in the region. The effort to reach out to temporary workers by providing new services and exploring new models of worker representation has helped build a constituency for Working Partnerships' other economic development initiatives as well, exposing people who first come into contact with the labor movement through their temporary placement services to the range of the organization's other initiatives.

With this broad set of activities as background, I will now turn to the range of economic development initiatives the South Bay Central Labor Council and Working Partnerships have pursued since the mid-1990s.

ECONOMIC DEVELOPMENT INITIATIVES

Subsidy Accountability

Working Partnerships first got involved in economic development policy in the summer of 1995 with an initiative to increase the accountability of corporations receiving public-sector economic development subsidies. Two years previously, the California State Legislature had adopted the bill AB 1823, which allowed counties to offer a property tax rebate to manufacturing firms to encourage them to locate in or expand in the county. This bill emerged in response to the economic downturn in the early 1990s and was seen by the state legislature as a potentially important tool for local government to promote economic development. The policy, however, had no guidelines for how to evaluate companies for receiving this subsidy and no mechanism to ensure that companies would follow through on job creation plans once they received the tax benefit. Building on a growing national movement to challenge these free subsidies (LeRoy, 1997), Working Partnerships developed a set of proposed guidelines requiring tax rebate recipients to provide jobs with health insurance and a minimum wage level of $10/hour and requiring them to refund the rebate if they failed to generate the number of jobs promised. Under the guidelines, companies had to ensure a history of fair labor practices and adequate workplace health and safety policies. The South Bay Central Labor Council organized a broad coalition in support of these provisions, and over the opposition of the Silicon Valley Manufacturing Group, the Santa Clara County Board of Supervisors unanimously approved the new requirements.

Urban Land-Use Decisions

This subsidy accountability effort was followed up almost immediately with an innovative initiative designed to promote high-road economic development by leveraging San Jose's zoning authority. The issue in this case was a proposal from K-Mart to build a new Super K-Mart store that would also sell groceries. To build the store, K-Mart needed a change in the zoning regulation to allow for large, "big-box" retail development to take place on the site. The expansion was opposed by the United Food and Commercial Workers Union (UFCW), who were in a representation battle with K-Mart at a store in Oakland. Union leaders feared that K-Mart would actively oppose unionization in the new store and that the nonunion grocery would undermine nearby unionized grocery stores. From the point of view of local economic development, Working Partnerships was also concerned about the Super K-Mart for several additional reasons. First, the jobs that would be created at the site were likely to be part-time and pay low wages. With land a scarce resource in Silicon Valley, Working Partnerships wanted the city to consider using the site for other uses that might create higher-quality jobs. Working Partnerships also questioned whether the city of San Jose was right in anticipating that the Super K-Mart would result in additional sales tax revenue. The city had failed to conduct any assessment of whether an expansion in sales at Super K-Mart would simply come at the expense of other local retailers in San Jose or even from the neighboring city of Milpitas, in which case an expansion in San Jose's revenue would simply come at the expense of Milpitas, resulting in no net gain for the region.

In response to this, Working Partnerships and the SBCLC pursued a two-pronged strategy. First, they argued that, prior to making the zoning change to benefit Super K-Mart, the city of San Jose should conduct an Economic Impact Analysis, similar in concept to an Environmental Impact Analysis, to assess the impact of this changed zoning on equity, job creation, and revenue generation. Second, Working Partnerships and SBCLC argued that the zoning change should be made contingent on Super K-Mart's signing an agreement providing job quality guidelines similar to the guidelines they proposed in the AB 1823 battle over tax rebates for job creation. Unfortunately, the proposals were not adopted for several reasons. Super K-Mart refused to sign any agreement, but apparently gave verbal assurances that they would use union workers in the construction of the store and would remain neutral in any subsequent unionization efforts among their staff. In addition, the San Jose City Attorney argued that the city didn't have the legal ability to make zoning linked with a particular *user* (e.g., Super

K-Mart), only with a particular *use* (e.g. big-box retail). Although the labor council obtained other legal advice that such a consideration was indeed legal, the concern about litigation swayed some of the city council members. Finally, the city council member who represented the district in which the Super K-Mart would be located was clearly in favor of the development, arguing that his district, which was quite poor, required job creation regardless of the quality of the jobs. Although hundreds of residents turned out at the meeting opposed to the development, the city council voted in favor of the zoning change.

Despite being a losing effort, the struggle over these land-use decisions has had at least two important lasting impacts. First, the eventual outcome of the development increased the labor movement's credibility in the city council. Two years after the development was approved, K-Mart developed the building with a significant amount of nonunion labor and took a clearly antiunion stance in relation to its retail employees. When the SBCLC returned to the city council to ask for its endorsement of a UFCW-led boycott against Super K-Mart, the council agreed. This vote was only symbolic—the city didn't do any business with Super K-Mart—and it came at a high political price.[5] It did, however, help serve notice to other developers that the labor movement could play a significant role in shaping land-use decisions, which became important in subsequent developments. Second, the concept of an Economic Impact Analysis, though not applied in this case, clearly was attractive to a wide constituency, and Working Partnerships is still working to get it accepted in principle as part of future land-use decisions in the city.

Living Wage Ordinance

Following the struggle over the Super K-Mart, Working Partnerships turned their attention to getting a living wage ordinance adopted in the city of San Jose. The basic concept of living wage ordinances— ensuring that publicly subsidized or contracted-out jobs pay wages sufficient to enable workers to be self-sufficient—and the growing nationwide living wage movement are well described elsewhere (Pollin and Luce, 1998; Brownstein, 2000). There are a number of significant aspects about the ordinance in San Jose. At the time it was passed, it had the highest wage level in the country—$9.50/hour with health benefits, or $10.75/hour without. It also contained two significant elements important to labor organizations. The first was a worker retention clause designed to protect employees of contracted service firms. If the city decides to change recipients of city contracts, the new firm is required to retain the existing employees for a period of time after the contract is switched. The second provision was a "labor peace" clause that allowed the city to consider the potential consequences of unstable labor relations, including nonunionized firms, when it evaluated individual bidders for contracts.

As in all living wage initiatives, the specific number of workers affected in this case was small, perhaps fewer than one thousand. More importantly, though, the living wage campaign contributed to strengthening a progressive alliance in the community. The labor movement in this case was advocating for the broader interests of working families in the region, since most of the workers directly affected were not union members. Furthermore, their argument appealed to all taxpayers, since it is clearly a waste of public resources to have workers in publicly contracted jobs paid so little that they have to depend on public health and social services at an often greater cost to the public sector than would be the case if they were paid living wages in the first place. The broad mobilization built around the living wage ordinance was evidenced in the large numbers of people that jammed the city council chambers on the night of the decision and in the fact that the ordinance passed by a surprising 8 to 3 margin, as even one of the most persistent opponents of the ordinance eventually voted yes (Brownstein, 2000).

Community Economic Blueprint

At the same time that the K-Mart and living wage campaigns were moving ahead, Working Partnerships also initiated a program to involve working families and representatives from numerous sectors of society in developing a broad economic development vision for the region. This process was designed to prioritize economic issues and develop specific policy proposals to address these concerns. The "Community Economic Blueprint" process began in 1997 with a series of focus groups including activists, experts, community leaders, representatives of local organizations, skilled workers, service providers, and service recipients, discussing both broad economic concerns and issues of particular concern to their constituency, including health care, the environment, neighborhood issues, childcare, housing, and other concerns. Out of these meetings came a series of ideas, priorities, and potential policies to address urgent economic problems of Silicon Valley residents. Two specific issues—children's health and affordable housing—are discussed in the next section.

The process of developing the Community Blueprint was important for a number of reasons. Clearly, the issues that emerged were not limited to narrow economic issues, but included a range of social policy issues as well. By bringing all these issues together under a broad strategic vision of the region's economy, Working Partnerships attempted to shift the economic development debate away from simply a focus on growth toward issues of equity and the quality of the region's economy. Clearly, despite some temporary downturns, sustaining the growth of Silicon Valley's regional economy has not been the major challenge for the region. Instead, the major challenges are ensuring that the by-products of success—including skyrocketing housing prices, increased traffic congestion, environmental damage, and increasing inequality—don't undermine the long-term competitiveness of the region. The Community Blueprint process helps redefine the goals of economic development policy to include this broader set of social policy issues, while trying to ensure that the benefits of economic growth are more widely shared. Furthermore, the consultative process involved a wide-ranging constituency and helped them get involved in campaigns to improve the region. As Amy Dean argues:

> Perhaps most of all, [the Community Blueprint process] attempts to determine not only what people would like to have handed to them but what they would be willing to organize and if necessary, struggle, to achieve. The last point identifies the heart of the Community Blueprint ethic. Working Partnerships performs research and popular education. Political and social change requires people to organize and act. The test of Community Blueprint projects ... [is] the extent to which and manner in which members of the community respond to the information and ideas we have generated. If they discuss the analysis, establish objectives, and organize campaigns to achieve a more just society ... the Blueprint model will have demonstrated its worth. (Bhargava et al., 2001)

The success of these efforts is evident in the large number of people who have turned out in support of two major policy initiatives that have emerged out of this process—the Children's Health Initiative and the Affordable Housing policy.

Children's Health Initiative

In 1999 Working Partnerships, in cooperation with People Acting in Community Together (PACT—an organization made up of thirteen local faith-based congregations), began promoting a countywide

Children's Health Initiative that had the goal of providing universal health insurance coverage to all children under the age of five. Initial data indicated that two-thirds of the 71,000 uninsured children in Santa Clara County were eligible for existing public programs (Healthy Families and MediCal), but were not taking advantage of them either because they were unaware of the programs or unaware that they were eligible. Part of the strategy was to get Santa Clara County to increase efforts to reach these children. The remaining children, many of whom were undocumented immigrants or whose income levels made them ineligible for existing programs, would be served through a newly created subsidized local insurance plan. This plan, called Healthy Kids, was to be funded by three sources: from the city of San Jose and Santa Clara County primarily through funds they had received as part of the national tobacco settlement; from Proposition 10, a tax on tobacco products the proceeds of which must be used for children under the age of five; and additional funds from philanthropic foundations, which Working Partnerships helped raise.

By June of 2000, Working Partnerships and PACT had mobilized hundreds of supporters to attend a city council meeting to request that the city of San Jose dedicate its tobacco funds for this initiative. Although they were initially unsuccessful at the city level, they persisted, receiving unanimous approval at the county level, receiving additional foundation support, and eventually convincing the city to follow suit. Within six months, they had raised $7.4 million. The Children's Health Initiative began enrolling new children in January 1, 2001, and by all accounts it has been a tremendous success (Long, 2001). By September 26, 2001, the program had succeeded in enrolling an additional 19,982 children in the different programs, including 6,800 in Healthy Kids and was receiving on average one hundred fifty calls a day from people interested in the program (Children's Health Initiative, 2001).

Aside from the success in providing health insurance to needy children, the campaign was a tremendous success in building public backing for the labor movement. The goal of 100 percent coverage helped galvanize extraordinary support for this project, as the slogan "We will leave no child behind" became broadly adopted by elected officials, clergy, community organizations, and local leaders throughout the region. The fact that the labor movement was visibly one of the key leaders of this initiative clearly increased its credibility and support in many circles.

Affordable Housing

The other major issue that emerged out of the Community Blueprint process was the critical housing crisis facing working families in Silicon Valley. The signs of this crisis are everywhere. Between 1990 and 2000, only 48,700 new housing units were created in Santa Clara County compared to a total of 211,000 new jobs.[6] This ratio of 4.3 new jobs for every new housing unit is substantially more than the ratio of 1.6 that experts estimate is sustainable, and the resulting imbalance of supply and demand resulted in dramatic increases in housing prices. The median sale price of a single-family home skyrocketed to $565,000 in 2001, up more than 130 percent from only five years previously, and a price that only an estimated 18 percent of Silicon Valley families could afford.[7] By 2000, an estimated 90,000 Santa Clara County residents were paying more than 30 percent of their incomes in rent, and a full 43,000 residents were paying more than half their income in rent (Bhargava et al., 2001). The lack of affordable housing forces an estimated 133,000 Silicon Valley workers to live outside Santa Clara County, resulting in traffic congestion that now costs an estimated $1.25 billion in extra commuting costs and lost work time. The housing crisis has become a critical problem for many firms in the area who have a difficult time recruiting new employees.

In June of 2001, Working Partnerships issued a major policy report on housing in Silicon Valley (Bhargava et al., 2001) that helped document the scale of the problem and proposed solutions that included both increasing the supply of affordable units and preserving the supply of existing affordable units. These proposals have yet to be implemented. Nonetheless, simply the fact that the labor council would take on such a difficult and complicated issue as affordable housing further enhanced its role in representing a broad constituency in the region and engaging in local land-use and economic development decision-making processes.

Temporary Worker Employment Project

Working Partnerships also developed an interesting program aimed at addressing the growing problems of temporary workers in the regional labor market. The goal of this project is simultaneously to help temporary workers gain access to better employment and to upgrade employment practices within the staffing services industry as a whole. This project began in 1997 and has three basic components:

1. The creation of a best-practices temp agency in an effort to set high standards for the industry, which provides access to higher-paying jobs; holiday and vacation pay; affordable, portable health insurance; and fewer barriers for conversion to permanent employment.
2. The formation of a temporary workers' membership association to enhance workers' voice and advocate for change in the industry.
3. Improved access to training for workers who are clients of the staffing service and the membership association with a longer-term goal of creating recognizable cross-firm skill ladders.

Developing this initiative turned out to be more challenging than Working Partnerships originally anticipated. Trying to operate as a new small business, the staffing service had problems at the outset because there are significant barriers to entry into the temp industry including developing specialized brokering skills. As a result, Working Partnerships eventually switched from relying on their own staff to hiring staffing industry professionals who have worked to implement more of a "business model" to ensure financial stability. This approach has shown signs of success with the agency now very near the break-even point despite meeting the higher standards. The temp workers membership association has grown rapidly with over one thousand members. A portion of these have become involved in advocacy efforts that were focused initially on establishing a code of conduct for temporary agencies. Like living wage campaigns, the code of conduct campaign involves lobbying public agencies to give preferential treatment to temporary agencies they hire from that sign and abide by the code of conduct. The membership association is also now attempting to reform the unemployment insurance program in the state to allow temp workers more reasonable access.[8]

Overall, this temporary worker employment initiative is an ambitious program that aims to upgrade employment opportunities and business practices in a difficult area. It is an exciting initiative, but one that is still in the process of implementation and testing. Some of the challenges are due to the usual stresses and strains of start-ups, but others are implicit in the model itself. Since organizing for worker leverage is difficult in an occupation spread across many industries where skill requirements vary widely, union strength is low, and employer collective action problems are severe. Nonetheless, this program builds access for the labor movement to new constituencies and clearly shows that the labor movement is trying to deal with one of the more intractable problems in the regional economy.

ECONOMIC DEVELOPMENT INITIATIVES, LABOR REVITALIZATION AND HIGH-TECH WORKERS— SOME IMPLICATIONS

The labor movement in Silicon Valley has gained significant visibility and strength since the early 1990s. By 2000, the San Jose Mercury News included Amy Dean in a list of the forty most powerful people in the valley, on a par with high-tech executives such as Larry Ellison (Oracle), Carly Fiorina (Hewlett-Packard), Andy Grove (Intel), and Steve Jobs (Apple) (Bartindale and Ostrom, 2000).

The economic development initiatives described in the previous section, of course, are only one component of labor's resurgence in the region. The labor council and local unions have also been involved in a whole range of more traditional organizing and political activity aimed at increasing the labor movement's influence at local and statewide levels. The economic development initiatives, however, have been a critical component of labor's resurgence in the area.

The clearest contribution of these initiatives is in the area of the labor movement's *political base and influence*. Obviously, much of the labor movement's political influence in the valley has come from more traditional means, including political endorsements, phone banks, and door-to-door get-out-the-vote initiatives, which have become highly effective in leveraging the strength of union membership in the region. The economic development initiatives, however, have been critical for expanding the labor movement's influence to a much broader constituency. By leading popular campaigns, like the living wage ordinance and the Children's Health Initiative, the local labor movement has been able to build new allies and, particularly, to help build a strong labor-community coalition that has played a strategic role in supporting both particular policy initiatives and a broad progressive economic agenda. These initiatives have increased the capacity of Working Partnerships' staff to be effective on a variety of issues, not just those of immediate benefit to unions, and thus have increased their credibility among a broad set of allies. The economic development initiatives have also been important in building labor's credibility among a range of nontraditional constituencies, including foundations, small business owners, ethnic business leaders, university researchers, and many policy analysts. By building such a diverse set of relationships and networks, the labor movement has increased its influence far beyond its membership base.

The initiatives described above have also had a direct *economic* impact, though here the contributions have been more modest. Clearly, there are some success stories to point to. The Children's Health Initiative resulted in tens of thousands of children in Silicon Valley receiving health insurance that they wouldn't have had otherwise. The living wage ordinance and the Temporary Worker Employment Project have resulted in higher wages for hundreds of workers and have created new mechanisms for influencing economic trajectories related to both public-sector contracting and the use of temporary workers. And the subsidy accountability policy has, at least in principle, increased the accountability of public-sector economic subsidies, though no firm has yet decided to apply for the tax abatement. Even in the losing struggle over the new Super K-Mart store, there are positive outcomes in terms of future development decisions in the valley, as the concept of an Economic Impact Analysis is now being promoted in a subsidy-accountability campaign aimed at promoting Smart Growth.

These initiatives, however, have had only minimal impact on the information technology industries that are at the heart of the regional economy. By and large, firms in the information technology sector have been unaffected, either positively or negatively, by the economic development initiatives of Working Partnerships. Opportunities do exist to intervene in issues of critical importance for these firms. One of the most obvious is to help these firms solve a classic collective actor problem around skill development in information technology occupations. All employers need to have a well-trained workforce, but individual employers have little incentive to contribute to training on their own when high levels of turnover mean they are unlikely to reap the benefits of increased training investments. This dynamic has been particularly evident in the "shortage" of information technology workers that firms experienced in the late 1990s. Many detailed examinations of this phenomenon made it clear that management practices and the institutional framework of skills development were a key part of the problem (Cappelli, 2000; National Research Council, 2001). Unions and other workers' associations organized on an occupational or industry level could help solve this problem by negotiating with employers to invest in regional training programs and collaborative learning networks. Workers would gain from improved career opportunities, while employers would be able to capture many of the same gains from investment in human resources in organized regional labor markets that they used to capture in internal labor markets.

Nonetheless, for the labor movement to effectively develop that role in Silicon Valley would require deep ties with workers in the high-tech industry and the ability to help these workers organize around these kinds of issues. Given the difficulties of developing training programs in complex and rapidly changing technology fields and the difficulty in organizing in an industry with high levels of turnover and a highly diverse workforce, the SBCLC has not prioritized targeting high-tech industries in the valley. Instead, it has chosen to focus on areas where it has more strength and a much greater likelihood of success. The hope is that this will help develop significant power and influence, enabling it to ultimately have a more significant impact on activities of high-tech firms in the region. Whether this will happen remains to be seen and will ultimately depend on the organizing strategies pursued by local unions in the area.

In the arena of *membership expansion*, however, there is little clear evidence that the economic development initiatives have contributed significantly. To be sure, there have been some significant organizing victories in the 1990s, including public health services, retail grocery sales, and the cleaning services industry. The significant influence of the SBCLC has been a factor in building political support for these organizing drives, and this increased influence has come in part from the experience gained in economic development initiatives. This influence, however, is no substitute for direct union organizing, which ultimately resides in the capacities and strategies of local unions in the region, not in the SBCLC. There are no detailed statistics available on unionization levels just in Silicon Valley, but the trends evident in the larger San Francisco Bay Area metropolitan area are not encouraging. Public-sector unionization rates have declined slightly since 1994, after having increased substantially in the prior decade. Private-sector unionization rates have declined steadily since 1986, declining from 18.2 percent to 10.8 percent of the private-sector labor force. Obviously, membership is only the most basic indicator of labor's strength, and the labor movement in San Jose has the ability to mobilize a large number of nonunion members in support of common goals. Without the additional strength a union contract provides, however, social mobilization is limited in its ability to influence employers and, particularly, high-tech employers in the region. Thus, while economic development initiatives have been critical for building a broad labor-led progressive coalition, they cannot substitute for direct worker organizing. The labor movement still faces the challenge of translating this social mobilization into specific organizing efforts that can expand formal union recognition in strategic industries in Silicon Valley.

NOTES

1. Between January 1996 and January 2001, the median house price in Santa Clara County, the core of Silicon Valley, more than doubled, rising from $251,000 to $577,500. Source: www.penwest.com, accessed May 2001.

2. Prominent examples include the New York–based Garment Industry Development Corporation (www.gidc.org), the Wisconsin Regional Training Partnerships (www.wrtp.org), and the Michigan-based Labor-Management Council for Economic Renewal, and are described in more detail in AFL-CIO Working for America Institute (2000).

3. Obviously, state and federal funding and policy play a critical role in shaping regional economic development.

4. Of the eighty-one that no longer appeared in the top one hundred list in 2000, thirty-nine were acquired or merged into other companies, twenty-two were still independent public companies but were too small to make the list in 1994, thirteen more entered bankruptcy proceedings, six more moved out of the area, and one became private through a management buyout. Data from *San Jose Mercury News* Annual Reports on Silicon Valley 150.

5. Winning the boycott vote required heavy lobbying of city council members and ended up postponing a campaign over a living wage ordinance.

6. Housing data: California Department of Finance County Profiles. Available at http://www.dof.ca.gov/HTML/FS_DATA/profiles/pf_home.htm, accessed February 27, 2006. Employment data: CA EDD LMID. Available at http://www.labormarketinfo.edd.ca.gov/cgi/databrowsing/?PageID=4&SubID= 166, accessed February 27, 2006.

7. Silicon Valley Association of Realtors, http://www.silvar.org/stats/ stat_page.html. Page no longer available.

8. Currently, if a worker affiliated with a temporary agency turns down employment because of poor wages or working conditions, this makes him or her ineligible for unemployment insurance. This ties the worker to the agency and forces him or her to accept any offer, no matter how inadequate from the point of view of career building.

9

The New Media Union: What New Media Professionals Can Learn from Old Media Unions

John Amman

The experience of entertainment industry unions offers many lessons for organizing the new economy workforce. Many new media professionals share common professional goals and concerns with their counterparts the "old" media of film and television. Both groups have very high degrees of professional identification, and work primarily on a freelance basis. Within both groups there are people who are at different times both employer and employee. But while the new media workforce is almost exclusively nonunion, the old media workforce has one of the highest union densities in the United States. I first outlined the similarities between these two groups in an article in *Working U.S.A.* (Amman, 2002).

That article was directed, more or less, to persons within the sphere of the U.S. labor movement who might be in search of an appropriate union model for the new economy workforce. I have concluded since that it makes more sense for me to address this chapter for the new media workforce itself. After all, new media professionals will have to decide what type of representational structure, if any, is appropriate for them. Danielle Van Jaarsveld, Immanuel Ness, and Derek Schultz have already pointed out that new media professionals have every reason to band together to address common workplace, professional, and political concerns, and they are capable and willing to do so. But new media professionals have not gravitated toward traditional AFL-CIO unions nor have they seen them as the structures through which to organize. For example, Laurie Milton (2003) in interviews with programmers, systems engineers, and software engineers found that when asked "if they had ever thought of joining a union, every high-tech worker interviewed responded with silence, and in several instances prolonged silence." She went on to state that respondents viewed union membership as something antithetical to high-tech culture. Derek Schultz, who is now an advocate for a white-collar, high-tech union, admitted to me in an interview that he was not initially drawn to the labor movement nor did he see then its relevance to the high-tech workforce. For new media professionals, professional identity is crucial in their decision whether or not to unionize or to create any kind of community of interest. If AFL-CIO unions are seen as largely blue-collar organizations representing the interests of workers in manufacturing, construction, or blue-collar service jobs, it is not likely that freelance new media professionals will have an interest in them.

For a labor union to be effective it must represent the interests of a majority or substantial minority of workers in a particular set of related occupations in the economy. For a labor movement to be effective it must be totally integrated into the economy itself. When Samuel Gompers and his associates created the AFL in the 1880s, they focused on highly skilled craft workers, a blue-collar elite, that were essential to the manufacturing economy prior to mass production. When mass production took over and manufacturers no longer relied as heavily on skilled craftsmen, the AFL unions lost members and power. In the 1930s John L. Lewis helped to create the CIO when the U.S. manufacturing economy relied on armies of unskilled workers employed in workplaces that utilized mass production work models. With manufacturing jobs outsourced to Mexico and China, the industrial unions have also lost members and clout. The new media professional does not fit comfortably in either the craft or industrial worker mold, so an industrial or craft union may be no more equipped to represent freelance computer programmers and software designers than the International Cigar Makers Union would have been at representing autoworkers seventy years ago. New media professionals must have a representational structure appropriate for the mercurial and global twenty-first century economy.

Old media unions still offer lessons for new media professionals who have an interest in creating representational structures. The film and television workforce is well trained, highly skilled, and largely freelance much as new media professionals are. They also rely heavily on similar types of networking relationships with employers and co-workers in order to maintain their careers. It is also important to note that these older media rely on new technologies. The film and television industries are steeped in the same computer technologies as those found in new media. In fact, in areas like editing, computer graphics animation, and special effects, the old and new media workforces overlap a great deal. Since the workforces are so similar to one another, they also share very similar challenges. Access to affordable health insurance and retirement plans are two principal concerns of any freelance worker, regardless of the industry. Training and professional credentialing are another concern. Both old and new media professionals are subject to intense work schedules that often demand that they work long hours at the expense of their physical and emotional well-being (see Batt et al., 2001).

This chapter begins with an examination of the broad similarities between "new" media professionals (for example, computer programmers, Web site designers, and computer graphics animators) and "old" media workers in entertainment industries. I then outline those elements of the Motion Picture and Television Industry union structures that best complement high-tech industries. While presenting this model, I also include the pitfalls that currently plague the film and television industry unions that any high-tech union would be wise to avoid.

PROFILE OF THE NEW MEDIA PROFESSIONAL

In their analysis of high-tech workers in New York City's "Silicon Alley," Batt and her coauthors (2001) use the term *new media* to describe Internet-oriented activities. I would broaden Batt's use of new media to include a somewhat wider array of computer-related technologies that are not limited to the Internet per se. The same technologies are used to create Internet Web sites, computer games, educational CD-ROMs, and animation and special effects for the motion picture industry. The use of the technologies used in new media technologies is growing and is clearly not restricted to just one sector of the economy. The old media of television, film, and telecommunications are being changed by new information technologies. These similarities along with the similarities between the workforces make the comparison of these two industries meaningful.

The authors in this book have already described the characteristics of the high-tech workforce. While I have already made mention of some of these characteristics, it is worth reviewing some of the observations found by Batt and her coauthors:

- New media professionals are rarely "employees" in the way the term is typically understood. Most work by moving from project to project, providing specialized inputs to the creation of products such as movies, advertisements, and Web page designs.
- Full-time employment does not necessarily mean long-term employment. Even full-time workers averaged about six months in any given job. As a consequence, career paths are organized around the acquisition of a marketable portfolio of specialized skills and prestige projects rather than tenure with long-term employment.
- New media workers rely heavily on social networks in order to obtain work.
- Only 11 percent of new media workers employed on a freelance or a project-by-project basis receive comprehensive health coverage.
- New media professionals are concerned with obtaining and improving skills necessary to be competitive in the job market.
- New media professionals have high levels of commitment to their professions. (Batt et al., 2001)

New media professionals rejected the notion of an industry in favor of a community of new media artists and professionals that encompasses employers and employees alike (Batt et al., 2001). This echoes Andrew Ross's (2001) observations about Silicon Alley professionals, no doubt the very same people surveyed in "Networking," that they believed that they were partners in a new, more humane form of capitalism that would break down traditional barriers between management and labor. In reading both *No Collar* (Ross, 2001) and Batt et al.'s *Net Working* (2001), it is clear that new media professionals share a sense of community both in the workplace and within the broader high-tech industry. This dream of community did not hold up well after the dot-com bubble burst and investor pressures forced companies to behave like old-time capitalists. On the West Coast, employees at Amazon and ETown flirted with unionization, but it never went past the handholding stage. The CWA supported these drives and both were similar in their organizing targets and results. WashTech/CWA attempted to organize Amazon's customer service representatives in Seattle, Washington. Ninety out of the four hundred employees targeted by the union signed authorization cards. The nascent union threatened National Labor Relations Board charges when

Amazon.com laid off a large number of its Seattle-based customer service representatives, including those known to be active in the organizing effort (Johnston, 2001). The Northern California Media Workers Union's (NCMWU) efforts to organize Etown seemed to be gaining momentum until that company announced cutbacks after the first of the year. The NCMWU called off its plans for an election. Since then, Etown itself has gone out of business, a casualty of the dramatic reversal of fortunes in the high-tech industry.

PROFILE OF MOTION PICTURE AND TELEVISION WORKERS

The profiles of the new media professional could be easily applied to a description of their unionized counterparts in traditional media. The following profile is based on my own experiences in representing film and television technicians for the last fifteen years and from my discussions with other union representatives in the old media:

- Employment is contingent in nature. Employees must work for and maintain relations with various companies.
- People working on crews, whether they are cinematographers, editors, grips, electricians, video engineers, animators, or any other worker, must be highly trained and skilled in order to be successful in the industry. They must maintain and upgrade their skills if they are to remain competitive.
- Professional identity is essential to professionals in old media, and it also is central to union identity.
- Professionals in old media are also concerned about credit for their work. They rely on past successes to create future work opportunities. Screen credit is vital to their careers and is negotiated in union agreements.
- The nature of their work and employment requires that old media professionals know how to network and create opportunities. They also rely on social networks in order to get employment.
- A number of old media professionals work at times as employees, vendors, or employers in different settings.
- Traditional media union agreements allow members to negotiate wages and conditions superior to those negotiated by the union.

As stated earlier, a central difference between the old and new media workforces is their comparative levels of unionization. Put simply, most old media professionals belong to unions and most new media professionals don't. While there are no hard figures on union density in old media, I would still argue that it is very high, perhaps the highest of any other U.S. industry. Nearly all U.S.-produced feature films from both the major studios and the independents as well as television movies, specials, and commercials are produced with union directors, writers, performers, and crew covered by union agreements. The last fifteen years in particular have seen an expansion of union agreements in new areas of production. This is particularly true for the International Alliance of Theatrical Stage Employees or IATSE, which launched several successful organizing efforts in new entertainment sectors such as cable television, low-budget independent feature film-making, and, most recently, music video productions. This means the creation of new collective bargaining agreements as well as an increase in union members. For example, in 1995 total membership in the IATSE was under 75,000; in 2001 membership was estimated at over 100,000 (Gray, 2001).

While not every old media union has organized as aggressively as the IATSE, many have seen a steady growth in membership. The Directors Guild of America (DGA) had a total membership of 9,000 in 1989 and has over 12,000 members today. The Writers Guild of America East and West represents screen writers as well as news and television writers, and membership grew from 9,900 in 1989 to 11,829 in 2001 (Gray and Seeber, 1996; Gray, 2001).

Identity plays a key role in the growth of these unions, regardless of whether that growth comes through organizing drives or membership applications. Professionals in old media see the unions as more than a vehicle to increase wages and handle grievances. Union membership in the entertainment industries is a major career move that will hopefully open doors to more regular freelance employment. So for the old media professional, union membership has a utility in and of itself. Union membership helps to identify the true professional in the motion picture or broadcast community; it is more than a union card, it is a credential.

One could argue that history has played an important role in the strength of the old media unions. The entertainment unions have been around for a long time; they have developed long-standing relationships with major companies in film and broadcasting that date back to the 1920s and 1930s, so they are industry institutions. But the same can be said for any number of other industrial or craft unions that have seen dramatic drops in membership and have seen their collective strength diminish over the last thirty years. Yes, the old media unions have benefited from having a historic presence in the old media industries, but they have also benefited from structures that allowed them to represent the core interests of freelance professionals even when their industries went through corporate restructuring and technological change.

New media professionals interested in building representational structures could examine the structural aspects and experiences of almost any old media union. However, if they are looking for unions with members working in occupations most closely related to their own, I would point them to two guilds within the IATSE: the Animation Guild, Local 839; and the Motion Picture Editors Guild, Local 700.

The Animation Guild and Affiliated Optical Electronic and Graphic Arts, IATSE Local 839

In the 1990s a number of optical effects and animation houses switched from the old optical effects (i.e., stop motion) to computer or digital effects. The 1993 film *Jurassic Park* was the first major motion picture to make complete use of computer graphics animation. Many cell animators found themselves working alongside computer graphics animators and designers. Eventually, the screen cartoonists began to incorporate these new occupations into their collective bargaining agreements. I briefly represented these same crafts at a special effects house on the East Coast and noticed the similarities in work stations, work lives, and the spirit of individuality of animators and computer graphics animators, designers, programmers, among other members. Local 839 was one of the first entertainment industry unions to create its own Web site and use it to communicate with both members and nonmembers. It founded the American Animation Institute in 1980 to teach classic animation, again to members and nonmembers, so the guild is seen as a source of knowledge about the industry. The Screen Cartoonists Guild provides training for members in these new computer-related forms of animation.

The Motion Picture Editors Guild, IATSE Local 700

Up until the 1980s and 1990s, film editing largely involved physically cutting and pasting celluloid to make a story cogent in much the same way book editors cut and pasted narrative. Initially, video technology and, later, computer technology changed the face and the pace of editing. Now editors use almost all of the same tools found in the new media arsenal, particularly as they have taken on the additional responsibility of adding special effects in the editing process. It is no wonder an issue of *Editors Guild Magazine* features the film editor Anita Brandt Burgoyne holding a keyboard. In the same issue, there is an article critiquing Siggraph 2005, one of the nation's oldest societies for computer graphics and one in which the Editors Guild actively participates. The Editors Guild has invested in high-tech training for its members. It showcases the skills and abilities of its members through the magazine and its participation in two professional societies for the editing profession, the ACE (American Cinema Editors) and the CAS (Cinema Audio Society). And, as we shall see from Tris Carpenter's chapter in this book, the Editors Guild has been organizing employees with a foot in both old and new media production.

Other IATSE guilds, like the International Cinematographers Guild, have similar programs to train members and provide them with professional recognition. The International Cinematographers Guild showcases members through the *International Cinematographers Magazine*. It also has a very close relationship with the American Society of Cinematographers (ASC). In fact, it would be fair to say that, like the ACE and the CAS, most of the members of the ASC also hold union cards.

Other entertainment unions like the Directors Guild of America, the Writers Guild (East and West), the Screen Actors Guild, and the American Federation of Television and Radio Artists have very similar attributes. All these old media unions celebrate their members' successes by calling attention to industry awards they've received (such as the Academy Awards, Emmy Awards, and Cable Ace Awards, to name but a few), or by having their own awards (for example, the Screen Actors Guild sponsors the annual SAG Awards). Plus, all of these unions have either as a practice with employers or in their contracts language that requires that employers give members' proper credit for their work. The general public may largely ignore credit roles at the end of films, but for performers, technicians, writers, and directors, these credits are essential elements of their resumes.

MEMBERS AS EMPLOYERS; EMPLOYERS AS MEMBERS

The freelance nature of employment and the project-to-project nature of productions within entertainment industries create an atmosphere that promotes and even calls for entrepreneurship among union members.

As a consequence in some corners of old media there are overlaps between people who hold union cards and who also own companies. Scan the list of company owners who are members of the Association of Independent Commercial Producers (AICP), the employer association that represents commercial production companies in negotiations with the IATSE and DGA, and you will find a fair number who are union directors and cinematographers. John Wells, the former president of the Writers Guild of America West, is the president of John Wells Productions, which produces the television series *The West Wing*. In the field of animation, union animators strike out on their own to open small animation studios. These moves from "worker" to "employer" do not necessitate the loss of union membership in entertainment unions. Many entrepreneurs hang on to their union cards in the event that larger companies hire them to work as employees. Union membership also allows producers to continue to work in their craft on projects they produce. By owning a production company a writer, director, cinematographer, or actor can not only choose the production that he or she wants to be involved in, but can also create the project itself. In an industry driven by "creative energy," this type of freedom is desirable.

For their part industry unions accept the notion that some members will move on to become company owners and that some small company owners may wish to hold union cards. The unions do, however, guard against the abuse of freelance members by employers who attempt to treat them as independent contractors in order to avoid payroll taxes, workers' compensation, and other benefits. Some benefit plans established under Taft-Hartley Act rules have severe restrictions on when and how participants can make contributions via their own companies. These considerations aside, do members owning companies or company owners becoming union members in any way undermine the union? Does it create an inherent conflict of interest within the union, or does it weaken the union's ability to represent members who are not company owners?

Since the unions seem to have managed potential abuses so well and since they have established themselves as important institutions in the old media industry, conflicts of interest seem to be kept to a minimum. The professional identification that the union provides is just as powerful and as necessary to creator-producers as is company ownership. John Wells may own a production company, but he is still a writer and he still has a vested interest in his profession as a writer. The same is true for any director, cinematographer, or editor who owns a company. Many company owners holding union cards will still work as freelance employees for larger production companies in order to make ends meet. They often utilize the same health and retirement plans as other rank-and-file members, so, in spite of occasional increases in employer contributions, they will have an interest in seeing that these plans are well maintained and taken care of. In short, many company owners still believe that union membership is valuable.

FREELANCE HEALTH AND RETIREMENT BENEFITS

Health and retirement benefits are among the chief benefits of membership in entertainment unions. They are key to motivating nonunion employees to sign union authorization cards and to getting union members employed on nonunion productions to cooperate in organizing efforts. All of the old media unions have some form of health insurance and pension plan funded through direct employer contributions. The ease of obtaining health benefits or vesting in the union pension varies by plan, but essentially it depends upon the amount of work done under contract. Each plan has a minimum qualifying threshold before an employee can qualify for health insurance or begin vesting in a pension. Essentially, the more difficult it is to qualify, the better the quality of benefits for those who do make the threshold; the easier it is to qualify, the more likely it is that employees have to pay higher deductibles or share the cost of health benefits.

These health and pension plans have been around for decades and were designed, more or less, with freelancers in mind. For example, there are multiemployer benefit plans that allow any employer signed to a collective bargaining agreement to make contributions. This would certainly solve the problem new media professionals face of having a handful of employers who provide health insurance, or only provide it for staff employees. These plans are also federally protected. Participants who vest in a pension in an old media union would not have the same worries of fund mismanagement as Enron employees. The bad news is that the laws governing these plans such as the Taft-Hartley Act and Employee Retirement Income Security Act (ERISA) were written in the era of more permanent employment relationships. In the more traditional plans the portability of benefits is limited or non-existent, especially if an employee leaves the industry or occupation. An editor may accumulate employer contributions into the Motion Picture Industry plans. However, should he or she get the opportunity to work as a director, contributions would have to go into the Directors Guild health and pension plans. Trust documents and the law limit or in some cases prohibit a cross-pollination of benefit contributions across different guilds and unions.

This system has created complications in the television industry that new media professionals would be wise not to duplicate. For
decades television technicians have been represented by the IATSE, the
National Alliance of Broadcast Engineers and Technicians (NABET),
or the International Brotherhood of Electrical Workers (IBEW). For the
first two decades of television broadcasting, most work was performed
by staff employees, and the existence of three rival unions created few
problems for technicians looking for lifetime employment. With the
shift from staff to freelance positions, technicians have found themselves forced to hold three or more union cards, and at times unable to
qualify for any of the benefit plans they see contributions going into.
The situation is not a happy one for the freelance members or the union
leadership. Freelance members who work regularly but don't qualify
for health insurance feel as though the system itself was designed to
penalize them. Efforts are underway by some of the unions to provide
more flexible benefits plans, which may help alleviate the worst of the
problems. Actors face a similar problem with the existence of three
national unions, the Screen Actors Guild (SAG), the American Federation of Television and Radio Artists (AFTRA), and Actors Equity. In
New York City it is not unusual for a supporting actor to work occasionally on a soap opera under contract with AFTRA, on a Broadway
play under contract with Equity, and on a commercial under contract
with SAG, with benefit contributions going to three different benefit
plans.

The fickle nature of freelance work can make obtaining health
insurance a feast-or-famine proposition. When jobs are plentiful, staying on the health plan is easy, but when it is slow, maintaining insurance is more of struggle. Some old media plans addressed this problem
by providing a bank of hours for employees who have more than
enough hours or credits to qualify for insurance. The extra hours stay in
the bank until they are drawn on when work is slow. Other plans allow
members to self-pay part of the amount necessary to help them qualify
for insurance. This latter feature is particularly common in benefit plans
created or revamped in the last ten years. Other unions have added
flexible retirement packages like 401(k) plans or other annuities that
allow for employee and, in some cases, employer contributions. In this
case unions are providing flexible retirement packages in which
participants can control investments in a structure that still maintains
some of the protections the older Taft-Hartley plans.

Other unions have looked into supplemental benefit plans for
members who cannot qualify for health insurance at all or coverage for

members who have temporarily fallen off their union health plans for whatever reason. This is, for the most part, experimental. Nonetheless, this level of flexibility may be a feature that a new media union would wish to look into incorporating into an overall benefit package for members.

APPLYING LESSONS FROM OLD MEDIA UNIONS TO NEW MEDIA ORGANIZATIONS

The question yet remains as to if and how new media professionals will come together nationally to organize. Still, if they succeed in any measure to create a bona fide nationwide representational structure, whether it is in or out of the current labor movement, their effort will have major implications for the growing number of professional and nonprofessional workers worldwide who work on a contingent basis. History has shown us time and time again that there is strength and safety in numbers. But how those numbers come together, and in what form or organizational structure, is essential to maintaining and increasing that strength. The more solid the foundation of this yet-to-be-conceived new media organization, the better chance it has to weather the external assaults and internal political struggles that lie ahead. It is likely that as a freelance organization it will have to decide, should it take on the union mantle, to contend with labor laws that were written to address industrial worker issues. It will have to decide what aspects of law and past practice are useful to its members and structural growth and what aspects should be avoided. The experiences of old media unions, both good and bad, provide important lessons for those interested in creating this new media organization.

Currently, there are a number of organizations created to represent specific concerns of new media professionals dealing with everything from professional identification to lobbying. As of yet, it appears that no national organization has been formed to address the many broad concerns of this workforce. If and when these organizations do, they would be very wise to examine and understand the experiences of the old media unions. Based on my own experience in the old media, I have outlined what I believe are key lessons for new media professionals to learn if they wish to create their own representational organization, including organizing around the profession, celebrating members' accomplishments, allowing for individual negotiations, leading in training and education, providing for the coordination of benefits, and facing the challenge of the employer-member.

Organize Around the Profession, not the Workplace

Members must identify with the profession over and above who they work for. This means that, as with old media, union membership in the new media organization must be seen as an essential component to one's professional career. This will mean that, as much as possible, the organization should also facilitate the kind of social networking that old media union members use to promote their careers. As with old media unions, membership can also come to signify professional standing within the industry.

Celebrate the Members' Accomplishments

Old media unions have done a good job of using magazines and Web sites to promote the accomplishments of their members. Other ways might include awards or other formal recognition of members' accomplishments. Such mechanisms are invaluable to underscoring the creation of a wider professional community. These forms of recognition also demonstrate to those outside the organization such as potential members or employers that the new media organization is the place to go for the most highly skilled professionals.

Allow for Individual Negotiations

Most old media union collective bargaining agreements allow members to negotiate "better terms and conditions." While to an industrial union this may appear to be antithetical to good trade unionism, it has been a practice in entertainment industry unions for decades. The practice allows members to excel, at least in terms of compensation, beyond what the minimum scale is in the agreement. This keeps the high earners, the old media stars, engaged in the organization. Keeping this group happy is vital to maintaining the professional integrity of the organization. If all the ingredients are right, there is no reason why a top-compensated professional would not see some value in belonging and supporting the new media organization, further enhancing the organization's prestige. Individual negotiations are also used by less prominent members who, in some circumstances, may use it to address issues the contract does not cover.

Be a Leader in Training and Education

Representational organization must be the center for training and skills

enhancement. This is a key component to the professional identification. We've already seen how the entertainment industry unions have
well-established training programs for freelance members. The more
the organization can take on the role of teacher and mentor, the more it
will succeed in maintaining the loyalty of a freelance workforce.

Health Insurance and Retirement Benefits

The organization must provide a method of health insurance and
retirement benefits geared to a freelance population. As I have stated, a
balance between a solid benefit plan and one that has some flexibility
and portability is vital. The old media and new media workforces move
around a lot among jobs by choice or by necessity. This means travel
between cities and states, creating enormous challenges for maintaining
insurance coverage. In an ideal world the new media workforce would
create a national benefit structure, at least for health insurance that
would be funded through some combination of employer and partici-
pant contributions. Members could then maintain insurance anywhere
in the United States. With respect to retirement benefits, it may prove
more appealing to new media professionals to have 401(k) plans over
traditional Taft-Hartley pensions. Personally, I see great value in federally protected pensions, but I am not certain how they will be received
by this workforce. Nonetheless, 401(k) plans that have similar protections as traditional union pensions might be a way of combining the
best of both. Providing for the coordination of benefits will be the new
media organization's single greatest task, but it will be its most important, which is why close study of old media union plans will prove vital
to creating new media representation structures.

The Challenge of the Employer-Member

What happens with members who own companies? Many new media
professionals consult or plan to consult at some point in their career.
This means that they will not be paid as employees by firms and could
hire their own employees. I would recommend that the new media take
the bold step of including independent contractors and these kinds of
employers because, based on my own experiences with freelance film
and television professionals, they are part of the professional community. Including employer-members also shows new members who plan
to consult themselves someday that membership in the new media
organization is not temporary. Membership is a career decision with
lifetime benefits. This may complicate aspects of the benefit plans

depending on how the organization sets them up, but I feel it would be worth the effort.

As work relations have become more temporary and economies more global, it is time, perhaps, to take a new look at the way in which workforces should be organized and represented. Is it possible that a mass effort of new media professionals to join together and create a representational structure would also lead to the creation a new type of labor movement, one that can rapidly address the challenges of this new global economy? It is possible, however, it would require enormous coordination and commitment, and a willingness to address problems creatively yet practically. As Tris Carpenter points out in his chapter, organizing is a key to the lifeblood of any new union or organization. Understanding how old media unions face the challenges of aggressive employers and indifferent labor laws will be the first and most important lesson that the new media professionals can learn.

10

What Works: Organizing Freelance Professionals in the New Economy

Tris Carpenter

If we are to delve deeper into the idea that the entertainment industry union model may be better suited than the "traditional" union model to represent people in the high-tech world, the next logical step is to examine union organizing in that industry. In historical terms the entertainment industry model, an industry-centered model of organizing union representation, is actually older than the so-called traditional model of organizing centered on specific companies. Calls within the U.S. labor movement to develop a "new" model for organizing high-tech workers seemingly ignore the fact that a successful model has existed in the entertainment unions for well over a century already.

There are some interesting questions that arise from a comparison of entertainment industry and high-tech organizing efforts. Does the difference in structure translate into a very different experience in terms of conducting organizing campaigns and bringing new members into the union? Are there certain debates and issues that are common to environments with many freelancers that do not occur in "regular" employee organizing campaigns? Answers to these questions should prove very instructive for would-be high-tech organizers who want to use this not-so-new approach.

In the past five years I have successfully organized several hundred entertainment industry employees working for dozens of companies. In most of these campaigns the key components of working life are virtually identical to those experienced by high-tech employees. To elaborate, the downsides and the upsides of postproduction work and high-tech work are strikingly similar. Both suffer from the insecurities of the freelance nature of work, long hours, and lack of employer-provided health insurance and retirement benefits. Both enjoy the social aspects of "group" projects, the potential for excellent wages, the status of being involved with a very "hip" industry, and the chance to work creatively. Both require a very specialized understanding of the work, usually involving several years' worth of training and honing of skills. And in both cases, staying employed means keeping abreast of rapidly changing technology and making and maintaining contacts in the industry.

Prior to working in the entertainment industry, I organized employees in many diverse professions, including sheriffs, medical school doctors and professors, social workers, teaching assistants, road maintenance workers, day care workers, and juvenile corrections officers. While organizing professionals, particularly doctors, has some similarities to postproduction employees, nothing from these prior campaigns was particularly helpful in preparing me for the challenges of organizing a freelance workforce that does not—and never expects to—stay in one place for very long.

By explaining the peculiarities of organizing freelancers in the entertainment industry, I hope to shorten the learning curve for those who might attempt to do some organizing in high-tech sectors. To that end, I will describe five major issues in organizing campaigns that I have conducted at the Editors Guild. In explaining these issues I hope to provide some firsthand experience in how these campaigns develop and what I think is a unique twist on the usual debate over whether to unionize. Finally, I will point out several different issues that high-tech organizers may encounter and offer advice on how these problems might be overcome.

ORGANIZING EDITORS

Discussions about postproduction employment issues are made more confusing simply because several terms are used synonymously when in fact they should not. Even among industry veterans, the term *free-lance* is often confused with *independent contractor*. Workers in the entertainment industry are primarily freelance employees, meaning that they have no regular job in the way that most people do. For them, work means having to string together several jobs with separate and distinct companies, sometimes a dozen or more in a calendar year. Freelance workers are real employees, with all the usual constraints of being an employee—a reporting time, an hourly wage, most if not all necessary equipment provided by the employer, and close supervision of many aspects of the job. By contrast, independent contractors set their own hours, provide their own equipment, and are paid per job, not hourly. Independent contractors are paid without tax and other payroll deductions, as opposed to being on the regular payroll with the rest of the company's employees. As has become clear through several high-profile cases such as the one brought against Microsoft, a company using independent contractors improperly may stand to gain several financial advantages, such as not having to pay overtime, unemployment, or workers' compensation.

Picture editors rarely have anything that resembles regular work with a single workplace. They are the purest freelancers in our business, stringing together several gigs with different employers each year. Sound editors and re-recording mixers, the other two "top-level" categories in the Editors Guild, are more likely to work regularly, maybe even year-round, for a single "sound house," "post house," or studio. In these cases they may work on various projects as they come in, but the house is their primary employer. However, the more ambitious of sound editors and re-recording mixers might pick up short-term work at other houses when things are slow at their main job.

In the nonunion world those working regularly at a post house, or postproduction studio, are said to be "on staff." They get the same benefits as the other regular employees, such as sales and office staff. The short-term freelancers or "day players" fill in on an as-needed basis and simply get a paycheck. The term *day players* refers to people who are working freelance somewhere, but it is not uncommon to find a day player working what most of us would consider a regular, full-time job but without any benefits whatsoever and otherwise indistinguishable from employees on staff doing exactly the same work. To make things more complicated, several post-production professionals, especially the more successful ones, form their own companies and have their wages paid through these companies in an attempt to reap certain tax advantages. These are called *loan out* arrangements, which usually look like independent contractor arrangements but may have provisions, such as overtime pay, that resemble traditional employment. A person working through a loan out is usually freelance, but could conceivably be on staff.

All of these arrangements make for some interesting organizing. A nonunion company might be staffed with nothing but independent contractors (a situation that is usually illegal and will be addressed in the next section) or it might be all freelance employees. Or the company might have some staff employees with some basic health benefits and some day players who get nothing more than their paychecks. A company might have mostly staff, a dozen day players, a loan out or two, and even an independent contractor.

The union postproduction scene is very different. With very few exceptions everyone working union is a freelance employee, and everyone gets prorated (daily or hourly) contributions toward their health and retirement benefits. These benefits begin when those contributions reach certain thresholds.

Organizing campaigns in postproduction often begin when Motion Picture Editors Guild members work on nonunion shows. Unlike several of the entertainment industry unions, the Editors Guild does not prohibit its members from working on nonunion productions. Therefore, someone in the campaign may have firsthand experience in what working union really means. This, of course, gives the guild a certain advantage. In several cases, though, the first contact comes from someone who is not a member and simply wants a better deal.

Hours

It has become an increasingly common practice among nonunion employers in the entertainment industry to hire postproduction employees as independent contractors. In spite of their sometimes-flexible hours, postproduction employees are rarely anything but true employees, as the equipment and work location are provided by the employer and final decisions about the show come from the director, producer, or the network or studio. Yet many producers who are anxious to reap the savings on payroll taxes and overtime refuse to hire anyone as a true employee—preferring to violate the law and call free-lancers by the term *independent contractors.*

The slightly more aboveboard counterpart to the independent contractor arrangement is the "flat rate." In this system, employees are hired for a weekly salary, regardless of the number of hours or days worked. Paychecks remain the same from week to week, regardless of the hours.[1]

Postproduction employees are nonexempt under the Fair Labor Standards Act, and are thus entitled to pay for all hours worked, but individual enforcement usually involves a Department of Labor claim. For permanent employees, there are "whistle-blower" protections that can make it difficult for an employer to retaliate, but for freelancers, a "lukewarm" reference from their last job (particularly if it has been a longer-running one) can be difficult to overcome. While the question of getting paid for the work done is important, most industry veterans agree that the larger issue is long hours. Without overtime premiums, there is no brake on a producer who wants to work an editor late into the night and over weekends. Even on union shows, long hours are typical, except that on those shows the overtime premiums do have some financial disincentive, and the "turnaround" penalty for an insufficient amount of time off between shifts also makes some difference. Without these provisions, however, a show can quickly become a nightmare that envelops one's entire life for weeks or months on end.

Editors who were fed up with losing weekends and nights due to producers who took full advantage of the flat-rate work began several Editors Guild organizing campaigns. Once a show is organized, the producers tend to become much more adept at prioritizing work that needs to be done; when every hour counts in real dollars, downtime needs to be eliminated and overtime avoided.

The *New York Times* Television campaign, in particular, is a good example of how the issue of long hours can drive a campaign. NYT-TV considered its editors to be independent contractors and even required the editors to sign an agreement acknowledging this. By refusing to pay overtime, labor costs at the company would remain constant from week to week, and managers had no incentive whatsoever to limit the amount of overtime worked. The vast majority of the editorial workers routinely put in more than sixty-hour work weeks, and some reportedly topped eighty hours. While a couple of editors had the clout to get their overtime paid, most did not and their assistants certainly didn't either. A major change on overtime policy required collective action, and the contract that was finally negotiated had premiums for weekend work and excessive hours.

The pressure to work for free is tremendous, yet the freelance nature of the work makes many people tremble in fear of losing a contact or a reference. Remember, the infamous quote, "You'll never work in this town again!" was said about the film biz. Of course, with a union contract there is at least some relatively expedient way of preventing such retaliation.

Benefits

Health insurance is extremely rare in nonunion jobs in this industry. The very few who do get insurance of some sort work for post houses; even then coverage is often just for the individual and requires a co-payment of the premium. As for retirement, even the most generous of post houses will only offer a 401(k) to staff employees, usually without any matching contribution from the employer. For day player jobs, insurance and retirement benefits are simply nonexistent.

The health insurance plans that cover most Motion Picture Editors Guild members who work enough union hours to qualify are extremely generous, with full family coverage provided without any copayment of the premium and an extensive schedule of benefits. The beauty of this plan is its portability. Most union employers pay into a centralized fund for hours worked by the employee, and when an employee reaches a certain threshold, health insurance is provided for a certain period of time, usually six months. If the employee can work enough hours before the six months run out, he or she can earn another six months of coverage. These plans are constructed in a way that recognizes the ups and downs of the industry. The largest of the plans allows extra hours beyond the threshold to be banked so that the employee can weather long stretches without union employment. In the second largest plan, the employee can pay a discounted rate for extended coverage during slow periods when the threshold is difficult to reach.

Retirement plans are similarly extensive. The main plan provides a defined benefit pension plan and a defined contribution annuity, both paid for by employer contributions. There is even retiree health insurance for those who accumulate enough union hours over a predetermined period of years.

Because of the high rate of unionization in this industry, it is not unusual for a nonunion show to have a union member or two working on the crew. While nonunion work might pay the bills, it does not contribute to the member's health insurance or to any accumulation of the member's pension. Often, members working nonunion are interested in organizing simply because they need to get enough union work in order to qualify for their next cycle of health insurance, or they need a limited number of hours to secure permanent pension and retirement benefits. Those that don't know about the benefits are usually astounded to hear about their extent and portability.

Wages

Campaigns that center around a general wage increase usually come from true "sweatshop" gigs where everything is awful—pay, benefits, hours, and the treatment of employees. More commonly, however, the existing wage rates on shows are acceptable to the editors and/or mixers at the top of the skill ladder, but could be improved for those at the bottom, such as assistant editors, recordists, tape operators, or other postproduction support personnel. Nonunion assistant editors tend to make about one-half to one-third of the full editor rate; other support staff make even less.[2] By contrast, union assistants tend to be far better compensated on jobs, often receiving 30 percent to 40 percent more than their non-union counterparts for far fewer hours. Post house campaigns are more like traditional organizing campaigns where wages are more generally an issue. In these cases, the wage rates may be fine at the top, but there are far more assistants and support personnel who may not have had an increase in several years. Often, wage rates at various nonunion post houses are widely known, as it is common for people to hop from post house to post house to get an increase. Also, since the union rates are easily found online, nonunion employees know full well what the people at the studios get paid—providing another incentive to push for unionization.

Equity Within the Industry

In the last several years, there has been some significant conglomeratization in the postproduction world. With few exceptions, acquired companies that had a union contract have kept it, while their sister companies under the same corporate umbrella do not provide the same benefits. The idea that working for one subsidiary means getting a better deal than at another subsidiary pushes some people to think about organizing.

Another example of inequality within the industry is the case of "reality" television. Virtually every major feature film, nearly all lower-budget films, and most prime-time television shows are union productions. The major exception has been "reality" television, which until recently has been a much less organized arena. In the past few years I have conducted several campaigns with picture editors who were looking to organize reality television shows. Often, these jobs are not the sweatshop gigs that people sometimes assume are the key targets for organizing. In many cases, the pay is excellent, the hours decent, and the environment friendly and professional. What brings some people around to organizing, however, is the fact that the "scripted" shows that the reality programs compete with have union benefits and protections. Why should the people who edit reality television earn less when their shows bring in as many viewers, if not more, than the traditional scripted shows?

The counterargument has been that reality television is simply a lower-budget medium. That may have been true in the early days, but in the last few years the product placement craze has created a whole new revenue stream for the producers of these shows. In fact, an episode of the reality television show *The Apprentice* with Donald Trump revolved around Burger King, which paid a reported $2 million for the privilege. Compare that to the fact that even the most expensive scripted television show rarely costs over $2 million per episode, and the placement craze has not yet taken full effect in scripted shows. Reality television is cheaper with no or very few actors and/or writers to pay and, with the product placement revenue, makes more money even before the shows hit the airwaves. Reality television is all grown up now as a genre and can afford to pay the same benefits as scripted television. Beyond reality television, however, the equity argument is usually not central to the start of a campaign. Rather, it tends to be voiced later, often in response to a heavy-handed management campaign. Eventually, it becomes a matter of respect—people start asking themselves why their employer won't give them the same deal that the best and brightest in the industry get.

Training

Access to training is an issue felt by all postproduction professionals because expanding technologies affect postproduction quite dramatically. For example, five years ago most prime-time television shows used Avid for their picture editing system and only a fraction of them used Apple's Final Cut Pro. Now, due to a much lower cost, Final Cut Pro has gained a significant share of the market and many editors are finding it necessary to learn how to use both systems in order to broaden their employment opportunities.

   Producers are not interested in training their editors on these new systems; rather, the editors must know the platform in order to get hired. The Editors Guild places a very high emphasis on training, especially in the last twenty years as various technologies have completely changed the craft. The guild provides free and subsidized training to its members through several outlets such as free seminars, discount rates at training facilities, and classes subsidized by federal and state grants. There are also free "practice rooms" in its East and West Coast offices so that the members can come and work through the things they learned in their classes.

   In my opinion, the training program is not a reason people organize, but it comes to be seen as a "bonus" in virtually every campaign I have run. Every editor out there already knows that he or she will have to keep up with new systems; a couple of free or subsidized classes can easily add up to what they'd spend on a year's worth of dues. Also, the training program fosters a sense of craft. The fact that the guild is a leader in the editorial community and spends real money on its members to help train them for the future has a very positive impact in the minds of folks that are thinking about joining the guild, and does a great deal to dispel the "thug" stereotype that many union busters try to perpetuate in order to derail a campaign.

LESSONS FOR THE HIGH-TECH ORGANIZING EFFORT

Other contributors to this book have written at length about what high-tech workers want—shorter hours, better pay and benefits, networking opportunities, training assistance, and a chance to celebrate their craft. Looking at the organizing campaigns I have run, we can see all of these aspects in the entertainment industry. Unions in the entertainment industry have found a way to improve the working lives of freelancers by using a union structure that recognizes the transient nature of the work. In the high-tech world, a few of these issues have been addressed by small professional organizations. But the difficult ones—involving pay, benefits, and hours—will require far more extensive organizing. Although the issue of uncompensated hours can be dealt with by strong individual negotiation and/or litigation, the most effective and expedient method is usually found in collective action. Other issues such as training, health care, and retirement have no real redress other than through some form of organizing and working collectively to move employers and to change government policies.

But can it be done? In spite of the success freelancers have made in the entertainment industry, it is not ensured that the same "freelance union" approach can be translated effectively to high-tech work. The high-tech workforce may have similar problems, but studies seem to indicate that, by and large, they do not see themselves as potential union members. Anything that smacks of "old" unions will likely be a burden in terms of persuading people to act collectively. So far, the "old" unions have been mostly rebuffed or ignored by those who would be organized by them.

My advice would be to mimic parts of the underlying entertainment industry union structure—including a portable benefit system that can be carried over during slow times, restrictions on long and/or unpaid hours, and assistance for people who wish to train on new systems—yet stay away from the union tag. Essentially, I would suggest trying to appear to be something new in a world quite unresponsive to the old methods of collective redress.

Of course, there will be people who wish to thwart any such movement and will make every effort to brand any such collective action as a union wolf in sheep's clothing. And any major union that sponsors such an attempt will quickly lose that spin battle. While not necessarily fatal, such a battle will present certain challenges for the organizers. Another challenge that will come up for high-tech freelancers that does not have a parallel in the entertainment industry is that most of the original organizing of the studios was done before people were freelancers and at a different point in U.S. history. Attempting to organize now may be less physically dangerous than in the 1920s and 1930s (we certainly have far fewer shootings by the Pinkertons these days), but there is no shortage of other obstacles. Furthermore, depending on the situation and the goals, there are major advantages to be gained by organizing more broadly than company by company. In some ways, a broad-based movement with more limited goals may be easier to achieve than an old-fashioned unionization effort at a single company. I also suspect that the "old" unions are more susceptible to the quagmire of the National Labor Relations Board (NLRB) process. Nearly every campaign I have directed has utilized this process in some fashion, and very few of my attempts to circumvent the process have worked. In the opinion of virtually every organizer I know, the NLRB is not helpful to organizing efforts, and the time-killing maneuvers by management representatives are often fatal to organizing drives. "Old" unions, including the IATSE, can and do weather this process, but groundswell groups who wish to organize should avoid it like the plague.

A regionally based health insurance collective for high-tech industry would be an excellent example of this new approach to collective organizing. Apart from the worker-organizing effort, there would likely need to be a political campaign since such an idea might require, say, the creation of a central fund with public grant seed money to buy insurance at a group discount. The idea would be to get workers across the industry to persuade their employers to make some payment to the central fund to subsidize health care for all participants. Employers who participate would be at no disadvantage so long as their competitors participated as well.[3]

Yes, the problem with this scenario is that, without a true union contract, enforcement will be difficult. This will be a common complaint from nearly everyone who believes that, unless there is a contract, the whole effort is for nothing. I agree that a full contract is the best situation, but in this industry without any union history, getting some rough coalition victories that provide some results may be the best way to begin. And we need to remember that the original deals the trade guilds struck back in the 1800s did not have much legal standing either. In the case above, the enforcement mechanism could be part of the political action component; for example, companies that want certain tax breaks must contribute to the fund. I have no doubt that creative problem solvers like high-tech workers can figure out these issues in real-world situations. Far less brilliant people have been doing just that for several decades.

The fact is that freelancers can organize. If they wish to move forward collectively, there are several examples of success, and plenty of creative avenues available, many of which may be adapted to avoid the pitfalls the "old" unions face. The organizing campaigns run by the entertainment industry unions should prove instructive to those who wish to take up the challenge, so long as the new organizers pay attention to the landscape differences, particularly in terms of union preference.

NOTES

1. In these instances, the number of hours listed on the check changes, but the wage rate is back-calculated to leave the total unchanged (e.g., $1000/week equals $25/hour for a 40-hour week, or $14.29/hour for a 60-hour week).

2. The current "on-call" minimum rate for picture editors, which covers most feature film and prime-time television, is $2,458.85 for a five-day week.

3. And all of this could be done without the NLRB process.

Conclusion

Strategies and Structures for the New Economy

John Amman, Tris Carpenter, and Gina Neff

In the introduction we examined the events that led to the emergence of the new economy and how the lack of social infrastructure embedded in the workplace (such as health insurance and pensions) make the U.S. workforce more vulnerable and less certain now than during the boom of the industrial era. In spite of the new economy celebration of individual initiative, this sense of uncertainty only grows stronger. The promise of the new economy has not clearly been kept for many of those who are working under changing conditions, facing greater risks, and shouldering more responsibility for their own security.

The U.S. economy has weathered many such major transitions over its history—from agrarian to industrial, industrial to post-industrial, and now to an intensification of the postindustrial economy that Castells (1996) has called "informationalization," as information technologies are utilized across the entire economy. While most of the chapters in this collection have focused on how those in high-technology industries have or can cope with these changes, surely their responses have implications for all workers in the new economy. Surviving the new economy is not a challenge restricted merely to high-tech work, as these changes have deep reverberations throughout the economy and implications for all workers across the spectrum of skills and pay. Massive economic restructuring is not new in American history either, nor will the shift to an informationalized new economy be the last transition that U.S. workers will ever face.

In this sense there is much to learn from history. As Simon Head pointed out in his chapter, many of the problems of the new economy are rooted firmly in the old industrial practices of Taylorism and scientific management. Another historical examination may be warranted: Do the problems of the new economy require different solutions to the problems than those workers faced in other economic eras? Do the old strategies and structures make sense in the new economy? Given that the social movements for change are influenced by existing legal, political, and organizational structures, might it be time to rethink those structures and their relationship to the movement for better working conditions in the new economy?

In other words, what are we to make of the changes that have accompanied the advent of the new economy, and will any of the prior methods of dealing with the instability caused by such cataclysmic changes work this time around? Can unions save the day as they did in the last major upheaval, when the manufacturing economy took full flight? Early evidence does not seem too promising. As the dot-com bubble began to burst, a few national unions entered the fray and began trying to organize high-tech workers. The results ranged from dismal to disastrous with few victories, none of which turned into long-term gains. Ultimately, workers simply were not interested enough to make a serious go of organizing. Or the unions had the wrong message. Or the corporations had finally eviscerated the laws regulating organizing. Or all of these and many more.

For a number of reasons, the United States has not been amenable to the same type of mass organizing that took place during the transition from an agrarian-based economy to the ascendancy of American industrial prowess. For one, the new economy workforce is far more mobile, both in terms of high employee turnover within single companies and in terms of regional, national, and international mobility. As Neff points out in her chapter, people working in the new economy have learned to accept risk as necessary to doing their jobs and sometimes even welcome this risk, making organizing collective responses to economic insecurity even more difficult. Small, less-hierarchical high-tech firms are much more difficult to organize than factories. Politically, unions have lost clout within the Democratic Party as union membership and union density decline. Although Democratic candidates may boast pro-working family credentials, little or nothing has been done in terms of leadership on legislative efforts to support workers' rights to organize, we would argue, since well before the Reagan administration. This lack of legislative support is in spite of the AFL-CIO's yeoman efforts to get out the vote for Democratic candidates. Conservative politicians have been more aggressive in their efforts to limit labor's political influence and place restrictions on the right to organize. As a consequence, corporations like Wal-Mart are able to get away with their very open contempt for labor unions and existing labor laws, along with their all-out efforts to block union organizing.

Yet, the need for collective solutions to the challenges of the new economy is clear. Every one of the contributors to this collection has discussed the role that unions or similar associations could play in the new economy. Derek Schultz, the only contributor who works in the high-tech sector, is perhaps the most vocal advocate of the positive roles that unions could play in the lives of tech workers. Still, while the need for collective solutions to these problems is clear, so, too, are the problems with the existing union structures. For Simon Head, the political agenda for the new economy seems clear: "to reform the National Labor Relations Act (NLRA) so that the rights of employees to organize are properly protected and so that ruthless, union-busting corporations like Wal-Mart can no longer flout the law with impunity." Surely, it is a worthwhile goal, but is it achievable—and worth the incredible time and effort necessary—in the new economy where traditional unions seem to be losing all relevance?

To understand the challenges at this transition of the U.S. economy, it is important to place them in the context of the story of the U.S. trade union movement. The following overview of the labor movement will examine how unions came to play such an important role in maintaining economic security and identify key structural considerations for representing the needs of high-tech workers based on the observations of the contributors to this collection. This sort of analysis of labor has become, for better or worse, an oft-told tale in labor relations and economic circles, but it is, we feel, a necessary examination. If a new labor or social movement is to succeed in the new economy, it will need to stand upon the history of American labor, understanding why unions are now marginalized and why collective bargaining as a means of addressing economic concerns is less effective now.

The last three decades of labor history have seen the U.S. labor movement continuing to lose density and political influence; unable to keep up with a rapidly changing economy; and finding it increasingly difficult to fight the more aggressive capitalism of the informationalized postindustrial economies. In the words of Bennett Harrison and Barry Bluestone (1988), American labor was "zapped" by corporations and conservative lawmakers who minimized unions' effectiveness through aggressive bargaining and plant closings and who limited their reach through increasingly conservative interpretations of labor law. Labor laws and regulatory systems that were highly effective in protecting the rights of industrial workers in the mid-twentieth century have proven ineffective (and at times detrimental) to protecting high-tech workers in the new economy. Any movement that arises to deal with these challenges will have to free itself from elements of the past to a large degree, while retaining some sense of continuity and history with the concept of employee representation.

UNIONS AS ASSOCIATIONAL

In *The New Unionism*, Charles Heckscher (1996) outlines two competing visions of worker representation that have existed in labor unions since their founding in the late nineteenth century, "voluntary associations based on the active participation of their members" and "disciplined organizations managing a long term battle with employers." This tension between the associational model of unions runs through the history of the American labor movement. American labor unions have been principally interested in the economic and workplace welfare of the members they directly represent, and for over a century, they have relied on collective bargaining, negotiations with specific employers, as the principal means to raise wages, provide benefits, and provide a safe workplace. Heckscher was the first to begin to advocate that unions look beyond workplace organizing and collective bargaining protected under the National Labor Relations Act (NLRA) as the principal vehicle to address worker concerns. Heckscher described efforts by the AFL-CIO to create associational unions for people working in places without union agreements. Essentially, associational unionism seeks to create a more fluid type of labor movement, one that could reach out to a broader constituency than simply to members represented at specific workplaces. Unions largely have confined themselves by the paradigm of collective bargaining and the strict notion that there is a line of demarcation between management's role to create workplace policy and the union's role to react to it. Unions, Heckscher argued, suffered from their own inability to reach out to the greater public and position themselves as social advocates for the greater society and not for just a narrowly defined group of workers.

We see the associational union in action in WashTech and other new organizations to benefit high-tech workers. In her case study of WashTech van Jaarsveld shows us a worker association that by necessity did not organize around collective bargaining, but around a wide range of issues and concerns. Heckscher tied the notion of the associational union with the broader call for employee rights. In the new economy, a broad movement using the associational model might be more successful in securing workers rights than a few loosely connected "organized" high-tech workplaces. Being locked into what we might argue is a losing proposition of focusing exclusively on collective bargaining may blind the labor movement to more viable strategies and structures.

THE CRAFT UNION AND CORPORATE CAPITAL

The history of the labor movement holds many valuable lessons for organizing in the new economy. Struggles won over the course of time were rooted in the challenges of particular economic moments and of particular transitions within the U.S. economy. As we will see below, these transitions shaped the structures and models used by the labor movement, which in turn had significant influence on the trajectory of organizing.

The concept for the modern American trade union began in the late nineteenth century with the founding of the American Federation of Labor (AFL). The AFL was a federation of craft unions, which represented skilled trade workers, the blue-collar elite of the early industrial economy. The AFL might not have come into existence at all were it not for the rise of corporations after the Civil War (Heckscher, 1996). Controlling all major U.S. industries, concentrating enormous wealth and power into the hands of their founders, and governing the workplace through a top-down management bureaucracy, corporations represented an organizational form that was a far cry from the farms of America's agrarian roots. Populist and social reform movements sought to put an end to corporations through grass-roots action.

Samuel Gompers, the founder of the AFL, felt that these popular movements could not match the organizational power and discipline of corporate capitalism. The AFL created a trade union bureaucracy that did not challenge the existence of corporations, but sought instead to protect its members from corporate excesses. Eschewing broad social agendas, AFL unions concentrated on meeting their members' workplace needs through collective bargaining with management. Rather than using the strike as a mass call to arms against all of American capitalism, trade unions used it instead as a strategic weapon to achieve specific benefits. These early unions were structured around the craft or occupation of their members, which the AFL saw as crucial for creating solidarity and instilling a sense of a common purpose. At the time the craft unions did not feel that it was possible to organize unskilled workers who lacked a common and consistent identity.

The AFL itself was not a union but a federation of the craft unions across the country. Membership for unions in the AFL was voluntary and, thus, the AFL could only guide member unions by influence. Although the AFL did not see a role for government in collective bargaining, it did engage in political action. The AFL pledged to support any candidate, regardless of party affiliation, that supported labor's agenda and lobbied lawmakers at the state and national levels.[1]

Since the founding of the AFL, its member unions have fought corporate efforts to wrest control of work from their members. The core of craft union strength and solidarity rested in the skilled union worker's knowledge of how to do his job. The more complicated the task, the greater the ability to command high wages. For that reason the craft union like their guild predecessors carefully controlled the flow of craft training and knowledge. By the 1920s, though, the principles of scientific management and Henry Ford's mass production techniques provided management with more control over the work process in industrial settings. By breaking down complex tasks into simplified units, corporations were able to deskill a wide range of jobs. In doing so, they could employ cheap, nonunion, unskilled workers while eliminating more expensive, unionized craft workers.

This transition from craft-based to assembly line production caused one of the first crises for U.S. organized labor. The AFL lost members as craft workers were replaced with less skilled workers, and, as a result, craft unions significantly lost bargaining strength. Yet, even with these challenges and in spite of the desire by many unskilled factory workers to be represented by a union, most unions in the federation refused to launch organizing drives of industrial workers—the craft unions simply could not break out of the established strategies and structures. The AFL did have an industrial organizing committee at the time for reaching out to unskilled factory workers. However, John L. Lewis, the committee's chair, felt that the federation's efforts were halfhearted at best.

THE INDUSTRIAL UNION AND
THE NATIONAL LABOR RELATIONS ACT

New models and structures emerged from this crisis. Lewis was also president of the United Mine Workers, and in 1935 he led an exodus of like-minded unions out of the American Federation of Labor, forming the Congress of Industrial Organizations (CIO) to organize industrial workers. Rather than using occupation as the unifying force among workers, this new model of industrial union used the workplace to unite employees across different crafts and occupations. Strength in the CIO unions came from their ability to represent the majority of workers at a single workplace, rather than a particular group of craft workers. Otherwise, the CIO shared common traits with the AFL: it was a federation, membership by unions was voluntary, and its member unions focused primarily on workplace benefits for their members through collective bargaining.

Social and political context goes a long way toward shaping union structure. Just as the rise of corporations gave birth to the AFL, the Great Depression played a crucial role in the rise of the CIO. The economic devastation of the depression, the social unrest that came out of it, and the growing appeal of radical political ideologies on both the extreme Left and Right forced the hand of the Roosevelt administration. John L. Lewis argued that free-trade unionism was a safe middle ground for working people, the government, and for the economy, compared to the communist and fascist organizations that were gaining in popularity at the time (Dubofsky and Van Tine, 1986), an argument that won support from mainstream political officials.

The political response was a series of social legislative initiatives, including the National Labor Relations Act. The NLRA broke through decades of federal court rulings that limited the right to organize to a handful of workers. Until that point, corporations could utilize any means at their disposal to keep unions from organizing employees. While the new legislation provided workers with the right to organize and prohibited employers from punishing workers for union activities, the act did so only under the rubric of creating "industrial peace." The NLRA only guaranteed the right to organize in order to have stability in the economy and not because of the inherent value of union representation. This historic piece of labor legislation was, in effect, a result of the crisis of the year it went into effect—1935. Previous attempts at similar legislation had failed, and according to Heckscher, it is unlikely that any other period of U.S. history could have produced such a law. All the Roosevelt administration had to do was to point to the rise of fascism in Europe and communism of the Soviet Union to convince the Congress and the courts of the need for a compromise with workers.

The NLRA gave stronger legs to the fledgling CIO unions, which then embarked on the most impressive series of organizing drives the United States has ever seen. The accelerating increases in union members helped to bolster the political clout of the CIO's leadership, which was already proving to be more willing to use the power of the labor movement to advance broader social issues than the federation of craft unions was. In the 1940s the CIO experienced further gains in membership and influence, as the government needed their good will and industrial peace during World War II. By the late 1940s the CIO and the AFL combined represented 35 percent of the U.S. workforce.

SETBACKS AND INDUSTRIAL STABILITY

This strength, bolstered by a new model that fit the country's industrial expansion, began the first of a long series of legislative setbacks in 1947. A Republican-led Congress aided by conservative Southern Democrats passed the Taft-Hartley Act, which made union organizing more difficult. The legislation passed over Truman's veto and was a body blow to the labor movement, from which, in many ways it has never recovered. Efforts to repeal or amend the Taft-Harley Act failed, and legislation to date has only further regulated the behavior of labor unions. By 1954 the CIO merged with the AFL creating the present-day AFL-CIO in an effort to have a truly united labor front (see Lichtenstein, 1995). This front was formidable, but more conservative.

In spite of these legislative setbacks, the 1950s still proved to be the high-water mark for the tide of the American labor movement. The AFL-CIO unions saw themselves as an integral part of the U.S. economy and democracy. Collective bargaining not only allowed working people to address issues and redress working conditions directly with management, but union agreements included health and retirement benefits along with minimum wages. Based on the proliferation of this model of compensation and benefits established by strong unions, American workplaces still provide the bulk of social benefits for working families. Unions achieved these victories through relatively healthy labor-management relations. America's brand of free-trade unionism did not rely on government intervention or state-controlled unions, as U.S. unions were quick to point out. Collective bargaining allowed the parties to address issues with the government's playing only a refereeing role, usually through mediation.

THE INDUSTRIAL ECONOMY, UNRAVELED

Although scholars noted a drop in union density by the early 1960s, overall union membership in blue-collar industries like manufacturing remained constant through the 1960s and early 1970s. With the challenge of international manufacturing competition in the 1970s and the subsequent rise of the service economy in the 1980s, the American workforce faced yet another transition. The difference between the strong industrial and unionized industries and fledgling service work was striking in terms of compensation, job security, and benefits for American workers. The new service economy brought with it an even more aggressive form of capitalism than the industrial economy. The new smaller, service-oriented firms seemed less rooted in local communities and less responsive to workforces than the old manufacturing companies. As a result, collective bargaining and labor unions were seen as anachronisms of an older, less successful economy and as an unnecessary and expensive burden to fast-growing companies.

Unions responded slowly to new economic trends and proved vulnerable to both the antiunion tactics of the nonunionized firms and the ultraconservative free-market philosophy of the Reagan administration. New structures and new strategies were needed. By the late 1980s and early 1990s, within the American labor movement there were widespread calls for a shift away from the prevalent "servicing" model of unionism toward an "organizing" model. Many people argued that the servicing model, in which the workers brought complaints to the union officials and they in turn fixed workers' problems, was disempowering. The organizing model, on the other hand, encouraged workers themselves to solve problems and worked together to organize and create change. To some people within the labor movement this organizing strategy seemed to be unions' best savior.

And yet, in essence, the division between organizing and servicing models reflects the differences in the very structures on which unions formed the AFL-CIO. Rooted in older craft and industrial paradigms, these structures—the historic AFL approach to servicing existing members and the CIO investment in broader organizing—still shape the tools and strategies of the labor movement. These structures, developed and honed within very different political and economic contexts, continue to be used to respond to the challenges of the new economy. We might begin to ask ourselves when new structures, new strategies, and new models will emerge for the contemporary challenges of the American workforce.

PROMISES AND FAILURES OF THE NEW ECONOMY

By the early 1990s, during the congressional battle over the North American Free Trade Agreement (NAFTA), economists assured us that the information technology sector was developing and that U.S. manufacturing would never be the same as it was in the 1950s and 1960s. However, what form these changes would take or exactly how average American workers should prepare for them was not clear. The NAFTA battle was a watershed moment for U.S. labor, as the Democratic Party refused to support its old manufacturing union allies and instead, directly or otherwise, supported the massive offshoring of manufacturing jobs. The ability of labor to respond to the exportation of jobs was finally crushed. The political and social strategies that had worked so well during the rise and expansion of industrialism failed in the face of the transition to a globalized information economy.

From the ashes of the U.S. manufacturing losses, the new economy was supposed to rise with more, better-quality jobs. The new economy promised a highly skilled and educated workforce that could help create new companies and new industries by working smart, not hard. Millions of dollars in "retraining" money for displaced workers was tied to NAFTA legislation, as if the transition from manufacturing to high tech would be as simple as obtaining new skills. What use were unions, similar logic held, if laid-off factory workers became high-paid computer programmers and if lucrative stock options replaced stodgy old pensions? This new economy did not seem to need unions, as rhetoric about individual initiative replaced that of collective social problem solving. If the slogan for the 1930s was a chicken in every pot and for the 1950s a car in every garage, then by the 1990s sloganeers declared stock options and 401(k)s for all. Of course, we now know what became of the promise of the new economy and the sense of insecurity that remains.

The structures and strategies that worked so well for unions in previous eras have not been effective in the new economy. Union organizing itself (and this is in our assessment as decidedly prounion authors) seems more like a throwback to the years before the National Labor Relations Act than anything even remotely resembling organizing in the late 1930s, 1940s, and 1950s. The NLRA is showing its industrial-era age, and it is not aging well.

The NLRA provides the right to organize to workers who have taken the considerable risk of signing union authorization cards and endured intimidation prior to elections held under the rules and auspices of the National Labor Relations Board. These organizing campaigns around union elections must, by definition, focus on workplaces with full-time and regular part-time employees. Left out of this strategy are temporary, contingent, short-term, and other "nonstandard" workers—one of the fastest-growing segments of the labor market and, in terms of health care and other benefits, often the most vulnerable (Kalleberg, 2000). In workplaces with flatter hierarchies, rights to organize have been limited by National Labor Relations Board decisions on "nonsupervisory employees," which also limit the effectiveness of such organizing drives for many new economy workplaces. Organizing temporary workers through the traditional union structure of NLRB elections is virtually impossible. NLRB elections can lead to huge casualties—workers are illegally fired or openly ostracized at work—and are costly in terms of time, money, and effort, resources in which corporations are often far richer than unions. For these and other reasons the NLRA has been criticized, and for many years, there have been calls to amend it to allow it to comply with the new mobile and professional workforce. With the exception of occasional lip service, lawmakers have yet to heed these calls. We doubt that even in the unlikely event that the Democrats win back both the Congress and the presidency in 2008, that any real effort would be made to amend the National Labor Relations Act, unless the United States faces a social and economic crisis on the order of magnitude of the Great Depression. In the meantime, the NLRA continues to carry out its legal mandate to ensure "industrial peace," even if it is at the expense of worker rights, and continues to function as if the economy were stuck circa 1953—as if worker mobility were not an issue; as if full-time, lifetime employment were the norm; and as if corporations were rooted within the confines of national boundaries. Breaking out of the mold of relying on National Labor Relations Board elections as organizing strategies will be difficult—but other transitions in the American economy brought the labor movement innovative approaches to workplace problems.

Efforts to lift the AFL-CIO out of its political and social malaise have been largely unsuccessful. The exodus of some of the most powerful unions from the AFL-CIO in 2005 to create a rival coalition, Change to Win, can be attributed more to frustration with the strategies and structures of the new economy than over real ideological differences. While the Democratic Party leadership urged the breakaway unions to rejoin the AFL-CIO, a significant number of Democrats broke ranks and voted for the Central American Free Trade Agreement, a controversial piece of legislation expanding free trade into Central America and the Caribbean. In a cruel irony of history, the vote took place the same week of the AFL-CIO convention during which unions announced their departure from the federation. The timing only underscored the dire straights the U.S. labor movement finds itself in.

A weakened labor movement is not likely to appear attractive even to a workforce that desperately needs a union. Workers in the new economy may suspect that AFL-CIO's efforts to organize them have as much or more to do with efforts to preserve the labor federation as they do with protecting the rights of the new economy workforce. This impression dooms any organizing effort before it even starts.

Perhaps the most serious flaw in these traditional organizing structures is that they no longer make sense to ordinary people working in the new economy. Rather than ask why disgruntled high-tech workers are not organically forming unions, perhaps we should be asking what kinds of structures and strategies they are using to survive the new economy. Rather than trying to fit old models to new problems, perhaps it is time to develop solutions that are attractive to the people working under these conditions. If history is any guide, a labor movement for the new economy will not come into existence to salvage the AFL-CIO—it will be organic and will develop its own unique sense of member identity and solidarity. Such a movement will also be responsive to the unique challenges that the workforce faces in this particular historical moment and within the contemporary political and social context.

SOLUTIONS:
STRUCTURES AND STRATEGIES FOR THE NEW ECONOMY

Given the rampant economic insecurity that people now face some sort of structure to protect their rights is desperately needed. The contributors to this collection have documented that all workers, even high-tech employees, are vulnerable to the vagaries of capitalism, and that they need collective solutions to the economic problems that they face. What structures, strategies, and forms would such collective solutions for the new economy require? The contributors to this collection identify elements necessary for creating structures to support the new economy workforce.

Organizing is already taking place. Ness writes in his chapter that collective action is taking the form of "micro-organizing," that is, occurring independently of labor unions and being driven by the actions of individual workers and connected through information technologies. Seán Ó Riain has found that employees in high-tech industries "create firm-crossing networks of workers who share interests, contacts and information," which conform "to common technical interests rather than a common employer." These networks have the power to "challenge transnational corporations even as they remain dependent on them." Ó Riain argues that if collective institutions ensure security of income and long-term learning, such as educational systems, welfare state support, and activist industrial policy, then "technical communities could emerge as an important alternative model of economic organization to increasing corporate dominance of the workplace"— surely, a model for workplace organizing rooted in the economic, political, and historical context of the new economy.

New economy jobs are "are not so different from 'old economy' jobs the need for representation and protection in the workplace remains," Danielle van Jaarsveld writes. But the needs of information technology workers and contingent workers in the new economy are "multifaceted and therefore, require an organizational structure that can deploy a variety of strategies to represent the demands" of these employees. The case of WashTech demonstrates that the associational model of worker representation can serve a function within the new economy; and such professional organizations and unions, van Jaarsveld argues, could play a bigger role in supporting broader labor concerns. WashTech already has aspects of the "citizenship" model of unionism in its focus on larger political issues such as immigration and offshoring. Such tactics could help to reinvigorate a broad-based movement around the quality of jobs.

To create the momentum necessary for political change, social movements, unions, and new forms of professional organizations must build broad political alliances, occasionally looking beyond members' immediate needs to take on battles within the larger social and political realms. Chris Benner shows that the South Bay Central Labor Council (SBCLC) plays this role at the local level in California's Silicon Valley. This structure of organizing allows employee organizations to join local political advocates to become active in community action. SBCLC's innovative activities may not be within the realm of traditional collective bargaining, but they advance members' concerns and address the needs of the industry in new ways. This type of social action is a redefinition of the role that unions and other employee organizations can play in redressing social concerns. The approach of combining workers' concerns with community concerns grounds industries and workers in specific communities. This viable tactic is one worth pursuing since it utilizes an existing associational strategy of unions and many nonprofit organizations to help solve local and social problems.

At the same time, the challenges of globalization cannot be solved merely by retreating to fantasies of a nativist or isolationist past. As Andrew Ross writes in his chapter on engineers in China, international linkages are perhaps more important now than ever. Organizations seeking to improve the quality of jobs in one country should follow Ross's advice to seek a "deeper fraternity of workers and employees sharing knowledge, tactics, and goals across national borders." China may indeed be "the biggest and weakest link in the communication network aimed at combating the trade in what economists euphemistically refer to as 'global labor arbitrage,' and what contrarians call 'the race to the bottom,'" but as Ross shows, it may not be for long as capital continues to seek lower wages around the globe. The challenge for those trying to improve work conditions in the new economy will be to address these global linkages while at the same time connecting jobs and industries to the laws and political jurisdictions that they are in. Imagine an organization that could combine the local political power that Chris Benner described with the global focus and networks that can speak to the work of high-tech workeres—be they in Silicon Valley, Shanghai, Mumbai, or any other global center of production.

In the end, however, the effectiveness, survival, and viability of any organization focused on addressing the concerns of workers in the new economy will depend upon how it is structured. This is why John Amman directed high-tech workers, or as he calls them "new media professionals," to the experiences of unions in the entertainment industries. These unions were built around the notion of providing wages, benefits, and decent working conditions through collective bargaining, and yet they do so with a workforce that is mobile, project based, and often contingent. As Amman and Carpenter both point out, entertainment unions have long had models for dealing with working conditions that we now see as rampant across the new economy. As for the blurred line between management and employees, entertainment unions allow their members who own production companies or are independent contractors to remain members in order to maintain their craft credentials. This overlap enables writers, directors, performers, and others to maintain artistic control over the projects that they work on. This aspect of the entertainment industry model speaks to new economy concerns over the support of entrepreneurial work and small businesses. Perhaps, looking at entertainment unions, it is time to think of people who run small high-tech consultancies as a new constituency for organizing—who have at least the same level of concern over economic insecurity as other people working within the new economy have. Key, too, is the ability of members within these unions to negotiate contracts that are better than the minimum standards for union contracts. By supporting and reinforcing a minimum wage standard within the industry, unions and other such organizations can help allay fears that they "hold back" successful members. In fact, within the entertainment industries, the opposite is true. Amman points to the role that entertainment unions play in establishing their members' professional identities, coordinating training for new systems and technologies, and providing recognition for their members.

Another vital purpose for unions in the entertainment industry is providing for the coordination of health and retirement benefits for people who work on multiple projects across the industry. Like many high-tech workers, the film and television editors that Carpenter wrote about are largely freelance workers, and they are hired based largely on the success or failure of their last project or two. Carpenter pointed out that while the concepts of professional identity are important in cementing editors' relationship with the union, the practical, tangible benefits members receive (like increased wages and benefits) encourage people to throw their lot in with a labor union. Taking this analysis a step further, a viable high-tech organization, union or otherwise, must provide its members this basic support in order to be successful.

So far high-tech professionals have not been drawn to labor unions; in part, it seems they view unions as passé. Perhaps traditional unions are passé within this particular context. While, on the face of it, such a suggestion may seem anathema to the larger labor movement, it is one that we believe follows more attentively the culture and concerns of the high-tech workforce.

Carpenter suggests, for example, that the labor movement's publicity problem be resolved by fostering an organization for high-tech workers that is not even called a union. Certainly, it would not be the first time that an association took on union aspects for professionals and later evolved into a labor union. One excellent example is the National Education Association (NEA), now the nation's largest teachers' union, which began simply as a professional organization and moved over time into a strong collective bargaining agent. Another example is the American Medical Association (AMA). In an effort to assist physicians who were struggling with the financial issues created by managed care companies, the venerable professional society began assisting groups of physicians who wished to use collective bargaining "to reclaim clinical autonomy and increase reimbursement."[2] While the AMA can hardly be said to be a powerhouse in the U.S. labor movement, the NEA certainly is.

Considering the history of the ways in which the U.S. labor movement has navigated economic transitions, developing new models for organizing would not be without precedent. The key is that associations and other types of worker support are already providing benefit to the high-tech workforce. As Ó Riain wrote, one of the strategies that will be successful for new economy organizing is to "organize through unconventional channels outside the boundaries of the firm—networks, technical communities and technical user and interest groups" in order to help "set limits to employer demands on their time and social lives" and "provide security without the straitjacket of corporate loyalty." Guild, social network, association, or union—there are existing channels through which knowledge workers, in Ó Riain's words, can become "valuable figures in a broader movement for fair, egalitarian knowledge workplaces" instead of "individualized 'knowledge capitalists.'" Such an organization—such a movement—will most certainly need to be built from the ground up. As Derek Schultz wrote, "We need a broad social movement of, by, and for *workers*—exactly what the labor movement started out as a century ago—and we need to get started right away."

This is not going to be easy in this political and economic climate, when there is a general lack of support for unions politically and outright hostility toward unions by corporations. An activist approach to surviving the new economy will not be received with open arms by the corporations that are already outsourcing jobs to Bangalore and Beijing. But the fact that such work will not be easy does not mean it will not be done. If the history of labor has taught us anything, it is that working people can be just as tenacious in their fight for economic security as corporations are in their effort to secure profits—and that they will and can create the structures necessary to protect their economic interests and to survive economic changes.

NOTES

1. Before then, government intervention was usually on the side of management. Worse, governors and municipal leaders even used state militias and local police to break up and arrest striking workers.

2. Sujit Choudhry and Troyen A. Brennan, "Collective Bargaining by Physicians—Labor Law, Antitrust Law, and Organized Medicine," *New England Journal of Medicine*, October 11, 2001. Available online at http://content.nejm.org/cgi/content/extract/345/15/1141, accessed March 1, 2006.

Bibliography

AFL-CIO Working for America Institute. 2000. High Road Partnerships Report: Innovations in Building Good Jobs and Strong Communities, Washington, D.C.: AFL-CIO Working for American Institute.

Amman, John. 2002. "Union and the new economy: Motion picture and television unions offer a model for new media professionals," *Working USA* (Fall): 112–130.

Amoore, Louise. 2004. "Risk, reward and discipline at work," *Economy and Society* 33(2): 174–196.

Andersen Consulting. 1997. "Changing Health Care: Creating Tomorrow's Winning Enterprise Today." Santa Monica, CA: Knowledge Exchange.

Anderson, Sarah, John Cavanagh, Chris Hartman, Scott Klinger, and Stacey Chan. 2004. "Executive Excess 2004: Campaign Contributions, Outsourcing, Unexpensed Stock Options and Rising CEO Pay." Washington: Institute for Policy Studies.

Angel, David. 1994. *Restructuring for Innovation: The Remaking of the U.S. Semiconductor Industry*. New York: Guilford Press.

Anonymous. 1999. "Idealized Design of Clinical Office Practice: An Interview with Donald Berwick and Chuck Kilo of the Institute for Health Improvement," *Managed Care Quarterly* 7(4): 62-69.

Anon. 2003. "City Rises as Hub for Software," *Shanghai Daily*, September 20

Anon. 2004. "China's Factories Face Labour Shortage," *Straits Times*, September.

Anon. 2004. "IAPE Members Approve Dow Jones Contract Imposing Premium Payments for Health Care," *Daily Labor Report* 154, A-2.

Barnes, William R. and Larry C. Ledebur. 1998. *The New Regional Economies: The U.S. Common Market and The Global Economy*. Thousand Oaks, Calif.: Sage.

Baron, J., M. D. Burton, and M. Hannan. 1996. "The Road Taken: Origins and early evolution of employment systems in emerging companies," *Industrial and Corporate Change* 5 (2): 239–275.

Bartindale, Becky and Mary Anne Ostrom. 2000. "Power in Silicon Valley," *San Jose Mercury News*, July 30, 1A.

Batt, Rose, Susan Christopherson, Ned Rightor, and Danielle van Jaarsveld. 2001. *Net Working: Work Patterns and Workforce Policies for the New Media Industry*. New York: Economic Policy Institute.

Beck, Ulrich. 1992. *Risk Society: Towards a New Modernity*. London and Thousand Oaks, Calif.: Sage.

Beck, Ulrich. 2000. *Brave New World of Work*. Oxford: Polity Press.

Benner, Chris. 1996a. "Growing Together or Drifting Apart? Working Families and Business in the New Economy." San Jose, Calif.: Working Partnerships USA, with the Economic Policy Institute.

Benner, Chris. 1996b. "Shock Absorbers in the Flexible Economy: The Rise of Contingent Employment in Silicon Valley." San Jose, Calif.: Working Partnerships USA.

Benner, Chris. 2002. *Work in the New Economy*. Oxford: Blackwell.

Benner, Chris. 2003. "'Computers in the Wild': Guilds and Next Generation Unionism in the Information Revolution," *International Review of Social History* 48: S11.

Benner, Chris, Bob Brownstein, and Amy Dean. 1999. "Walking the Lifelong Tightrope: Negotiating Work in the New Economy. San Jose, Calif.: Working Partnerships USA, with the Economic Policy Institute.

Bernhardt, Annette, Martina Morris, Mark S. Handcock, and Marc A. Scott. 2001. *Divergent Paths: Economic Mobility in the New American Labor Market*. New York: Russell Sage.

Bhargava, Shalini, Bob Brownstein, Amy Dean, and Sarah Zimmerman. 2001. "Everyone's Valley: Inclusion and Affordable Housing in Silicon Valley." San Jose, Calif.: Working Partnerships USA.

Bradshaw, Ted and Edward Blakely. 1999. "What Are 'Third-Wave' State Economic Development Efforts? From Incentives to Industrial Policy." *Economic Development Quarterly* 13: 229–244.

Brenner, Robert. 2002. *The Boom and the Bubble: The U.S. in the World Economy*. London New York: Verso.

Brownstein, Bob. 2000. "Working Partnerships: A New Political Strategy for Creating Living Wage Jobs." *Working USA* 4: 35–48.

Burton-Jones, Alan. 1999. *Knowledge Capitalism: Business, Work, and Learning in the New Economy*. New York: Oxford University Press.

Cappelli, Peter. 2000. "Is There a Shortage of Information Technology Workers?" Philadelphia: Wharton School, University of Pennsylvania.

Carnoy, Martin and Manuel Castells. 1997. "Sustainable Flexibility: A Prospective Study on Work, Family and Society in the Information Age." Paris: OECD.

Carnoy, Martin, Manuel Castells, and Chris Benner. 1997. "Labour Markets and Employment Practices in the Age of Flexibility: A Case Study of Silicon Valley." *International Labour Review* 136: 27–48.

Cassidy, John. 2002. *Dot.Con: The Greatest Story Ever Sold*. New York: HarperCollins.

Castells, Manuel. 1996. *The Rise of the Network Society*. Cambridge, Mass.: Blackwell.

Castilla, Emilio, Hokyu Hwang, Ellen Granovetter, and Mark Granovetter. 2000. "Social Networks in Silicon Valley," in Chong-Moon Lee, William Miller, Marguerite Gong Hancock, and Henry Rowen, eds., *The Silicon Valley Edge*. Stanford, Calif.: Stanford University Press.

Chet, Carrie Lane. 2006. "Like Exporting Baseball: Individualism and Global Competition in the High-Tech Industry," in Carrie Chet, ed., *The Offshore Outsourcing of White Collar and Professional Work: Culture, Labor and Capital in the Global Marketplace*. Albany, N.Y.: SUNY Press.

Children's Health Initiative. 2001. "Activity Report," 2001. Santa Clara County, Calif.: Children's Health Initiative, September 28.

Christopherson, Susan and Danielle D. van Jaarsveld. 2005. "Cultural Politics and the Evolution of New Media," *International Journal of Cultural Policy* 11: (1), 77-93.

Cobble, Dorothy Sue. 1991. "Organizing the Postindustrial Work Force: Lessons from the History of Waitress Unionism," *Industrial and Labor Relations Review* 44(4): 419–436.

Cooper, Marianne. 2000. "Being the 'Go-To Guy': Fatherhood, masculinity, and the organization of work in the Silicon Valley," *Qualitative Sociology* 23 (4): 379–405.

Dertouzos, Michael L., Richard K. Lester, Robert M. Solow, and the MIT Commission on Industrial Productivity. 1989. *Made in America: Regaining the Productive Edge*. Cambridge, Mass.: MIT Press.

Drazen, Erica and Jane Metzger. 1999. *Strategies for Integrated Health Care: Emerging Practices in Information Management and Cross-Continuum Care*. San Francisco: Jossey-Bass.

Dubofsky, Melvyn and Warren Van Tine. 1986. *John L. Lewis: A Biography*. Urbana: University of Illinois Press.

Dunlop, John. 1958. *Industrial Relations Systems*. New York: Henry Holt.

Ehrenreich, Barbara. 2005. *Bait and Switch: The (Futile) Pursuit of the American Dream*. N.Y.: Metropolitan Books/Henry Holt.

Eimer, Stuart. 2001. "Fighting for Justice Beyond the Contract: The Milwaukee County Labor Council and Sustainable Milwaukee," eds., Immanuel Ness and Stuart Eimer, in *Central Labor Councils and the Revival of American Unionism*. Armonk, N.Y.: M.E. Sharpe.

Ernst and Young. 1996. "Information Technology for Integrated Health Systems, Positioning for the Future." New York: Ernst and Young.

Florida, Richard. 2004. *The Rise of the Creative Class: And How It's Transforming Work, Leisure, Community and Everyday Life*. New York: Basic Books.

Foucault, Michel. 1979. *Discipline and Punish: The Birth of the Prison.* New York: Vintage.

Frank, Thomas. 2000. *One Market Under God: Extreme Capitalism, Market Populism and the End of Economic Democracy.* New York: Doubleday.

Freeman, Richard and Joel Rogers. 1999. *What Workers Want.* Ithaca: ILR Press.

Friedman, Thomas. 2005. *The World Is Flat: A Brief History of the Twenty-First Century.* New York: Farrar, Straus and Giroux.

Fuller, Thomas. 2005. "China Feels a Labor Pinch," *International Herald Tribune,* April 20.

Girard, Monique and David Stark. 2002. "Distributing Intelligence and Organizing Diversity in New-Media Projects," *Environment and Planning A* 34: 1927–49.

Gray, Lois. 2001. "Entertainment Unions Tune up for Turbulent Times," *New Labor Forum* 9, 122-132.

Gray, Lois S. and Ronald L. Seeber, eds. 1996. *Under the Stars: Essays on Labor Relations in Arts and Entertainment.* Ithaca, N.Y.: ILR Press.

Gregory, Kathleen. 1984. "Signing-Up: The Culture and Careers of Silicon Valley Computer People." Ph.D. dissertation, Northwestern University.

Hafner, Katie and Daniel Preysman 2003. "Special visa's use for tech workers is challenged," *New York Times,* June 1.

Harrison, Bennett. 1994. *Lean and Mean: The Changing Landscape of Corporate Power in the Age of Flexibility.* New York: Basic Books.

Harrison, Bennett and Barry Bluestone. 1988. *The Great U-Turn: Corporate Restructuring and the Polarizing of America.* New York: Basic Books.

Head, Simon. 2003. *The New Ruthless Economy: Work & Power in the Digital Age.* New York: Oxford University Press.

Hecker, Daniel. 1999. "High Technology Employment: A Broader View," *Monthly Labor Review* 122(6): 18–28.

Heckscher, Charles. 1996. *The New Unionism: Employee Involvement in the Changing Corporation.* Ithaca, New York: ILR Press. First published by 1988 by Basic Books.

Henwood, Doug. 2003. *After the New Economy.* New York: New Press.

Herzenberg, Stephen, John Alic, and Howard Wial. 1998. *New Rules for a New Economy: Employment and Opportunity in Postindustrial America.* Ithaca: ILR Press.

Hossfeld, Karen J. 1995. "Why Aren't High-Tech Workers Organized?" in Daniel Cornford, ed., *Working People of California.* Berkeley, Calif.: University of California Press, pp. 405–432.

Hyde, Alan. 2003. *Working in Silicon Valley: Economic and Legal Analysis of a High-Velocity Labor Market.* Armonk, N.Y.: M. E. Sharpe.

Ichniowski, Casey and Jeffrey S. Zax. 1990. "Today's Associations, Tomorrow's Unions." *Industrial & Labor Relations Review* 43(2): 191–208.

Johnson, Tim. 2004. "Chinese Factory Workers Begin Protesting Low Wages, Poor Conditions," *Monterey Herald*, September 7.

Johnston, Paul. 1994. *Success While Others Fail: Social Movement Unionism and the Public Workplace*. Ithaca, N.Y.: ILR Press.

JVSVN. 2001. "2001 Index of Silicon Valley." San Jose, Calif.: Joint Venture: Silicon Valley Network.

Kalleberg, Arne L. 2000. "Nonstandard Employment Relations: Part-Time, Temporary and Contract Work." *Annual Review of Sociology* 26: 341–65.

Kalleberg, Arne L., Edith Rasell, Ken Hudson, David Webster, Barbara F. Reskin, Naomi Cassirer, and Eileen Appelbaum. 1997. "Nonstandard Work, Substandard Jobs: Flexible Work Arrangements in the U.S." Washington, D.C.: Economic Policy Institute.

Kanter, Rosabeth Moss. 1995. "Nice Work If You Can Get It: The Software Industry as a Model for Tomorrow's Jobs," *The American Prospect* 6, 23 (September 21).

Kazis, Richard. 1998. New Labor Market Intermediaries: What's Driving Them? Where are They Headed? Conference on New Labor Market Intermediaries. Available at http://mitsloan.mit.edu/iwer/tfkazis.pdf. Accessed February 27, 2006.

Kenney, Martin, ed. 2000. *Understanding Silicon Valley: The Anatomy of an Entrepreneurial Region*. Palo Alto, Calif.: Stanford University Press.

Knight, Frank H. 1921. *Risk, Uncertainty and Profit*. Boston: Houghton Mifflin.

Kobayashi-Hillary, Mark. 2004. *Outsourcing to India: The Offshore Advantage*. Berlin: Springer-Verlag.

Kriesky, Jill, ed. 1998. Working Together to Revitalize Labor in Our Communities: Case Studies of Labor Education-Central Labor Body Collaboration. Orono, Maine: University and College Labor Education Association and the University of Maine.

Krugman, Paul. 2005. "The Oblivious Right," *New York Times*, April 25.

Kunda, Gideon, Stephen R. Barley, and James Evans. 2002. "Why Do Contractors Contract? The Experience of Highly Skilled Technical Professionals in a Contingent Labor Market," *Industrial and Labor Relations Review* 55(2): 234–261.

Lee, Ching Kwan 2000. "Pathways of Labor Insurgency," in Elizabeth Perry and Mark Selden, eds., *Chinese Society: Change, Conflict and Resistance*, 41–61. New York: Routledge.

Lee, Chong-Moon, William Miller, Marguerite Gong Hancock, and Henry Rowen, eds. 2000. *The Silicon Valley Edge: A Habitat for Innovation and Entrepreneurship*. Palo Alto, Calif.: Stanford University Press.

LeRoy, Greg. 1997. *No More Candy Store: States and Cities Making Job Subsidies More Accountable*, Washington, D.C.: Institute on Taxation and Economic Policy.

Levy, Frank and Richard J. Murnane. 2004. *The New Division of Labor: How Computers Are Creating the Next Job Market*. New York: Russell Sage Foundation.

Lichtenstein, Nelson. 1995. *Walter Reuther: The Most Dangerous Man in Detroit*. New York: Basic Books.

Lloyd, Richard D. 2006. *Neo-bohemia: Art and Commerce in the Postindustrial City*. New York: Routledge.

Lohr, Steve. 2004. "High-End Technology Work Not Immune to Outsourcing," *New York Times*, June 16.

Lohr, Steve and Matt Richtel. 2004. "Lingering Job Insecurity of Silicon Valley," *New York Times*, March 9.

Long, Peter. 2001. "A First Glance at the Children's Health Initiative in Santa Clara Country, California." Los Angeles: UCLA School of Public Health.

Luce, Stephanie. 2001. "Building Political Power and Community Coalitions: The Role of Central Labor Councils in the Living-Wage Movement," in Immanuel Ness and Stuart Eimer, eds., *Central Labor Councils and the Revival of American Unionism: Organizing for Justice in Our Communities*. Armonk, N.Y.: M.E. Sharpe.

Ludmerer, Kenneth. 1999. *Time to Heal: American Medical Education from the Turn of the Century to the Era of Managed Care*. New York: Oxford University Press.

Luria, Dan, Joel Rogers, and Joshua Cohen. 1999. *Metro Futures: Economic Solutions for Cities and Their Suburbs*. Boston: Beacon Press.

Lustig, Nora Claudia. 1997. "NAFTA: Setting the Record Straight." The Brookings Institute.

Magee, Bill. 2004. "India's Call Centres Losing Attraction," *The Scotsman*, August 17.

Maskell, Peter and Anders Malmberg. 1999. "The Competitiveness of Firms and Regions: Ubiquitification and the Importance of Localized Learning." *European Urban and Regional Studies* 6: 9–25.

Maskell, Peter, Heikki Eskelinen, Ingjaldur Hannibalsson, Anders Malmberg and Eirik Vatne. 1998. *Competitiveness, Localised Learning and Regional Development: Specialisation and Prosperity in Small Open Economies*. New York; London: Routledge.

Matthews, Glenna. 2002. *Silicon Valley and the California Dream: Gender, Class and Opportunity in 20th Century San Jose.* Stanford, Calif.: Stanford University Press.

Mattoo, Aaditya, and Antonia Carzaniga, eds. 2003. *Moving People to Deliver Services.* Washington, D.C.: The World Bank and Oxford University Press.

McClendon, John A., Jill Kriesky, and Adrienne Eaton. 1995. "Member Support for Union Mergers: An Analysis of an Affiliation Referendum." *Journal of Labor Research* 16(1): 9–23.

McKinsey Global Institute. 1993. "Automobile Assembly," *Manufacturing Productivity.* Washington D.C.: McKinsey Global Institute.

Milton, Laurie P. 2003. "An Identity Perspective on the Propensity of High-Tech Talent to Organize," *Journal of Labor Research* 24(1): 31.

Muehlbauer, Jen. 2001. "Labor to Etown: Union No!" *The Industry Standard*, January 9.

Nader, Ralph et al. 1993. *The Case Against "Free Trade": GATT, NAFTA, and the Globalization of Corporate Power.* San Francisco: Earth Island Press.

Nardi, Bonnie A., Steve Whittaker, and Heinrich Schwarz. 2000. "It's Not What You Know, It's Who You Know: Work in the Information Age," *First Monday* 5 (5).

National Center on Education and the Economy, Commission on the Skills of the American Workforce. 1990. *America's Choice: High Skills or Low Wages!* Rochester, N.Y.: National Center on Education and the Economy.

National Research Council. 2000 [2001]. *Building a Workforce for the Information Economy.* Washington, D.C.: National Academy Press.

Neff, Gina. 2005. "The Changing Place of Cultural Production: Locating Social Networks in a Digital Media Industry," *The Annals of the American Academy of Political and Social Science* 597: 134–152.

Neff, Gina, Elizabeth Wissinger, and Sharon Zukin. 2005. "Entrepreneurial Labor Among Cultural Producers: 'Cool' Jobs in 'Hot' Industries," *Social Semiotics* 15(3): 307–334.

Ness, Immanuel and Stuart Eimer. 2001. *Central Labor Councils and the Revival of American Unionism: Organizing for Justice in Our Communities*, Armonk, N.Y.: M.E. Sharpe.

New York New Media Association (NYNMA). 1997. Second New York New Media Industry Survey.

New York New Media Association (NYNMA) and PricewaterhouseCoopers. 2000. Third New York New Media Industry Survey (March).

O'Carroll, A. 2004. *In the Shadow of the Clock.* Unpublished Ph.D. diss., Department of Sociology, Trinity College, Dublin.

Ó Riain, Seán. 2000. "Net-working for a Living," in Michael Burawoy et al., *Global Ethnography*. Berkeley: University of California Press.

Ó Riain, Seán. 2002. "High-Tech Communities: Better Work or Just More Work?" *Contexts* 1(4): 36–41.

Ó Riain, Seán. 2004. *The Politics of High Tech Growth*, Cambridge: Cambridge University Press.

Orfield, Myron. 1997. *Metropolitics: A Regional Agenda for Community and Stability*. Washington, D.C., and Cambridge, Mass.: Brookings Institution Press; Lincoln Institute of Land Policy.

Osterman, Paul. 1999. *Securing Prosperity*. Princeton, N.J.: Princeton University Press.

Osterman, Paul, Thomas A. Kochan, Richard M. Locke, and Michael J. Piore. 2002. *Working in America: A Blueprint for the New Labor Market*. Cambridge, Mass.: MIT Press.

Papademetriou, Demetrios G. and Stephen Yale-Loehr. 1996. *Balancing Interests: Rethinking U.S. Selection of Skilled Immigrants*. New York: International Migration Policy Program, Carnegie Endowment for International Peace.

Parker, Eric and Joel Rogers. 1995. *The Wisconsin Regional Training Partnership: Lessons for National Policy*. Berkeley, Calif.: National Center for the Workplace, Institute for Industrial Relations.

Parker, Eric and Joel Rogers. 2001. "Building the High Road in Metro Areas: Sectoral Training and Employment Projects," in Lowell Turner, Harry Katz and Richard Hurd, eds., *Rekindling the Movement: Labor's Quest for Relevance in the 21st Century*, 256–73. Ithaca, N.Y.: ILR Press.

Pastor, Manuel, Laura Leete, Laura Dresser, Chris Benner, Annette Bernhardt, Bob Brownstein, and Sarah Zimmerman. 2003. *Economic Opportunity in a Volatile Economy: Understanding the Role of Labor Market Intermediaries in Two Regions*. San Jose, Calif.: Working Partnerships USA.

Pastor, Manuel, Peter Dreier, Eugene Grigsby, and Marta Lopez-Garza. 2000. *Regions That Work: How Cities and Suburbs Can Grow Together*. Minneapolis: University of Minnesota Press.

Perlow, Leslie. 1997. *Finding Time*. Ithaca, N.Y.: Cornell University Press.

Perlow, Leslie, and L. Bailyn. 1997. "The Senseless Submergence of Difference: Engineers, Their Work and Their Careers," in Steve Barley and Julian Orr, eds., *Between Technology and Society: Technical Workers in Modern Workplaces*. Ithaca, N.Y.: IRL Press.

Persky, Joseph and Wim Wiewel. 1994. "The Growing Localness of the Global City," *Economic Geography* 70: 129–143.

Pham, Alex and Stephanie Stoughton. 2000. "Dot-Com Firms Foster New Corporate Culture," *The Boston Globe*, August 6, A26.

Pink, Daniel H. 2001. *Free Agent Nation: How America's New Independent Workers Are Transforming the Way We Live*. New York: Warner.

PolicyLink. 2000. *Perspectives on Regionalism: Opportunities for Community-Based Organizations to Advance Equity*. Oakland, Calif.: PolicyLink.

Pollin, Robert and Stephanie Luce. 1998. *The Living Wage: Building a Fair Economy*. New York: The New Press.

Porter, Michael E. 2000. "Location, Competition and Economic Development: Local Clusters in a Global Economy," *Economic Development Quarterly* 14: 15–34.

Reich, Robert B. 2002. *I'll Be Short: Essentials for a Decent Working Society*. Boston: Beacon Press.

Reich, Robert B. 1991. *The Work of Nations*. New York: Knopf.

Ren, Fan. 2004. "Drought of Migrant Labour," *Beijing Review*, August 5.

Roberts, Dexter, 2004. "Is China Running Out of Workers?" *BusinessWeek*, October 25, 60.

Robinson, J. Gregg and Judith S. McIlwee. 1989. "Obstacles to Unionization in High-Tech Industries," *Work and Occupations* 16: 115–136.

Rogers, Joel. 1996. "Labor and Economic Development." Madison, Wis: Center on Wisconsin Strategy.

Rosner, Rachel and Chris Benner. 1997. *Living Wage: An Opportunity for San Jose*. San Jose, Calif.: Working Partnerships USA.

Ross, Andrew. 2003. *No-collar: The Humane Workplace and Its Hidden Costs*. New York: Basic Books.

Ross, Andrew. 2004. *Low Pay, High Profile: The Global Push for Fair Labor*, New York: New Press.

Ross, Andrew. 2006. *Fast Boat to China: Corporate Flight and the Consequences of Free Trade—Lessons from Shanghai*. New York: Pantheon Books.

Sassen, Saskia. 1996. *Losing Control? Sovereignty in an Age of Globalization*. New York: Columbia University Press.

Saxenian, AnnaLee and Jinn-Yuh Hsu. 2001. "The Silicon Valley-Hsinchu Connection: Technical Communities and Industrial Upgrading," *Industrial and Corporate Change* 10: 893–920.

Saxenian, AnnaLee. 1999. *Silicon Valley's New Immigrant Entrepreneurs*. San Francisco: Public Policy Institute of California.

Saxenian, AnnaLee. 1994. *Regional Advantage: Culture and Competition in Silicon Valley and Route 128*. Cambridge, Mass.: Harvard University Press.

Saxenian, AnnaLee. 1996. "Beyond Boundaries: Open Labor Markets and Learning in Silicon Valley," in Michael Arthur and Denise Rousseau, eds., *The Boundaryless Career: A New Employment Principle for a New Organizational Era*, 23–39. Oxford: Oxford University Press.

Schoenberger, Erica. 1997. *The Cultural Crisis of the Firm*. Oxford: Blackwell.

Schumacher, William C. 1999. "Give Peace a Chance," *Health Care Business* (July–August): 80.

Scott, Allen John. 1988. *New Industrial Spaces: Flexible Production Organization and Regional Development in North America and Western Europe*. London: Pion.

Scott, Allen John. 1998. *Regions and the World Economy: The Coming Shape of Global Production, Competition, and Political Order*. Oxford: Oxford University Press.

Sennett, Richard. 2006. *The Culture of the New Capitalism*. New Haven, Conn.: Yale University Press.

Shapiro, Carl and Hal R.Varian. 1998. *Information Rules: A Strategic Guide to the Network Economy*. Boston: Harvard Business School Press.

Sharone, O. 2004. "Engineering Overwork: Bell Curve Management at a High-Tech Firm," in C. Epstein and A. Kalleberg, eds., *Fighting for Time*, 191–218. New York: Russell Sage.

Shingo, Shigeo. 1985. *A Revolution in Manufacturing, the SMED System*. Stamford, Conn.: Productivity Press.

Slichter, Sumner, James Healy, and Robert Livernash. 1960. *The Impact of Collective Bargaining on Management*. Washington, D.C.: The Brookings Institution.

Smith, Vicki. 2001. *Crossing the Great Divide: Worker Risk and Opportunity in the New Economy*. Ithaca, N.Y.: ILR Press.

Solinger, Dorothy. 2004. "Workers of China Unite in a Paradox for Communism," *Straits Times*, February 14.

Srivastada, Snighda and Nik Theodore 2004. "America's High-Tech Bust." Chicago: Center for Urban Economic Development.

Steen, Margaret. 2003. "Pain From Layoffs Runs Deep in Valley," *San Jose Mercury News*, July 13.

Stiglitz, Joseph. 2001. *The Roaring Nineties*. New York: WW Norton.

Stone, Katherine Van Wezel. 2001. "The New Psychological Contract: Implications of the Changing Workplace for Labor and Employment Law," *University of California Law Review* 48: 519–661.

Stone, Katherine Van Wezel. 2004. *From Wigits to Digits*.Cambridge; New York: Cambridge University Press.

Storper, Michael. 1997. *The Regional World: Territorial Development in a Global Economy*. New York: Guilford Press.

Sum, Andrew, Paul Harrington, Paulo Tobar, and Ishwar Khatiwada. 2004. "The Unprecedented Rising Tide of Corporate Profits and the Simultaneous Ebbing of Labor Compensation; Gainers and Losers from the National Economic Recovery of 2002 and 2003." Boston: Center for Labor Market Studies, Northeastern University.

Christopher Swann, "US Real Wages Fall at Fastest Rate in 14 Years," *Financial Times*, May 10, 2005.

Sylvester, David. 2003. "Valley's Bust More Severe Than Other Regions' Fall," *San Jose Mercury News*, June 21.

Tonelson, Alan. 2000. *The Race to the Bottom: Why a Worldwide Worker Surplus and Uncontrolled Free Trade Are Sinking American Living Standards*. Boulder, Colo.: Westview Press.

van Jaarsveld, Danielle. 2004. "Collective Representation Among High-Tech Workers at Microsoft and Beyond: Lessons from WashTech/CWA," *Industrial Relations* 43(2): 364–385.

van Jaarsveld, Danielle. 2005. "Boom & Bust: An Analysis of Information Technology Work Patterns." Ph.D. diss., Cornell University.

Voelker, Rebecca. 1994. "Population Based Medicine Merges Clinic Care, Epidemiological Techniques," *Journal of the American Medical Association* 271(17): 1301–2 (May 4).

Voss, Kim 1993. *The Making of American Exceptionalism: The Knights of Labor and Class Formation in the Nineteenth Century*. Ithaca, N.Y.: Cornell University Press.

Webb, Sidney and Beatrice Webb. 1920. *The History of Trade Unionism*. New York: Longmans, Green (1894).

Weifeng, Liu 2004. "Labour Shortage Puzzles Experts," *China Daily*, August 25

Wial, Howard. 1993. "The Emerging Organizational Structure of Unionism in Low-Wage Services," *Rutgers Law Review* 45(3): 671–738.

Winslow, Ward, ed. 1995. *The Making of Silicon Valley: A One Hundred Year Renaissance*. Palo Alto: Santa Clara Valley Historical Assn.

Yang, Dali L. 2005. "China's Looming Labor Shortage," *Far Eastern Economic Review* 168, no. 2 (February): 19–24.

Yardley, Jim and David Barboza. 2005. "Help Wanted: China Finds Itself with a Labor Shortage," *New York Times*, April 3, A4.

Yuan, Yao. 2004. "China, Land of 1.3 Billion, Is Short of Labor," *Asia Times*, August 16.

Zuboff, Shoshana. 1988. *In the Age of the Smart Machine: The Future of Work and Power*. New York: Basic Books.

Index

About the Editors

John Amman is a business representative for International Cinematographers Guild Local 600, International Alliance of Theatrical Stage Employees. He has a M.S. from the New York State School of Industrial Labor Relations at Cornell University. John was a contributing author to the book *Under the Stars: Essays on Labor Relations in Arts and Entertainment* edited by Lois Gray and Ronald Seeber. He also wrote the article "Union for the New Economy," that appeared in *Working USA* in Fall 2002. John is the recipient of the IRRA's 2003 Outstanding Young Practitioner's Award.

Tris Carpenter directs the nationwide organizing activities for the Motion Picture Editors Guild, Local 700 of the International Alliance of Stage and Theatrical Employees. He has run organizing drives against several international media conglomerates, including The New York Times, Liberty Media, Lucasfilm Digital, 20th Century Fox, Time-Warner, Viacom, and NBC-Universal. In addition to writing the article "Organizing Technical and Artistic Professionals," that appeared in *Working USA* in Winter 2003-2004, Mr. Carpenter has a master of science in labor studies and a master of arts in philosophy from the University of Massachusetts at Amherst.

Gina Neff is an assistant professor in the Department of Communication at the University of Washington. Currently she is completing a book entitled *Venture Labor: Work and the Burden of Risk in Innovative Industries*, which addresses the experience of uncertainty within new economy jobs. Her research focuses on the relationship between changing technologies and organizational structures and on the commercial production of culture in contemporary media industries. She received her Ph.D. in sociology from Columbia University and has held academic positions at the Institute for Labor and Employment at the University of California, Los Angeles as well as in the communication department at the University of California, San Diego.

About the Contributors

Chris Benner is an Assistant Professor of Geography and Labor Studies at Pennsylvania State University and a research associate at the Center for Justice, Tolerance and Community at University of California, Santa Cruz and the Sociology of Work Program at University of Witwatersrand (South Africa). Benner's research focuses on the relationships between technological change, regional development, and the structure of economic opportunity, focusing on regional labor markets and the transformation of work and employment patterns. His book, *Work in the New Economy* (2002), analyzes processes of labor market restructuring in the information economy, documenting the impact on workers' livelihoods of the growth in flexibility and the rise of labor market intermediaries. He received his doctorate in City and Regional Planning from the University of California, Berkeley.

Simon Head is Senior Fellow in Rothermere American Institute at the University of Oxford. He was Director of Project on Technology and the Workplace at the Century Foundation from 1998 to 2004. Head is the author of *The New Ruthless Economy, Work and Power in the Digital Age* published by Oxford University Press in 2003.

Immanuel Ness is Professor of Political Science at Brooklyn College—City University of New York. Ness is completing a book on global labor migration and labor struggles. He is also working on a project examining worker self organizing and strikes in the United States. He is conducting research on revolution and social transformation. His recent books include *Immigrants, Unions, and the New U.S. Labor Market; Race and Labor Matters in the U.S.; Organizing for Justice in Our Communities; The New Urban Immigrant Labor Force.* Ness is editor of the peer-reviewed journal *WORKINGUSA: The Journal of Labor and Society.*

Seán Ó Riain is Professor of Sociology at the National University of Ireland, Maynooth. His research explores the social foundations of the information economy in the workplace, the firm and the economy. He has published *The Politics of High Tech Growth* (Cambridge, 2004), which shows the crucial role of state and social supports in Irish high tech industrial development during the "Celtic Tiger" years. His other research investigates the global evolution of high tech industry, changing forms of state development policies and institutions, the politics of the software workplace, and a life history analysis of social change in Ireland.

Andrew Ross is Professor of American Studies and Director of the Metropolitan Studies Program at New York University. He is the author of several books, including *Fast Boat to China: Corporate Flight and the Consequences of Free Trade*; *Low Pay, High Profile: The Global Push for Fair Labor*; *No-Collar: The Humane Workplace and Its Hidden Costs*; and *The Celebration Chronicles: Life, Liberty and the Pursuit of Property Value in Disney's New Town*. He has also edited several books, including *No Sweat: Fashion, Free Trade, and the Rights of Garment Workers*, and, most recently, *Anti-Americanism*.

Derek W. Schultz has worked in information technology for over twenty-five years. He holds M.A. and Ph.D. degrees in experimental/cognitive psychology and an M.S. in business administration specializing in research management, all from the University of Illinois. He started his career at Bell Labs working on usability engineering for software systems. In 1985 he formed Media Design Associates to consult in information design and business process analysis/improvement. His interest in research management focused on teamwork in R&D projects—creating environments where a team of talented people could excel—but this knowledge became moot as companies pursued policies that devalued and demoralized workers. The more he watched disturbing trends, the more he understood that unions—reinvented for the realities of the 21st century—are crucial for correcting misguided policies and restoring economic justice. That's why he became active in the labor movement, joined WashTech (CWA Local 37083), and served on the Board of Directors of the Programmers Guild.

Danielle van Jaarsveld is an Assistant Professor of Organizational Behavior and Human Resources at the University of British Columbia's Sauder School of Business. Her research seeks to understand workforce flexibility from the perspective of both employers and the workforce. She is currently studying working conditions in Canadian contact centers. She received her Ph.D. from the School of Industrial and Labor Relations at Cornell University.